the flap pamphlet series

Advice
for an Only Child

open, read, turn

Advice for an Only Child

the flap pamphlet series (No. 12)
Printed and Bound in the United Kingdom

Published by the flap series, 2014
the pamphlet series of flipped eye publishing

Cover Design by Petraski
Series Design © flipped eye publishing, 2010

First Edition

ISBN-13: 978-1-905233-46-5
Editorial work for this series is supported by the Arts Council of England

LOTTERY FUNDED

Advice for an Only Child

For Willi Kracher

But who may abide the day of his coming?
And who shall stand when he appeareth?
For he is like a refiner's fire.
— Malachi 3:2

und es listet die Seele
Tag für Tag der Gebrauch uns ab
— Friedrich Hölderlin

… und was sich reimt ist gut
— Pumuckl

Anja Konig

Contents | *Advice for an Only Child*

October

The world being
praiseworthy
I went
and in the early morning
bought a pen.

Battersea

Fog on the railroad track,
black brick, buds
bursting there, and here
the broken frontwheel just near
the holly and the red piece
of plastic left for color, syringes
and a rubber glove: light blue,
thumb missing, between blades
of grass newly green. So much
to celebrate – cigarette butts
and daffodils arranged
just so, the gray unquenchable
river tide, embedded pebbles,
April ! the oil-slick sand
with its silver Heineken cans.

Triple Negative

We always met at Cafe Blunt -
latte, eggs, Moroccan tiles.
Your hair was growing back
more wiry and wild.
      You said that it had spread –
brain, liver, bones,
a butcher's plate.
You looked afraid. We talked
      of other things,
that we should get out more,
enroll in match dot com, how hard it was
to make new friends.

Outlook

The grass is brighter today,
a cup of perfect silver needle
tea, the air less agitated,
a sharper chair, sink, sill,
less desperately, this morning,
in love, three dogs with varied
interests on the sidewalk, slick
and still.

Sight Seeing for Two

Here is the muddy meadow
where we couldn't hike because of rain but kissed instead.
Down there you can see the lakeshore where I said *so, I love you.*

Here is the pontoon.
Here is the tram where we sat silent, bitter, surprised after a fight.

Other important places:
a sleep clinic, Pier One, my bathroom cabinet with your allergy pills.

Here is the tree under which you lay and here the back
of your shirt where you found gum had stuck.
Here is Henrici's, where we had the argument, where I find now
that a whole flammkuchen is too large for one person.

Here is the pedestal of the equestrian statue
where we ate falafel and you got hit with pigeon shit,
here is where we still laughed about such things.

Here are the steps into the Seine where we had too much champagne.
Here is the ice cream shop on the rue St. Louis where we escaped from
            hail
with a bowl of sorbet.

Here is the spot on your living room wall at which I threw a book,
            where I wept,
and here is the book itself, left on your shelf.

Dump

I don't accumulate,
chuck everything
out. You were a pack rat,
kept your Tesco card
just in case.

At the dump they weigh the car
on the way in
and out,
charge for the difference, the weight
left behind.

I remember - we argued
about holding on to papers,
training manuals for defunct operating systems.

I carry your desk chair across.
Someone unscrews
its only wheel.
Aluminum is the most
precious scrap.

The pillow where the cat slept
goes into a container
connected by conveyor belt
directly to the furnace.
The sign says *don't jump in*.

Belaubt Geglaubt

And the fog half
hanging trees still
beleaved some yellow there
left over: two ice
cream spoons in the sink
from where you were
lilies blue vase pink
one closed one
curled, a pair.

Radiocarbon Dating

It's no longer done –
comparing a woman's body to a landscape -
buttock hillocks, dales and deltas –

politically incorrect. But I want you
in charge of manning up an expedition to undefined
white spaces on my map. I want you

to use your scientific training, evaluate
my forestation, measure the circumference of both
polar caps. You can examine drilling cores

to reconstruct my seismic history. The tectonic
fault positions, degree of liquefaction
of the crust and mantle imply tremors

are possible and could be more
than model settlements can handle.

You can still shift your paradigm, embrace
a post-colonial sentiment, and keep your footprint light.

Darwin at the Car Museum

Some rich guy collected
vintage cars and stored them
in a big fridge, their fluids
drained as from slabbed corpses
labeled and drawered. Immense
acquarial quiet, so many
specimens, we dart like golden fish
between the underwater
fossils, there is one like a pram,
here are tanks and sharks,
bugs, mammoths, the little
red Spiderferraris next to huge
30s Benzes, the globulous
blind frontbulbs, one body
teak and shipshaped, original
wax intact. We float by, picking
at the bones, veering together.
This ancient Bugattimonster
spawned viable offspring you can
see on the streets today, Phaetons
perished whole in the skycrash,
the fittest can hope, the others
are encased for memory only.
You and I, too, a curious new
mutation among obsolete shapes, trial
and error, if you have a hundred
million years, what are a few

false starts? Trial and eros, we have
this life, today - so let me quickly
kiss you, between the extinct whale,
a lesser Levassor, breakable
mahogany spokes, dense rubber,
brass, pendulous soft horn,
and the sleek silverfitted Cadillac
from the streets of Chicago
spickblue and good as new.

She's Good with her Hands

She jacks up my frame
unclenches my wheel
loosens my chain
strips my inner tube off the rim
pumps in the air - hissing -
she runs her thumb along the inside of my tire
bloodied by a speck of glass
missed in there
she licks it
fixes the nick in my rubber
inflates it
puts it together
she greases my gears
tightens my spokes
caps my valves
and charges only fifty.

Six Nineteen

On a bus or a train
alone, looking out
at night in the rain
she forgot why it ended.
She called him again -
and remembered.

Weather Forecast

For the 8th
they predict
the last
nice day
for a while
maybe
all fall.

I watched
as
a wistful
chestnut
fell.

I passed
all
the places
where
I lied
to you.

I ate
fifteen
plums
for lunch.
They were
on sale.

I Nearly Took the Twenty Four Today

Remember, once it just stopped,
the driver got out and walked off.

Remember, on the left side of Lupus
a pedestrian might get hit by an empty beer can.

Remember the mould, the leak, the water bills,
the boiler. I thought we were unhappy then.

Remember gooseberry pickles, like eyeballs
in a jar, you said they help a person relax.

Remember when it snowed for three days and
I did not have to go to the airport.

Saturday 6am

Having just
come in
from the already
bright terrace
together
with traces
of meadowy air
and hyacinth
sitting down
on the chair
with the one
plate and the one
cup in front of me
I see the day
is mine
entirely.

Inner Ear

They have shaved you
except for one strip of brown coat along your flank.
The have stripped you
for the axe,
made you clean and slick.
Your voluble ears move.
They have cut
your mane. You are trimmed.
You are readied. You are winnowed.

Still, the world addresses you.
The clang of the knacker
drums your ear's delicate hammer,
beats the anvil,
stirs the smallest bone.
Stirrup pistons against cochlea.
The whinny. The shiver.
The snow. The thick sound of the slick floor.

The neigh.
Your breath.
The noise.

Fear
shaking
your shaven flank.

The hammer.
The silence.

Suicide

Do it by leaping
off a mountain, one with a cliff.

From where you live,
take the train (change once) and then a bus to the meadows.

Start early in the day to reach the trailhead before eight.

The cows are out and it's a weekday, so there is silence enough.

If there is another walker share the map you bring,
but don't talk about too many things with him.

Farms   ferns   waterfalls

The mist lifts and you see the end of the trees and the place
up above, its sheer face.

By this time

after hours of walking and grime you crave the water in the flask,
warm from the sun, delicious
as it goes down.

First It's Just a Couple of Bricks

First it's just a couple of bricks off the top.
The tower looks out: winter horses, warriors

shouting for show. I have seen you hacked at,
one eye at a time, have seen stalks and snow,

pigeons in and out of the bell house, owned
as it is by ghosts. In the last room only fire

where we dry and shiver, hips unscrewed,
swollen fingers fretting horn buttons. We find

we can live without hearing or hair,
we do not remember, we never needed any of it.

We rock in the tapestry bower, waiting
for the catapults. On the ramparts no archers:

when rams batter, slide back the bolts, step
aside and lightly invite what comes through.

Not the Last Chapter

I'm up all night,
trapped
like a bottled bug.
London is hardest.
The broken escalators
we used to mock
can bring it on.
The Twenty Four is stalled
opposite the curry house.
The driver smokes one outside,
passengers look on.
Attachment is suffering.
At Southbank
pedestals are crammed
with trash. Planks jut
into the river where I took
the call. The bridge,
the brink, the wall.
Cats don't get insomnia.
We can learn from that.

Tissue, Bone

My grandmother
whom nobody liked
with her own shit encrusted

fingernails holding on
to the triangle above
the automatic bed:

wiping her fingers when
she barely knew it,
the only kind thing

I ever did for her. She had lost all
the weight and was nice
and thin for death when it came.

Number Five is Alive

The soul is a subtle
automaton, not like
the seedy inside
of the tomato,
but it's made of
wheels of titanium,
turning and ticking.
A robot, a small one,
started as a human child
transformed in search
of perfection, reached
the fragile precision
a Swiss citizen
could respect. Open up
the back and look
at the ruby coil spring,
but don't shake or put
your finger in.

Advice for an Only Child

Go out to play they say - but you
can sit in the tidy garbage shed
until it's time to go to bed.

In the suburban summer the dozing roads
unglue - scratch off the plastic tags
and smell their toxic backs.

When you see a matchbox car
left in a sandbox, take it.
Run it against your bedroom door.

When they are loud downstairs go
to the bathroom with a book. No one
knows: a coin will open any lock.

When someone angry and grown up
says *you are not even human,*
say: *I am a little robot then.*

At night look at the albums in the attic.
You'll find, in black and white: a bald girl
in her smock, four boys in sailor jackets.

The Storks

are back,
ten of them
piercing frogs
in the mud.

As kids
we were taught
they were
extinct.

Things
may be more
resilient
than we think.

We are the Bees of the Invisible

says Rilke, of poets (I think) I thought I could never
be a bee: all that peer pressure, the hum
and hustle of the hive. Who can relax
when the next bee is doing her urgent dance?

But the bees of the invisible live wild,
solitary lives - in bee hotels in botanical gardens,
hollows of reeds, holes in baked bricks,
a kind of Manhattan at the edge of a wood.

Each singular bee in her cell makes
honey, so transparent that it looks like nothing.

But a hungry tongue can just detect its mix
of tastes, its texture, tough and sweet, like love.

.

Acknowledgements & Thanks

Grateful acknowledgement is made to the editors of the publications in which the following poems first appeared.

Cimarron Review: "Dump"
The Cortland Review: "Belaubt, Geglaubt"
The EmmaPress Anthology of Mildly Erotic Verse: "Radiocarbon Dating"
Magma: "October"
The Moth: "Triple Negative"
Orbis: "Six Nineteen"
Poetry London: "Darwin at the Car Museum"
Poetry Review: "Advice for an Only Child"
Smiths Knoll: "Tissue, Bone", "Suicide"
The Stand: "Outlook", "Battersea", "I Nearly Took the Twenty Four Today"
Under the Radar: "Not the Last Chapter"
Washington Square Review: "First it's Just a Couple of Bricks"

Thank you to Nii Parkes for giving this small book a home. Thank you to Jacqui Saphra for her help with the manuscript and above all for her friendship. Friendship is the stuff of life.

EunJoo and Russ Thompson, you are my first call, and love to Audrey. A bear hug for Carole Allamand. Thank you to Jyothish George for emergency kottu roti and all his wisdom ("how come if you've got all this wisdom, your life is so fucking hard") and to Purvi Harlalka. Thank you to Zia Rahman for walking together. Thank you to Frank Eberlein and Gerald Personnier. Thank you to Ursi Kracher.

Thank you to Ruth Wiggins, Cheryl Moskowitz, Liane Strauss, Claudia Daventry, Len Joy, Shifra Sharlin and David Sorkin, Marion Kaplan, Lucrezia Zappi, and the wonderful Barry and Lorrie Goldensohn for sharing poems, essays, novels, cups of tea, udon noodles and masala dosas.

Thank you to New York City for having an Anja-shaped slot to fit into, no matter how odd the angles.

Thank you to Nell Nelson, Anne MacLeod, George Szirtes, and Michael Laskey. Thank you to Maggie Dietz for telling me to make it better.

Special thanks to Robert Pinsky, who often nudged me into the right direction. Thank you to Alice Oswald for her kindness. And a special thank you to John Glenday for believing in my work and for being a mensch.

Thank you to Gilda Waelzel and Hubert Kalf for adopting a wolf cub. And thank you to Willi for everything you are still teaching me.

Lightning Source UK Ltd.
Milton Keynes UK
UKOW03f0648161014

240181UK00001B/102/P

THE PONY EXPRESS TRAIL:
YESTERDAY AND TODAY

THE PONY EXPRESS TRAIL:
YESTERDAY AND TODAY

WILLIAM E. HILL

CAXTON PRESS
Caldwell, Idaho
2010

ISBN 978-0-87004-476-2

Library of Congress Cataloging in-Publication Data

Hill, William E.
The Pony Express trail : yesterday and today / William E. Hill.
    p. cm.
Includes index.
ISBN 978-0-87004-476-2 (pbk.)
    1. Pony Express National Historic Trail. 2. Pony express--United States--History. 3. West (U.S.)--Description and travel. I. Title.

F593.H554 2009
917.804'33--dc22

2009048073

Lithographed and bound in the United States of America

CAXTON PRESS
Caldwell, Idaho
178229

DEDICATION

Dedicated to the Pony Riders in the Sky –
Seeing the Truth in their Stories and Tales!
And Wishing We All could Follow their Trails!

TABLE OF CONTENTS

ILLUSTRATIONS

xii

Introduction

The recent resurgence of interest in the American West has brought increased attention to the Pony Express Trail. As people focus on it and learn about its history and significance, it is important to first place it in perspective with the other great western trails. The Lewis and Clark Trail was a trail of exploration of the newly acquired Louisiana Purchase. It was intended for future commercial use, but never used as such. The Santa Fe Trail originated as a commercial trail in the 1820s. It went southwest to Santa Fe which was then part of Mexico. The Oregon and California trails were emigrant trails, forged in the 1840s as part of the fulfillment of Manifest Destiny. The Mormon Trail, also an emigrant trail, was used by the Mormons as part of the quest for religious freedom that brought them to Utah.

But, what was the Pony Express Trail? It was not a trail of exploration, but relied heavily on Captain James H. Simpson's exploration route in the Central Basin to the Sierra Nevada. It was not a commercial trail, but it carried important commercial and political communications. Freight wagons and stagecoaches used it. For owners of the great freighting firm of Russell, Majors, and Waddell, it was a way to bring them future mail and commercial contracts. It was not really an emigrant trail, but it followed them and was heavily used by emigrants, especially in the eastern half and then again over the Sierra Nevada in the far west. The trail was a communication line. But most of all, today it is a part of our history in which the absolute facts are hard to discern, but whose story is worth knowing.

Today, the Pony Express is often referred to as "a successful failure." The founders realized that the Pony Express, commonly referred to as "the Pony," would not be financially successful, but they hoped it would prove the success of the central route, and thus, result in additional government contracts for them. The reality was that the Pony Express lost money and it did not bring the failing Russell, Majors and Waddell successful contracts. It actually drove them further into debt and brought about the financial collapse of what was once considered the biggest and mightiest freighting empire of the West.

There was no government bailout for them. Some could argue that the government or some officials did the opposite by making sure there were no government contracts for the firm. However, it did succeed in proving the practicality of the central route. And that route was almost instantaneously used by the telegraph, emigrant and freight wagons, and much of it later by the Lincoln Highway, the first cross-country auto road in the early twentieth century. It also succeeded in relation to our broader American history regarding the Civil War by keeping California in the Union. These secondary consequences by themselves were actually more important than the success or failure of the firm of Russell, Majors, and Waddell.

HISTORICAL CONCERNS

Many of the books on the Pony Express include detailed stories accepted as fact by some, but considered folklore by others. A few of these stories will be mentioned briefly, but it is the reader's exposure to the route, the stations and the words of those who used the trail that is the primary goal of this author. Sufficient basic information will be presented to foster an understanding of its history and to put it in its historical perspective.

The Pony Express has a unique place in American history and in the hearts and minds of Americans. In many ways the reality and perceptions of the Pony Express don't match. Everyone has heard of the Pony Express, but what do we really know? When told how long the Pony Express existed, many people can't believe its duration was really measured in months, not in years; nor that it did not carry most of the mail that was sent west, but only a very limited amount. And regarding Buffalo Bill, Pony Bob Haslam and Bronco Charlie, all are considered by some to be the most famous riders. The stories about their heroic deeds, how other riders were killed, their young ages and their long rides have been repeated over and over. However, when people find out that some historians have real concerns and doubts about them, they are very surprised. How can this be explained?

In one of my favorite classic Hollywood westerns, *The Man Who Shot Liberty Valence*, starring John Wayne, Jimmy Stewart and Lee Marvin, there is the classic line about the press. The conversation involves an interview between a young reporter and the hero, the man (Jimmy Stewart) credited with shooting Liberty Valence (Lee

Marvin), the town bully. The reporter is told the factual story about the incident and the identity of the real shooter (John Wayne), but the reporter decides not to print the truth. When asked why, his response was, "When the lie becomes bigger than the truth, you print the lie." In some ways that line best represents the recounting of the history and the problems associated with it.

Much has been written about the Pony Express, but how much is true? It seems much is written based on what is believed to be true, what is possibly true, and what comes from stories told and retold. The point is, is that due to the wide range of the possible data and how much has been corroborated, the more one uses material that could be further from the known truth, the greater the probability of having an inaccurate view of the Pony Express. Because of the type of materials used, historians and writers have provided different descriptions of the same event. Even in stories and legends there is often some truth. If one wants to appreciate something, perhaps the big picture is most important. My Dad gave me some advice one time that seems apropos. He said that you don't have to know how to hold, crack and serve a hardboiled egg like colonists did in order to understand what a breakfast was like in Colonial America.

Historians tell their story based on the study of the materials and records that are available. Availability is an important factor. A historian cannot use what cannot be obtained. Some material may be known to some individuals, but not to others. It may be known to exist, but it may be unavailable or its location unknown. Other material may not be known to exist, but does, in fact exist, and may someday be found. Records can take many forms. They may be physical artifacts; or written and oral materials based on primary and secondary sources, both biased and impartial. When using these sources one must be aware of the differences between perception and reality, journals and reminiscences, individual biases or motivations, and the skills of the observers. The objectives and cultural biases of the writers or historians should also be considered.

The documents related to the Pony Express are varied, and there should be many records. It existed only a century and a half ago. Government agencies are known for their records. The company was one of the largest and most important firms in the country. There were hundreds of people involved. It was an important event in its own time. Newspapers were increasing in numbers. It was a major interest of the public. Therefore, it would seem that there should be lots of primary materials.

While it may be true that governments tend to keep volumes of records, the Pony Express was a private operation, not a government agency. The government contracted out much of the mail transportation and delivery system. The firm of Russell, Majors and Waddell was the largest freighting company in the nation. The Pony Express was part of the Central Overland California and Pikes Peak Express Company. However, the Pony Express was only a small part of their business concerns. The partners were involved with a number of other business enterprises. As individuals they were also involved in other business ventures with other individuals and companies. Sometimes these businesses overlapped and shared equipment such as their stage line and Pony Express. The overlapping nature also made it difficult to identify or separate costs. Since the Pony Express spanned the country, there were large numbers of employees. Offices and records were spread out. Record keeping was subject to the skills and dedication of the particular employee.

Even though the Pony Express was a significant event, there was another event that quickly overshadowed all other concerns— the Civil War. It became the primary focus of citizens, businesses and governments. It dominated the news of the time. Unrest, demonstrations, riots and fighting broke out in some of the areas of the Pony Express, including St. Joseph and Lexington, Missouri. Buildings were destroyed or burned and records were lost. During the Paiute War many stations were raided and what records existed there were destroyed.

The company went bankrupt and much of its equipment and supplies transferred to its new owners. The need to keep all its records became unimportant. The founders' interests and time became focused on other matters.

Some of the earliest stories about the Pony Express and riders were written as "dime novels." It would not have been uncommon for the writer to have had little real contact with the people and events described, yet those stories were the sources from which many people learned about the Pony Express. This was especially true of stories about Buffalo Bill Cody and Bill Hickok. Many of the individuals that have come to be associated with the Pony Express, such as Buffalo Bill, Pony Bob and Bronco Billy had reputations for being good story tellers.

By the time there was a rebirth in interest in the Pony Express, nearly a half century had passed since its founding. By then many of the people had faded memories and others had died. Among the founders, only Alexander Majors wrote a book. It was supposed to be 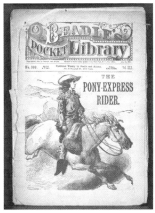 his autobiography, but it was written with the assistance of Bill Cody and Prentiss Ingraham. Commenting later about his own book, Majors remarked that Ingraham might have embellished the truth. Both Russell and Waddell died bankrupt within a few months of each other a decade after the Pony Express ended. With their deaths, so went their knowledge, perspectives, and insights into the dealings of the Pony Express. There were only a few riders and associates interviewed at length. And few

New York Public Library wrote extensively about their time with the Pony Express until late in their lives. Much of what is "known" comes from those few. Corroboration of stories is sometimes difficult to find, and over time some stories have changed. Newspaper articles are useful, most were short, but even the veracity of many of them is open to debate. They also suffered some of the same problems when the towns they served disappeared or suffered from destruction.

We have lists of riders, even though no authentic list from the time has been found. They are the result of research, a composite of sources, some old and some recent. There was no single employment office. The division superintendents were responsible. According to some stories, emergency situations led to on-the-spot hiring. It must be remembered that the amount of time between the inception of the Pony Express to its starting run was less than three months. The company did not have time to waste. The employees probably were not too concerned with the keeping and storage of records.

One hundred fifty years have now passed since the Pony Express had its run. We know more than we did 100 or 125 years ago. Documents have been uncovered, new approaches used to examine old materials, and archaeological studies have, and hopefully will continue to increase our knowledge or improve our interpretations.

One of the topics described in many books is the living conditions at the express stations. Most frequently noted is the description of the roofless stations. This is based on the comments about both Cold Springs and Sand Springs stations in Nevada by Richard Burton who traveled west and visited many of the express stations. That bit of information and his comments are reported and relied upon over and over again in many books on the Pony Express. Not mentioned are his comments that some of the stations were in the process of being rebuilt. It would also be reasonable to assume that a roof was needed in some form or other, especially during the winter in the mountains and in the Central Basin where the winters are severe. Those comments about holes in the ground and roofless stone walls may be accurate for that instant in time, but not necessarily applicable for later times. As a matter of fact, the archaeological evidence of the study of both Cold Springs and Sand Springs indicate something different. Post holes in the living quarters were found in the Cold Springs ruins which likely indicate supports for a roof, and evidence of a wooden floor was found in Sand Springs. Why install a floor and then not protect it? Also, the lack of wood or roof beams in the ruins by itself should not lead to the conclusion that there was no roof. Wood beams, doors, etc. were usually salvaged to be used somewhere else. A prime example of this is in the large ruins of Fort Churchill. The large fireplace in Cold Springs has a chimney and a peaked wall. Both would indicate the existence of a roof or that one was planned. These early descriptions are used to show the primitive living conditions at the express stations. I am not saying that conditions weren't hard, just that there were better examples to use to substantiate the point. In the same manner, if stations were used where the descriptions indicated good conditions, it would be equally as incorrect to imply they were representative of the stations.

As the story of the Pony Express unfolds and information is presented, it is important to keep these things in mind.

PREFACE

This book continues what has developed into my "Yesterday and Today" series about the Great Trails West. I credit my interest in the trails west to my Dad and Mom's encouragement and our family trips west every summer. Depending on the year there came to be five of us kids, plus other "adopted" youngsters. At first, we were "packed" into a car with a homemade trailer, then a station-wagon, and later, a house or travel trailer was added. They were our covered wagons.

We often went to Kansas to visit my grandparents. I still remember a cattle drive with the cowboys driving their small herd of cattle off the Flint Hills past my grandparents' small farm south of Manhattan. I was told stories about the young boys who were needed to "man" the Pony Express and their adventures and feats of courage and endurance. For a young eastern boy in the 1940s and 50s, the West was a real place. Its spirit was alive, and it was being caught by this Pennsylvania lad. As a family we went to see historic sites throughout the country. We started with visits to local sites in eastern Pennsylvania outside of Philadelphia where I was born and radiated out to locations across the country. Thus, not only were they places we read about or discussed at home or in school, they were real and touchable. Altogether they instilled a love and pride in our country's history which probably led to my career as a social studies teacher and author.

My Dad always talked about the National Road and its importance. We even have a model of a Conestoga wagon which he had made, but my interest was in a trail farther west. It was the Oregon Trail. I had become a high school social studies teacher in the late 1960s, and I had continued the practice of going west in the summers. By the early 70s I had been bitten by the "Oregon" bug and by the late 70s started some serious study. I finally had my book on the Oregon Trail accepted for publication and shifted my attention to its companion trail, the California Trail. My Dad still pushed for the National Road. I started it a couple of times, but other factors changed my focus. The Santa Fe Trail, full of it own romance, was a natural next choice, as it became the route of our honeymoon trip for my wife, Jan, and me. Over the next few years my friends encouraged me to write about the Mormon Trail, and then the Lewis and Clark Trail, and to tie them into their trail's respective celebrations which I did, but my Dad still pushed for the National Road. However, I still felt I had at least one more trail to write about—the Pony Express Trail. I started on that in 2004 and wrote two activity books for students and teachers, but soon events arose that took time and attention. Recently, I've been able to complete this volume, *The Pony Express Trail, Yesterday and Today*. Living in New York, however, has allowed me to use the route of the National Road as part of our pathway west. My Dad passed away a few years ago when I had started on the Pony Express, and my stepmother passed a little over a year ago. Perhaps now that I have completed my Pony Express project I can soon return to the National Road. It is always good to have one more thing to do.

The goal in each of my books has been to give the readers some basic information about the history of the respective trail, to provide different ways to experience the trail, to add to the field of knowledge, all in hopes of tweaking an interest in the reader to seek more information, to visit the sites, and to appreciate its chapter in our nation's history. To accomplish this, written and illustrative materials from those who had originally organized, experienced and traveled the trail are provided. By examining the sites and the trail as they existed during their historic period and comparing them with the views from today, a clearer picture of what it was like should emerge. Other books exist that go into much greater detail about some of the specifics, and they should be read, but no other exists that allows one to both view the old trail and also to see it in its present state as is done here.

This book is organized a little differently from my others. Although it has the sections on the history of the trail, significant maps, and museums, I usually also include separate pictorial and diary sections. While I still have an extensive number of "yesterday and today" illustrations, the diary section posed a major problem. Usually it highlights entries from three different emigrants/travelers traveling over a common section of the trail, enabling the reader to better understand what trail travel was like. That was almost impossible to do due to the lack of detailed diaries by riders over their route. I decided to combine the sections and to include more comments, quotes and related information than previously done with the illustrations. Hopefully, this will still provide the reader with a good understanding of what it was like for the Pony Express riders, and will also inspire an appreciation for the sites.

xxii

Numerous organizations have been formed to preserve and promote interest in trails. They are open to the public, and these groups are always looking for new members. Although each organization encourages its members to become active in its preservation efforts and events, even "passive" membership has many rewards, especially for armchair travelers! All have local or regional chapters, various publications that focus on both social gatherings of its members and also academic study, and national conferences or conventions.

For those interested in Pony Express history there is the National Pony Express Association (NPEA). It was organized in 1978 to re-establish, identify, and re-ride the historical Pony Express Trail. It works to preserve the history of the Pony and helps in marking the route. Each year this group sponsors a re-ride of the trail, alternating the starting point at St. Joseph, Missouri, in the east in odd years, and Sacramento, California, in the west during even years. You do not have to be a rider to participate in the organization. It has local chapters that sponsor and take part in local events and celebrations. Another organization is the Pony Express Trail Association. It has also been very active in identifying, preserving and marking the sites associated with the Pony Express. It uses monuments and aluminum stakes to mark the sites. Both organizations have worked with the National Parks Service in its work as guardian of the Pony Express National Historic Trail and the Bureau of Land Management and USDA Forest Service as guardians of public lands.

For some of the other historic trails there are the following organizations: The Oregon-California Trails Association is concerned, not only with the main Oregon and California trails and feeder routes, but all the emigrant/wagon trails of the Trans-Mississippi West. It has had a very active program in researching, identifying, and marking trails and significant sites. Many of those overlap with the Pony Express Trail. Another group that has been active primarily with the California Trail and its variants is Trails West. For those interested specifically in the southwest, there is the Santa Fe Trail Association. The Mormon Trail Association focuses on the Mormon experience to Salt Lake City and the Great Basin. Those interested in the adventures and explorations of Lewis and Clark can participate in the Lewis and Clark Trail Heritage Foundation.

And, for those interested in experiencing the Pony, the trail and what it was like, one can still partake in aspects of it. The National Park Service, using major highways, has identified and signed a Pony Express Auto Route. It tries to follow or closely approximate the trail, but because of the remoteness of sections of the trail, in those areas where there are no paved roads, the marked highways are many miles from the actual trail. In 2005 the park service started publishing a series of "National Historic Trails Auto Tour Interpretive Guides" for the Oregon-California-Mormon and Pony Express trails. Each booklet, which more or less covers a state, describes the routes and associated major sites. They are presently published as far west as Utah, but when finished are scheduled to have booklets to the ends of the respective trails. Considering the total length of the route, it is a good way to follow the trail. But, if you really want a closer experience, then a good four-wheel drive vehicle with detailed local maps and good weather would be needed for the remote areas.

Although I can't say that I ever rode horseback over sections of the Pony Express Trail nor at the speed they probably traveled, I have ridden by both horse and wagon on small sections of other trails at wagon speed. For most of our trips our pony has either been a four-wheel drive Blazer or Suburban, which like most of the original express horses proved to be up for the task.

Ponies threw shoes, fell and sometimes went lame. Riders would have to get to the next station for another horse or home station for smithing facilities. We certainly had similar experiences with flat tires in Nevada and Wyoming. Service stations today can be much farther away than were the stations for the express riders. On one earlier trip we had to leave the trail and drive more than sixty miles to Wendover, Utah, for a new spare. By the time one was obtained and put on, it was two days later. On our last trip we took two spares, which proved to be a wise decision.

The express riders frequently commented about the loneliness of their job and the trail. On some sections of the trail, except for the brief exchanges at relay stations, the riders were alone with no means of communications if they ran into trouble. We've had similar experiences while driving along in sections in Wyoming, Utah and Nevada. On our last trip during a sixteen-hour drive we saw only one person. One weekend we met a father and son who realized they were about to run out of gas. By then we didn't have extra gas. We tried our cell phone and even On Star, but we could not get through in this remote area. After a few hours we arrived at Wendover, Nevada, got connected and were able to get help.

Just as the riders could have problems with gullies and streams, it can still happen today. Once when I took my Father on part of the trail we just barely made it across the Sweetwater River. It was much deeper than we had determined. On a much smaller creek we got stuck half way. We got out, but had to go back and find another crossing area. On the last trip with my wife we also got stuck in what appeared to be a shallow little creek, but it turned out to have a very muddy bottom. With the addition of some large rocks, sticks and sage brush pushed under, in front, and behind the wheels, we were able to get going and across. We even got a chance to see where Dad and I had gotten stuck years ago, but now the creek was dry.

Riding in a saddle for hours certainly was hard on the rider. Ask anyone who has taken a cross country trip today and they will attest to the fact that even riding in a car with a soft seat and air conditioning can be extremely difficult and tiring. And, if you're driving on a dry two track or dirt corduroy road even for a short distance, the experience can really shake you up.

Riders kept going twenty-four hours a day in all kinds of weather. Riding at night under a full moon and the bright stars could be beautiful. Keeping to the trail could be done, but in bad weather, day or night, it could be difficult. One afternoon we had been searching for the alternate trail near Butte Station, Nevada. By the time we found it, it was nearly evening. We drove as far as we could, and then I got out and hiked. By the time I arrived at the top, it was sundown and no time to explore. It was dark by the time I returned to the car. We drove back through the tall sage and cedars to the main trail and then all the way back to Schellbourne, Nevada. Remaining safely on the trail that night was quite a feat. Even in the desert areas rain storms can occur quickly and make primitive roads and the trail muddy and slippery. A few times we were thankful the rain lasted for only a few minutes. In the eastern part of the trail you need to follow the section line roads to approximate the trail. On one spring trip, while driving in Kansas we decided to take the farm and section roads to better follow the trail back to this one site we had visited sometime before. We knew it had rained in that area earlier, but all the roads looked dry from the highway. That turned out to be a mistake. After a quarter mile the car started to slip and slide and we ended up stuck in the mud. It was the heaviest mud I'd ever encountered. We did not use our Suburban on that trip, but even the truck that finally arrived to pull us out had trouble.

On the other hand, one can also enjoy the wonders of the trail. There are areas of the route that have changed very little. While some parts are in what might be considered a hostile environment, the scenery is absolutely gorgeous. Over the years we have camped out along the trail and spent some very pleasant nights—enjoying the stars and hearing the howling coyotes. Sometimes it's been in campgrounds, such as Rock Creek Station in Nebraska, while at other times we've pitched our tent along the Sweetwater in Wyoming, or in the deserts in Nevada. We've seen eagles soaring, wild horses galloping, deer running, and antelope scattering across our path. There is a certain appreciation or excitement derived when one finds or stands in a specific historic place. That is exactly what happened when I located where Richard Burton was in 1860 when he sketched his view of Carson Lake, and I could still see the shape of the trail far below, just as he had drawn it about a century and a half ago; or when I climbed the hills above Lake Tahoe in California and found the spot where I believe H.V. A. Von Bechk was in 1859 when he made his sketch. Standing in the ruins of Cold Springs Station, or in a spot on the trail in Egan's Canyon, can almost make you see what unfolded as you read firsthand accounts of events that happened in those very places.

While one can't experience everything, there is still enough out there to excite you!

And now, it's time to saddle up!

THE PONY RIDER

The mail's got to go through, boy—
    got to go through.
Do you sense what that means?
There'll be deserts to dare and
        rivers to swim,
And canyon defiles where Redskins
        may lurk
To cut short your run with a flint-
        headed shaft;
And you can't stop to fight—
You must ride, boy.
    Just like the wind.

Spare your horse?—yes and no;
Treat him square, boy, of course;
But the mail's got to go through,
    And it's up to the horse
    To carry it through
Though his heart thumps his side,
Get the best he can give
If he drops on the trail
    Just grab up the mail,
Get another and ride,
    Just ride like the wind.

Another thing—mark me—
    Let the liquor alone.
You'll need all your brains
    To win in this game;
And don't curse and swear;
You'd better keep God right close by
            your side,
Then you never can fail to bring through
        the mail.
I've your word. Here's my hand!
    Now just ride, boy,
        Just like the wind.

HOWARD R. DRIGGS

Howard R. Driggs Collection,
Sherratt Library, Southern Utah University

Chapter One

It Begins

W riters sometimes focus on the issue of which historical figure should be given credit for the idea of the Pony Express. Many different people have been suggested. Some include Ben Ficklin, California Senator William M. Gwin, Frederick Bee, William H. Russell, John Scudder, A. B. Miller and John Butterfield. Perhaps the concern should really be about who took the idea and brought it to fruition. On that writers and historians agree—William Russell and Senator Gwin. Even Alexander Majors credited Senator Gwin noting, "It turned out that Senator Gwin's original idea with reference to running a pony express from the Missouri River to Sacramento to prove the practicability of that route all seasons of the year was well taken. . .as the pony proved. . ." (44:167)

It was sometime in December 1859 or early January 1860 that William H. Russell, one of the partners in the firm of Russell, Majors and Waddell, and California Senator William M. Gwin met to discuss the need to improve communications between California and the East and how it could best be achieved. Both men concurred that the need was real and immediate and that a horse express system could provide that service. Gwin hoped to gain favor politically. Even though he was a Southern sympathizer, he believed that bringing in a mail service over the shorter central route would increase his popularity and ensure his chance of re-election or higher office. Russell believed that a successful horse express over the shorter central route would result in needed government mail and freighting contracts. He thought that Gwin, a member of the Senate Committee on Post Offices and Post

Roads, could provide the needed political influence, and probably the extra "wheeling and dealing" if it were needed, so they would be awarded the government contracts. The deal was made on Russell's word, and the responsibility fell to him to get the service running by April.

Russell's first major hurdle was to gain the support of his partners, Alexander Majors and William Waddell. We know from Majors that both partners were initially opposed to the plan because ". . .it could not be made to pay expenses." (44:183) Yet, Russell asked they reexamine the idea reminding them that they ". . .should stand by him, as he had committed himself to Senator Gwin. . .assuring him he could get his partners to join him, and that he might rely on the project being carried through. . ." (44:183)

Russell also spoke of Washington's lack of support for the central route because it had not been shown to be practicable during the winter and explained, "That as soon as we demonstrated the feasibility of such a scheme he (Senator Gwin) would use his influence with Congress to get a subsidy to help pay the expenses of such a line. . ."(44:183-4). Majors and Waddell realized that their partner had given his word and in the world of business "a man's word was his bond." In addition, if it worked out, their firm should get new government contracts since the central route was faster to California than the southern route, which at that time carried the mail contracts. "we concluded to sustain him in the undertaking." (44:184)

Before they made their plan public, it seems that word about a venture leaked out. A dispatch announced that the government was to open a horse relay between Placerville, California and St. Joseph, Missouri. While the facts were wrong, the general idea was correct. On January 27, 1860, Russell had sent a dispatch to his son John, the secretary of the Central Overland California and Pike's Peak Express Company (COC&PP) stating, "Have determined to establish a Pony Express to Sacramento, California commencing 3rd of April. Time ten days." John contacted the newspapers, and on January 30 the Leavenworth Daily Times headlines read "GREAT EXPRESS ADVENTURE FROM LEAVENWORTH TO SACRAMENTO IN TEN DAYS. CLEAR THE TRACK AND LET THE PONY COME THROUGH." (61:35) At that time the eastern terminus had not yet been selected. Russell, Majors and Waddell had their work cut out if

2

William H. Russell
—Pony Express National Museums

they were to keep their word. The fact that they did complete their task on time is a tribute to their organizational skills.

William H. Russell was almost forty eight years of age at the time. He was an experienced, respected member of the prestigious freighting firm of Russell, Majors and Waddell with a reputation for financial dealings. He started working in a dry goods store at the age of sixteen and married into a socially prominent family at the age of twenty-three. His first few attempts at business resulted in failure but by twenty-five he was the owner of a successful store in Lexington, Missouri. After the Mexican War his interests turned to freighting, and he became involved in the Santa Fe trade first with commercial goods and then military supplies. His first enterprise was a great success, but his next a failure. His reputation as a socialite, a successful trader, and risk-taker was being established. By the early 1850s his wealth and influence had grown. He became a partner with William Waddell, another successful businessman from Lexington. Then in 1855, they joined with Alexander Majors, their biggest competitor. That did not stop Russell from sometimes

Alexander Majors
—Pony Express National Museum

forming partnerships with other men as was the case when the Leavenworth and Pike's Peak Express Company was formed. It was said that Russell had an ego and was most at ease when in comfortable surrounding in the East, in the bank, the halls of Congress, or at parties. When the Pony Express was formed he was happy to take on the political aspects of the company.

Alexander Majors was the youngest of the partners. He was forty-five years old when the Pony Express began. He had married young and originally was engaged in farming. After his service in the Mexican

3

War he became involved in freighting over the Santa Fe Trail. He quickly became a dominant figure in the Santa Fe trade. Before he joined with Russell and Waddell in 1855, he was said to have employed more than 100 men with wagons and 1,200 oxen. He was a religious man and required his employees to take an oath and be given a Bible. This practice continued when Majors became partners with Russell and Waddell. Because of his years of hands-on experience with freighting, his primary duty with the Pony Express was to handle its organization and daily operations. After the Pony Express, Majors continued with the freighting business for a few years and then tried other businesses with little success. He later moved to Denver. The last of the founders, he died in 1900.

William B. Waddell

—Pony Express National Museum

William B. Waddell was the oldest member of the partnership. He was fifty-three when the Pony Express was organized. He was married by his early twenties and engaged in farming, but soon opened a dry goods store. He decided to move from Kentucky to Lexington, Missouri, which had become a major commercial center. There he prospered and became acquainted with William Russell. In 1852 Waddell and Russell became partners and expanded into the freighting business. In 1855 they joined forces with Alexander Majors and quickly became the dominant company in freighting. Waddell was responsible for daily operations and purchases and finances of the firm's offices in Leavenworth and then in St. Joseph. Both Waddell and Majors had a more conservative approach to business than did Russell. They were initially opposed to joining Russell when he expanded into running a stagecoach line to Denver, and were also opposed to the idea of the Pony Express. However, in both cases they were maneuvered into each enterprise. After the Pony Express, Waddell returned to Lexington, Missouri. His business problems, the fighting in Lexington, Missouri, and his declining health all took their toll. In 1872 he became the first of the founders to die. Some of his papers were saved.

These were the men who took the idea, ran with it and organized the Pony Express. The operation was too large to be run effectively by three men in Missouri. They had a little more than two months to meet Russell's promise to have the Pony Express operational by April. The task was immense. Some of the jobs which needed to be accomplished were to: obtain financing; select the specific route; determine station sites; procure or build necessary stations; hire the needed employees— riders, station keepers, stockmen, teamsters; purchase the needed stock—horses, mules, oxen; purchase needed supplies and equipment for their employees, stations and stock; disperse the employees and stock along the route; obtain and provide for the continuous supply of food and equipment for the employees and stock; and establish a system for the collection of the mail. Fortunately, they had recently acquired ownership of a stage line and had incorporated as the Central Overland California and Pike's Peak Express. They were able to use it and overlap the two systems. The organizational structure they used had one overall route manager. Then the route was divided into five divisions, each with its own superintendent.

Benjamin Ficklin was appointed the general superintendent for the trail. He had served in a similar position for the Leavenworth and Pike's Peak Stage Company in 1859. When it was taken over by the Central Overland California and Pike's Peak Express Company, he was the natural choice for the position. He acted as the overall manager which included establishing the stations along the route. Some stations had to be built, while in populated areas he could buy or rent the stations. He was also responsible for overseeing the five division superintendents. By July 1860, Ficklin was replaced by J. H. Clute.

The division superintendents were responsible for the hiring and firing of the riders and station keepers and stockmen, the stock for all their section stations, the food for both the men and the stock, and other supplies and equipment needed for the stations. Their pay was about ninety dollars a month which was less than the riders received. (43:15)

A. E. Lewis served as the Division I superintendent. His territory included the stations from St. Joseph to Fort Kearny. His office was probably at the Patee House. Little is known today about him. He was said to have traveled over his district using an odometer to check the mileage. It was based on this that J. H. Keetley's ride may have actually been the longest in the history of the Pony Express. (11:11-3) Many of the firm's documents may have been lost when some parts of St. Joseph were burned during the start of the Civil War.

Division II from Fort Kearny to Horseshoe Station was under the watchful eye and what might have been described as the iron handed rule of Joseph (Jack) Slade. By the time he was employed as Division II superintendent his reputation as a hard, no nonsense, fair—to those he liked, mean—to those who crossed him, skilled shooter and stage driver, and alcoholic was well established. [A new book that sheds new light on the facts and myths associated with Slade's life is Rottenberg's *Death of a Gunfighter.*] Slade had been earlier appointed division superintendent for the Leavenworth and Pike's Peak Express Company, and continued in the similar position once the Pony Express was established. His division's major problem was the actions of rustlers and thieves and was centered in the Julesburg area. It was his job to rid the area of them. The man thought responsible was Jules Reni who ran a local ranch at Overland City (Julesburg.) The stories of their feud, Slade's near death, his recovery, and the shooting and death of Jules was the talk of the West. Slade succeeded in bringing order to his division. He lived with his wife Maria Virginia (Dale) at the Horseshoe Station. After the demise of the Pony Express, Slade was retained in a similar position for the stage line. His drinking finally brought about his downfall, and he was hanged in 1864.

James E. Bromley was responsible for Division III – from Horseshoe Station to Salt Lake City.

He had driven stagecoaches for many years. He had been a driver for the Hockaday Company and served as its general superintendent before it was acquired. He continued working with Russell, Majors and Waddell until he was put in charge of Division III. After Benjamin Holladay took over in 1861, he continued in the same capacity.

Major Howard Egan was in charge of Division IV – Salt Lake City to Roberts Creek Station. Egan had been living in Utah for thirteen years. He had explored much of the area west of Salt Lake City in the early 1850s and had opened the route known locally as the Egan Trail. He also was employed as a stagecoach driver. He worked with George Chorpenning as superintendent for the section over the Egan Trail. When Chorpenning's company was taken over by Russell, Majors and Waddell in 1860, Egan was an obvious choice to be their manager.

Egan did "double duty." He served as division superintendent and station keeper at Deep Creek, and at times served as an express rider. When the Pony Express ended he continued to serve as the station keeper at Deep Creek for the Overland Mail Company. Some of the major problems in his section were associated with the Indians and the hostile conditions in this remote region.

Division V from Roberts Creek to Sacramento was supervised by Bolivar Roberts. He had come to Utah in 1850. He became familiar with the territory of the Great Basin. He had problems similar to Division IV, and the additional one of severe winter snows in the Sierra Nevada that could easily stop the mail. He resided at the Carson City Station.

TO SAN FRANCISCO IN EIGHT DAYS,
—BY—
THE CENTRAL OVERLAND CALIFORNIA
—AND—
PIKE'S PEAK EXPRESS CO.
—:o:—

The first courier of the Pony Express will leave the Missouri River on Tuesday, April 3, at 5 o'clock p. m. and will run regularly weekly thereafter, carrying a letter mail only. The point of departure on the Missouri River, will be in telegraphic connection with the East and will be announced in due time.

Telegraphic messages from all parts of the United States and Canada in connection with the point of departure will be received up to 5 o'clock p. m. of the day of leaving, and transmitted over the Placerville and St. Joseph telegraph wire to San Francisco and intermediate points, by the connecting express in eight days.

The letter mail will be delivered in San Francisco in ten days from the departure of the express. The Express passes through Forts Kearney, Laramie, and Bridger, Great Salt Lake City, Camp Floyd, Carson City, the Washoe Silver Mines, Placerville, and Sacramento.

Letters for Oregon, Washington Territory, British Columbia, the Pacific Mexican ports, Russian Possessions, Sandwich Islands, China, Japan and India, will be mailed in San Francisco.

Special messengers, bearers of letters to connect with the Express of the 3d of April, will receive communications for the courier of that day at No. 481 Tenth street, Washington City, up to 2:45 p. m. on Friday, March 30, and in New York at the office of J. B. Simpson, Room No. 8, Continental Bank Building, Nassau street, up to 6:30 a. m. of March 31.

Full particulars can be obtained on application at the above place and agents of the company.　　W. H. RUSSELL, President.

Leavenworth City, Kansas, March, 1860.

Office in New York, J. B. Simpson, Vice President.

Samuel & Allen, Agents, St. Louis.

H. J. Spaulding, Agent, Chicago.

New York Herald, March 26, 1860 (56:107)

William H. Finney served as the general agent for the Central Overland and Pikes Peak Express in San Francisco. His area was between San Francisco and Sacramento, but some say it extended into the Sierra Nevada which was generally under Bolivar's jurisdiction. He was responsible for the early advertisements for men, stock and equipment, service and organization during the first few months. He was replaced in September 1860 by W. C. Marley from Buckland's Station.

The horse and rider made up the team that was in possession of the mail as it crossed the country. Each was crucial and required certain characteristics. Majors recalled that initially ". . .the services of over two hundred competent men were secured. Eighty of these men were selected as express riders." (44:174) It has been estimated that about

Daily Evening Bulletin, March 18, 1860

Pony Express National Museum

MEN WANTED! The undersigned wishes to hire ten or a dozen men, familiar with the management of horses, as hostlers, or riders, on the Overland Express Route via Salt Lake City. Wages $50 per month and found. I may be found at the St. George Hotel during Sunday, Monday and Tuesday.
WILLIAM W. FINNEY

This notice in the *Sacramento Union* is reportedly the only authentic ad uncovered by the 1990s (4:12)

200 men, perhaps more, were employed as riders during the Pony's history.

THE RIDERS

Perhaps one of the most recognized "documents" of the Pony Express is the advertisement for riders with "orphans preferred." It is the basis for comments by writers about how orphans were sought and preferred. However, it appears that this ad is more "folklore" than fact. No evidence of the ad has been found from 1860. It seems to have made its appearance in the twentieth century. It appears more like a composite of things that represent the ideas often thought of as desirable. The figure was drawn by artist Aaron Steindel. (It was used by writer Mary Pack in a 1923 article about riders in *The Union Pacific Magazine*.) (43:105) Bronco Billy, who asserted to have been a rider, at times claimed to have been an orphan. Based on the names and records of known riders, it seems few were true orphans. It should be noted that at the time life expectancy rates were low, and it would not have been uncommon for a person to have lost one parent by the time they were in their twenties. Majors did not state that they preferred orphans, but he did refer to "the thin, wiry, and hard pony-riders." (44:174) Perhaps that was the origin of the "young, skinny, wiry fellows.

Describing the individuals Majors recalled, "Light-weights were deemed the most eligible for the purpose; the lighter the man the better for the horse.(44:174) Billy Campbell had been employed by Russell, Majors and Waddell as a teamster and was working on the Platte. Campbell also had a good reputation as an expert rider and Charlie White, the station keeper at Cottonwood Station suggested Billy apply. He recalled, "They turned me down at first. They wanted strong lads of one hundred to one hundred twenty pounds at the most,

Rider Richard "Ras" Egan. - *International Society of Daughters of Utah Pioneers*

whereas, I weighed one hundred forty pounds, which wasn't much for a six-footer. But they had a place for me soon." (25:54) "Not only were they remarkable for their lightness of weight and energy, but their service required continual vigilance, bravery, and agility. Among their number were skillful guides, scouts and couriers, accustomed to adventures and hardships on the plains—men of strong wills and wonderful powers of endurance." (44:175)

Age was another consideration. Young men were considered to be the most physically fit. They were also more likely to fit the weight requirements. David R. Jay, age thirteen, was probably the youngest rider. Bronco Billy, who claimed to be a rider, was only eleven when he said he started. Based on a limited sampling of fifty-six riders, the mean or statistical average was 21.4 years. While the youngest was thirteen, the oldest, Major Howard Egan, was forty-five. The mode/median was twenty, with the majority twenty or under.

Riders were expected to be good horseman. Thomas O. King recalled that the express "required the best riders and physically able to stand the strains of endurance by day or night and in all kinds of weather and other dangers. (14:203). Elijah Maxfield, who rode in Nebraska, recalled how they separated the tenderfoots from the riders.

The applicants were given a horse to ride, "Old Roane," a mean old horse. If they could stay on for three minutes, they were hired. (43:93)

Majors wanted "hard" young riders who had stamina and endurance. King recounted, "In those days I did not know what it was to be tired. I rode the 145 miles in 13 hours and can very well remember taking a lady out to see Friends that evening." (14:204) The riders were expected to be hardy and honorable. Billy Campbell commented that the severe winter storms and blizzards really tested them. He remembered riding through storms. He remember coming to the relay stations noting, "we generally jumped off and grabbed up a few cookies and a cup of hot coffee to thaw us out a bit for the next freezing stretch; then off we would go again." Another time he arrived at his home station after riding through the trail covered with three feet of snow. He just wanted to warm up and sleep, but the relief rider hadn't arrived. He noted, "I had given my word of honor to put the mail through; so I mounted a fresh horse and struggled on, until I finally reached the next station and turned it over to another rider." He had a good meal and slept for eighteen hours. (19:178)

The pay for the riders was $100 to $150 a month plus room and board. Based on of some stories the company may have given a bonus for extra or dangerous rides. (6:55) Sometimes bonuses were provided by California businesses for record times. These were usually tied to significant events about the Civil War or presidential speeches. Sacramento businessmen provided $300 to be split among the riders for the faster delivery for the news about the Battle of Antietam. (56:111) San Francisco newspaper men offered a gold watch to the rider with the best record in the western division when Lincoln's speech was delivered. (56:117)

The trail was hard on the riders. Wilson noted "Not many riders could stand the long, fast riding at first, but after about two weeks they would get hardened to it." (76:141) Very few of the riders initially hired were still with the express when it ended. Jack Keetley was one who rode during the whole time.(73:22) Theodore Rand was another one. (73:25) and Bill Cates who rode out of Cottonwood Springs was another. (12:232) Most riders' employment lasted only a few months. Perhaps only a dozen or so were employed from its start until its finish. The conditions the riders faced were hard—hard on both the body and the mind. They took their toll on the men. The conflicts with the Indians, primarily those in the West—the Paiutes, the Goshutes, Bannocks and the Shoshoni, led a number of riders to resign. While the Sioux sometimes caused problems for the riders in the central plains sections, Campbell remembered, "they didn't bother me at all. . . .It was three or four years later that they broke out. . ."(19:177) Some Indians had been hired and worked faithfully as stockmen at the stations. Campbell noted, "In fact several Sioux were employed as stock tenders at some stations. The men at the stations never failed to have a horse ready

William "Billy" Fisher. - *International Society of Daughters of Utah Pioneers.*

when a rider arrived." (12:231) Charley Cliff, who was stationed farther east, recalled, "Not a bit. You see the only Indians we came in contact with at this end of the trail had been tamed. . .I had to cross the Kickapoo reservation on my run; but they never gave me any bother at all. It wasn't until after the Pony Express. . . ." (19-163) Accidents and sickness caused some riders to quit, but there were also other reasons. Billy Campbell was hired November 1, 1860 as a replacement for a rider who had resigned. He rode in the Kansas – Nebraska area. He recalled, "Many quit rather than ride in winter both because of weather condition and on account of it being a lonesome job." (25:67-8) Winters were terrible. It was not uncommon for the riders to face blizzards and subzero weather. Sometimes they were forced to ride as long as twenty-four hours before relief.

The Pony Express rider is often portrayed as lonely, a lone figure riding in the middle of nowhere over long distances for long periods of time without coming in contact with other people. The riders themselves describe their position as such. Billy Campbell recalled, "it being a lonesome job." (25:68) However, their route followed the heavily trafficked trails. The traffic included: thousands of emigrants heading to new homes, thousands of miners off to the rich mineral fields in California, Nevada, Colorado, and Montana; freighters bringing hundreds of wagons loaded with supplies for the military, the mines, and civilian stores; stagecoaches with passengers off to visit another part of the country; men and wagons hauling telegraph poles and wire; and herds of animals as additional teams or headed to distant markets. Riders mentioned how they were forced to cut off the trail or to slow down because there was no space left on the trail to keep up their speed. These accounts seem to be at odds with each other, but they are not.

Most of the traffic described happened during the summer months. Rider Billy Campbell noted, "In the summertime the trail was thick with freight wagons, prairie schooners, and emigrants going to the mines and things were lively, but in the winter this westward trek stopped."(25:67-8) Even during the summer when traffic was heavy it was not congested equally over the whole length of the trail. The congested portion moved along the trail as did the traffic. Any particular section would be congested for only a month or two and then thinned out. Riders were not supposed to stop and talk with others. Emigrant and travelers' diaries and journals include accounts of riders passing quickly by, but not of conversations. During the winter the emigrants and miners which accounted for tens of thousands could not travel. The grasses that sustained their draft animals had died or were under several feet of snow. Most of the freighting companies stopped or severely reduced shipments and few animals were driven over the trail for these reasons. Traffic could still be heavy in the populated areas, but those were few. Severe snowstorms could blanket areas and make travel over the trail almost impossible and snow stations in for days.

The riders were assigned to specific stations and sections. The number of people residing at the stations was typically two, to perhaps five. Riders were not to go far. Nick Wilson recalled, "When we were hired to ride the express, we had to go before a justice of the peace and swear we would be at our post at all times, and not go farther than one hundred yards from the station except when carrying the mail." (76:140) That seems a little too restrictive, but the fact was they had to be ready to take their ride as soon as the other rider came. They could not be off visiting miles or days away. The stations and stock required constant care and vigilance especially during the period of Indian conflict. The men were dependent on each other. The variety of entertainment was limited to a few games such as checkers, cards and perhaps reading. Drinking probably occurred and may have contributed to the few recorded fights among employees.

Many of the stations were far from populated areas and a rider was acquainted only with the people at the station and those others on their run. When interviewed later in life, some riders commented on how they may have heard the names of others associated with the Pony Express, or met some later, but when they were employed they knew only of

Pony rider Johnny Fry.
— *Pony Express National Museum*

the ones near their stations. Charlie Cliff who rode out of St. Joseph was asked about how many riders he knew, he replied, "Not many. You see, we got acquainted only with the ones we chased out! But I was well acquainted with Jack Keatly. . . .I met Buffalo Bill here when we dedicated the monument to mark the spot where the first express started from." (19:162) Thus, it seems true, that amidst the crowds the job was lonesome.

In one sense travel today may be lonelier than when the Pony rode. In parts of Nevada where express stations were about ten to twenty-five miles apart, today gas stations and motels may be almost a hundred miles apart.

The Ponies

The horse, as the means of transportation, was the central element in the relay system. It was expected to withstand all sorts of conditions. It had to carry the mail and the rider safely in all kinds of weather, in the day or night, over all types of terrain, for long periods of time, and had to be strong and fast enough to outrun anything that might chase it. It was expected to act in concert with its rider. The horse had to be hardy, surefooted, swift, and reliable.

Alexander Majors noted, "Five hundred of the fleetest horses to be procured were immediately purchased."(44:173-4) On February 10, 1860, only about two weeks after the Pony Express became public John Jones placed an ad in the Leavenworth *Daily Times* for "two hundred grey mares, from four to seven years old, not to exceed fifteen hands high, well broke to saddle, and warranted sound, with black hoofs, and suitable for running the overland Pony Express." (62:79) Many of the ones selected were Army stock. Billy Campbell remembered, "along the trail through Kansas and Nebraska we had mostly good Kentucky stock. It was a joy to ride these intelligent animals," (19-176) In Utah, A. B. Miller purchased two hundred more horses.(58:47) and others were purchased in California. Majors noted, "The horses were mostly half-breed California mustangs, as alert and energetic as their riders, and their part in the service—sure-footed and fleet—was invaluable. (44:175). Root noted, "The ponies ridden. . .were California mustangs, in their day considered the fleetest of animals in that part of the country." On March 19 Finney left Sacramento to stock the express line to Eagle Valley with about 100 horses and twenty-nine mules. The average price for most horses at that time was about $50.00, but the express needed the best horses, and Russell was willing to pay more for them. He paid between $150 and $200 per mount. (61:44) For the estimated 500 horses purchased that would have cost about $87,500.00. Frank Root recalled, "A few of the steeds, however, were the some small, hardy Mexican animals, very fleet and particularly safe for mountain travel."(56:112) While swift horses were the norm, Billy Campbell remembered that he sometimes rode a mule. (25:70)

Campbell noted, "The men who brought the horses knew their business. Sometimes we used to say that the company had bought up every mean, bucking, kicking horse that could be found, but they were good stock and could outrun anything along the trail." (12:228)

The riders were not expected to stop or fight the Indians, but to outrun them. For that reason the express horses were also given grain and more hay to ensure their strength.

Thomas Owen King, one of the original riders recounted how reliable and dependable the ponies were. He recalled, "Many a time Henry Worley and I passed each other on the road both of us fast asleep. . . .our horse were so used to the road and the gait of going and we were so used to riding that it was easy for us to frequently doze

14

off. . ."(14:203) Nick Wilson understood the importance of his horses and fondly remembered them. One such was Black Billy who arrived carrying his rider and the mail, but also two arrows—one in his flank and another in his shoulder. Another mount, American Boy, was a "high-spirited" animal always ready to go. Once during the change of horses the rider was slow in getting on and American Boy took off running all the way to the next station with the mochila, but no rider. (19:63-4)

Just as the runs were hard on the riders and most lasted only a few months, the same was true for the horses. Nick Wilson noted, "Everything went along first rate for a while, but after about six or eight months of that work, the big, fine horses began to play out, and then the company bought up a lot of wild horses from California, strung them along the road and put the best riders to breaking them."(76:141) "Wash" Perkins, another rider, recalled the incident involving the horse that he rode while delivering Lincoln's inaugural message. Since some of the stations had been wiped out, a longer run than normal was required. "I had to put him through pretty hard to make the close schedule they had set for us. Well, we made it all right, but it cost the life of that horse." (19:109) It seems that even the horses were dedicated to getting the mail through, no matter what.

THE SADDLE, MOCHILA & THE MAIL

This sketch is of the type of saddle the Pony Express used as described by express rider William Cates. It depicts a rather bare boned saddle when compared with the western saddles associated with cowboys and cattle drives. No known Pony Express saddles are at present known to exist. Since speed was of prime importance, the saddle was meant to be sturdy but light, easy on the horse, and able to easily accommodate the mochila. The comfort of the rider was of secondary importance, but the saddle's construction was meant to keep the rider in the saddle and the mail safe. Nicholas Wilson described them, "Our saddles, which were all provided by the company, had nothing to them but the bare tree, stirrups, and a cinch." (76:140) In San Francisco, the April 3, 1860, *Daily Evening Bulletin* described the saddle as, "The broad saddle, wooden stirrups, immense flappers to guard the rider's feet, and the girth that knows no buckle, were of the sort customary in California for swift horsemen who appreciate mud."

Israel Landis of St. Joseph, Missouri, is believed to have been the maker of most of the saddles used. The horn was short and broad, the cantle was low and sloping, the skirt was minimal, and the stirrups were with or without tapaderas. (12:86) There are, however, some saddles made by Israel or his son John Landis that exist that fit the general description and may date from the time of the Pony Express. The modern reproductions used in many of the museum displays are based on the descriptions provided by some of the riders. There are some who question whether the holes on the cantle existed on the original saddles. There was a saddle for each relay horse and

From The Pony Express by Arthur Chapman

probably extras at the stations. Saddles were never changed. When a rider came in, the horse was saddled and ready to go. This saved an enormous amount of time.

The picture of the rider fording a stream is believed to be the earliest known drawing of a Pony Express rider. Notice that the depiction of the mochila with its two cantinas on the side. It seems to be quite accurate. Note also the inclusion of tapaderas on the stirrups as depicted on the sketch of the saddle and mentioned in the news article. In most of the other early depictions the riders are often shown with a large bag of mail hung over one side of the horse or with saddle bags behind the saddle on the pony.

The mochila doubled as the mantle over the saddle tree and the mail container. The whole system weighed thirteen pounds, about one-third as much as a regular western saddle. (12:86) Cutouts enabled the pommel or horn and saddle cantle to fit through. That allowed for its easy removal when the rider changed horses. Riders were given two minutes to change the mochila and horses. (44:175) That allowed only a few seconds for the rider to grab some needed food and water. However, Frank Root noted, "but so expert had the "pony" boys become in the business of changing animals that it was usually made in about fifteen seconds." (56-116)

Nicholas Wilson described the mochila as "Two large pieces of leather about sixteen inches wide by twenty four long were laced together with a strong leather string thrown over the saddle. Fastened to these were four pockets or cantinas, two in front and two behind; these hung on each side of the saddle. The two hind ones were the largest. The one in the front on the left side was called the 'way pocket.'

)L. V.   JULY, 1860.   No.

THE PONY EXPRESS.

SWIMMING THE STORM-SWOLLEN STREAM.

California State Library

All of these pockets were locked with small padlocks and each home station keeper had a key to the 'way pocket.' Only the keepers at the beginning and the end had the key for the other three. When the express arrived at the home station, the keeper would unlock the 'way pocket' and if there were any letters for the boys between the home stations, the rider would distribute them as he went along. There was also a card in the way pocket that the keeper would take out and write on it the time the express arrived and left his station. If the express was behind time, he would tell the rider how much time he had to make up." (76:140)

It was reported that keys were also kept in Salt Lake. When the telegraph line had been completed to Fort Kearny, it soon replaced St. Joseph as the telegram pickup and delivery point. They were sealed by the operator and placed with the mail not to be opened until delivered to the western end. It would seem logical that the station keepers at the two ends of the telegraph line also had a key or the dispatches were placed in the way pocket cantina.

The rider sat on the mochila holding everything in place. The mochila could carry about twenty pounds of mail. Majors stated, "The weight to be carried by each was fixed at ten pounds or under. . ." (44:175) However, most others put the weight at twenty pounds. Billy Campbell remembered, "We carried about twenty pounds of express. . . ."(25:68)

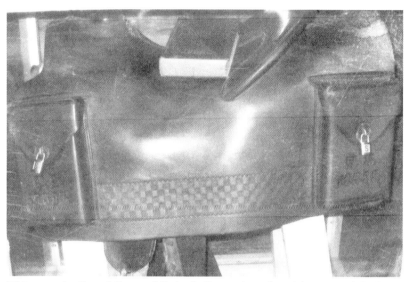

This reproduction of the mochila is similar to those found in many of the Pony Express related museums. No historic Pony Express mochilas are known to exist. In 1961 Harold Warp had the Wyeth Hardware and Saddlemaking Company of St. Joseph, Missouri, make this mochila, reportedly based on the same pattern that had been used for Majors and Waddell in 1860. Israel Landis was also the maker of the original mochilas. William A. Cates, an express rider in Nebraska, reportedly designed the leather mochila, or at least one that was made later for a celebration (52:104) - *Mochila display at Harold Warp's Pioneer Village -Hill*

It is estimated that the Pony Express made 308 trips and carried about 34,753 pieces of mail during its run. That would place the average at about 113 pieces per run. Billy Campbell remembered sometimes carrying perhaps 200 to 250. (25:68) Frank Root, the Atchison postal clerk reported the express delivered about 350 items on each run during the last few weeks. (56:117). Assuming those are accurate, some riders must have carried very few pieces of mail. The first mail west was comprised of forty-nine letters, nine telegrams, and several newspapers. Most went to San Francisco, while eight letters went to Sacramento, two for the newspaper *Daily Union* and one for Governor John G. Downey. The first east bound mail included eighty-five letters from San Francisco and more were added at Sacramento. The relationship of the volume of west/east mail continued. More mail came east than went west. Approximately 23,356 items were sent east, 18,456 items from San Francisco and about 4,900 from

Sacramento. Approximately 11,397 pieces of mail left St. Joseph, San Francisco received 9,553 and Sacramento 1,844. One mochila was lost. (61:196)

It is assumed by many that the mail carried by the Pony Express was comprised of letters from ordinary people to their friends and loved ones. That is not accurate. That's not to say that it never happened, it is just that it was generally too expensive for most people. When it began, rates were $10.00 per ounce or $5.00 for a half ounce or less. For that reason even business communications were generally short. Later, rates were lowered to $2.00 per ounce and $1.00 for a half ounce or less, but they were still expensive for ordinary people, and the volume of mail did not seem to change substantially to make it profitable. The charge for letters sent by sea or by stage cost much less, only ten cents per half ounce, the cost of the stamp. For the Pony special thin paper was used, especially for the newspapers in order to keep their weights down. Majors noted the cantinas "were filled with important business letters and press dispatches from eastern cities and San Francisco, printed upon tissue paper, and thus especially adapted by their weight for this mode of transportation." (44:174) Mail was wrapped tightly in oiled soaked silk to keep it dry during wet weather or stream crossings. Official government dispatches and letters, both state and national, going to or from California or the Orient were also carried. The new contract in the summer of 1861 also required the express to carry up to five pounds of government mail free of charge. (25:81) Some European nations also made use of the Pony Express in sending their dispatches to the Orient.

Newspapers such as the San Francisco *Daily Evening Bulletin* printed lists of those receiving mail so community members would know what was delivered. The names were sent by telegraph from Carson City. Here is the list for one of the last deliveries October 29, 1861.

Normal delivery time was set at ten days for letters and eight for telegrams. However, during the winter months the time was extended to twelve to sixteen days. The fastest delivery was seven days, seventeen hours when the Pony carried Lincoln's first inaugural address.

THE BIBLE & THE OATH

Alexander Majors was the partner most associated with both the Bible and the oath. It was a practice that he had used earlier before the existence of the Pony Express with his employees. It read: "While I am an employee of A. Majors, I agree not to use profane language, not to get drunk, not to gamble, not to treat animals cruelly, and not to do anything else that is incompatible with the conduct of a gentleman. And, I agree, if I violate any of the above conditions, to accept my discharge without any pay for my services." When the Pony Express was established and employees selected, they too were expected to take an oath. The version was very similar: "I, (name), do hereby swear, before the Great and Living God, that during my engagement, and while an employee of Russell, Majors, and Waddell, I will, under no circumstances, use profane language, that I will drink no intoxicating liquors; that I will not quarrel or fight with any other employee of the firm, and that in every respect I will conduct myself honestly, be faithful to my duties, and so direct all my acts as to win the confidence of my employer. So help me God."

Daily Evening Bulletin, October 29, 1861

During a later interview Billy Campbell said, "I took the pledge he extracted of all the boys; received my little leather-bound Bible (which I have yet), and after thanking him, went out walking on air—a full fledged pony rider." (19:175) Only a few of those Bibles are known to exist. The one shown here is part of an exhibit in the Lexington Museum in Missouri.

Based on the oath, one would assume that few employees ever drank alcohol or got drunk. However, the reality of the West would seem to lead to a different conclusion. First, note the slight

Majors presentation Bible - *Hill photo*

difference in the oaths. One says "not to get drunk," while the other says to "drink no intoxicating liquor." There is a difference between drinking and getting drunk. Even our state laws distinguish between them. Having a drink, being impaired or being completely disabled are not the same. Perhaps the employees interpreted it the same way.

Richard Burton met Alexander Majors in St. Joseph. He wrote, "His meritorious efforts to reform the morals of the land have not yet put forth even the bud of promise. He forbad his drivers and employés to drink, gamble, curse, and travel on Sundays; he desired them to peruse the Bibles distributed to them gratis; and though he refrained from lengthy proclamation commanding his lieges to be good boys and girls, he did not the less expect it of them. Results: I scarcely ever saw a sober driver; as for profanity—the Western equivalent for hard swearing—they would make the blush of shame crimson the check of the old Isis bargee." (9:8) It should be pointed out that Pony Express riders did ride on Sunday as did the freight wagon trains. As it will become evident, alcohol was always available at many of the stations. Since the water in many stations was so foul, perhaps alcohol was the only safe liquid to drink. Also, drinking or being allowed to drink was the

Daily Evening Bulletin, April 18, 1860

21

social norm, although this was truer for men than for women. The archaeological work done on the two stations in Nevada indicated that the greatest number of artifacts unearthed after animal bone fragments were liquor bottles. This finding tended to correspond to studies of two other sites in Nevada. (29:120) Perhaps this indicates just how difficult and lonely the conditions were for the employee on the stations.

Going back to the concept of degree of impairment, the example of Jack Slade is most relevant. Slade served in a number of significant positions with the C.O.C. & P.P and Pony Express. He served as an assistant and then as superintendent for one of the divisions. He successfully brought order to his region, was known for his skill at driving coaches, horses, and had the respect of most of his employees. Yet, it was known that he drank and drank heavily at times, yet he kept his job with the Pony Express. William Streeper, who delivered the regular mail and sometimes rode as an alternate, recalled at least one incident where one Pony rider was drunk on the job. Streeper, in fact, picked the rider up off the road and brought him in. Fortunately, the mail was recovered. He did note however, that after that incident he never did see the rider on the trail again. (18:162-3) The reality it seems was that if one fulfilled his responsibilities, stayed out of trouble and the mail got through, drinking was not a major concern, nor a threat to one's job. This does not, however, mean that every employee drank.

It is clear from comments that some riders did not use alcohol. Perhaps it was because of the oath, or because of their personal moral or religious beliefs or even a combination of all of them. Billy Campbell recalled, "Nebraska was pretty rough. . . .Often I heard . . .'Step up here, Pony Boy, and have a drink.' I never had any trouble when I refused. The only comment would be: 'Well, you're a funny feller to be runnin' around out here in this country.' Just the same, I was glad for my Presbyterian bringing up." (12:230)

It seems that there may have been an addition made to the oath that is rarely mentioned. James Bromley, the Division III superintendent recalled, "After the Civil War broke out an additional pledge of loyalty to the Union was added." (7:61)

The Stations

Over the years historians and writers have provided different figures for the number of Pony Express stations. While that may be troubling, arriving at a particular calculation is very difficult. The Pony Express enterprise was in an almost constant state of flux. Stations were often being added, some as replacements, some as new ones. Stations were destroyed and some abandoned. Sometimes those events occurred at the same time. A temporary station might be replaced by another structure in the same area, as occurred at Simpson's, or perhaps a mile away station as occurred at Canyon Station. Did that constitute one or two stations? If a tent such as the one at Simpson's, or a dugout or a wood station, was replaced by an adobe or stone structure such as at Simpson's, was that considered to be one or two stations? Government contracts usually identified the number of contract stations, but since the Pony Express used additional relay or swing stations, that posed a problem. If the names of stations were relied upon, they also seemed to have differed depending on who was writing about them and when. In addition, some people often used local names. Such is the case for Simpson's, Simpson's Springs, Lost Springs, Egan's Springs, or Pleasant Springs all of which refer to the same place. Sometimes stations were known by the name of the person who owned, occupied, or managed them. Thus, when ownership changed so did its name, e.g., Miller's became Reed's—or at least it did for some people. Travelers passing through and not being familiar with the area, have been known to incorrectly label a place. Later, stations were strengthened and their numbers increased for additional safety as happened after the Paiute War. Others may have been added for increased efficiency so the distance between stations was only about ten miles apart, as occurred in the summer of 1861 with the change in management/ownership. These are some of the problems encountered in the effort to determine the number of stations. The number of stations cited by the National Parks is eighty-six when it began and 147 by mid-1861. By the end of the express, the number could have grown to between 190 and 200, but some may not have been used.

The actual placement of a station was crucial to the smooth successful running of the express. One of the earliest stage lines to cross the country relied on the same coach and team to make the entire journey. It was cheaper that way, but the trip took longer. It necessitated the coach to stop every few hours to rest the horses or mules. The speed of the horses and their endurance was the key to the Pony Express. The environment and terrain had an impact on the horse's speed and how much fatigue it suffered. This was also true for the rider. Those factors influenced the placement of the stations. The more water and feed were nearby, the better it was for a station. If not they would have to be brought to the selected location.

Once the mail had been delivered to east and west terminuses and packed in the cantinas, that particular mochila was carried all the way across the route. It never changed, but the horse and rider carrying it did. This was accomplished by the use of two types of stations. One was the *home station*, and the other, the *relay* or *swing station*. At the onset Majors recalled, "The distance between relay riders' stations (home stations) varied from sixty-five to one hundred miles and often more. . . ." (44:175) "Relays were established at stations, the distance between which was, in each instance, determined by the character of the country." (44:175)

Home stations were usually larger, built stronger with better living accommodations than relay stations. There were usually two rooms, sometimes three or four, with perhaps a small kitchen area in the rear. Muslin was often used as room partitions. (56:605-6) These stations are where one rider ended his run, handing off the mochila to another rider with a new mount. The rider who completed his run normally was able to rest for a few days until the next mail came through. Besides the station keeper, there were two or more stock tenders and two or more riders who lived there while not on a run. If the station doubled as a stage station it would have additional stock tenders. Blacksmith facilities had to be on site for their own stock and for those of the nearby relay stations. They were usually located close to a good supply of water and meadows. Sometimes hay, and even water, had to be brought to the nearby relay stations.

The swing stations tended to be smaller with fewer hands than the home stations. This was where the rider changed horses and continued on with the mochila. The station, as with home stations, had a corral and a stable for its stock, hay stacks, and was near a water source or had water brought in. The men, usually no more than two, stayed in a variety of structures, frequently minimal in both size and furnishings. Most swing stations were one level and had only one room. (56:605-6)

Because the relay stations were usually manned by two individuals, the stations were harder to defend and were more vulnerable to attacks.

In the eastern section the stations tended to be of adobe or horizontal log construction, sometimes a frame building or dugout. West of Salt Lake to the Sierra Nevada they could be dugouts, adobe or horizontal or upright log construction, tents using canvas or brush, dry rock of local stones, or wooden frame structures as in the towns. West of the Sierra they tended to be of wooden frame construction.

By 1859 road ranches were beginning to be established in the Platte River Valley. Some of the owners were hoping to supplement the income from their newly acquired farm/ranch lands by providing some services, while others were hoping to make a living by serving the emigrant and growing commercial and stagecoach traffic that was starting to dominate the old emigrant roads. Most of these were not ranches as we know them today. One traveler, James Meline, explained "a ranche is not a dwelling, nor a farm-house, nor a store, nor a tavern, but all of these, and more. It is connected with a large corral, and capable of standing an Indian siege. You can procure entertainment at them. . .liquors, canned fruit, knives, playing-cards, saddlery and goggles . ." (46:271) Merrill Mattes puts the approximate number of ranches by the early 1860s as approximately thirty-five along the 200-mile stretch from Fort Kearny to Julesburg. East of Fort Kearny the area was also being settled with ranches and farms. Some of those ranches were quickly and easily incorporated into the relay station system without the great outlay of additional time, effort and capital. Since Russell, Majors, and Waddell had only about three months to organize the whole system, some of the established ranches were easily incorporated into their relay system. They were also able to incorporate some of the stage stations which they had acquired when they took over ownership of other companies.

In the western half of the trail fewer establishments of any kind existed that could be adapted for use. From Salt Lake City the Mormons had spread out into the surrounding areas of present-day Wyoming and Utah. Some of their dwellings came to be used as stations. But in the area west of Salt Lake City into the Central Basin areas of Nevada, few dwellings had been established or were available for easy inclusion into the relay system. This was also the most difficult area in terms of available water, timber, pasture, food and safety. Because of the various gold and silver rushes, once the Sierra Nevada was reached, sites were again available for inclusion and were usually pre-existing stage or freighting inns.

Because the stage and the Pony Express overlapped, many of the stations were used by both. Burton, commenting on the stage stations, noted that "at each station on this road, averaging twenty-five miles apart—the forks of the Platte they lengthen out by one-third—are three teams of four animals, with two extras, making a total of fourteen, besides two ponies for the express riders." (9:18) Mules were preferred over horses for use with the stagecoaches

It was up to the five division superintendents to establish, man, maintain, supply and repair all the stations within their jurisdiction. Although each had his own residence at a particular home station, each could be found moving back and forth, often unannounced, along the trail in their division. For them, their jobs were never done.

THE EQUIPMENT – WEAPONS & A HORN

For the Pony Express to be successful the mail had to go through and the riders and stations had to be protected. Attacks by Indians quickly became a major concern for the Pony Express and a problem for the riders and stations. The Paiute or Pyramid Lake War broke out five weeks after the Pony started. The physical station itself was expected to provide some of the needed protection. But the attacks proved how vulnerable the stations were, especially those that were quickly built. When it was determined they needed fortifying, improvements were made: walls added or thickened, gun-ports added, and sometimes stations moved. The military was called upon to provide and expand their patrols. Some soldiers were stationed at some of the stations.

All the riders and station hands had weapons. A rifle, two pistols, and a bowie knife were the typical arms for a rider when the Pony began. It seems the station keeper and hands had similar weapons. Rifles were more accurate over longer distances, but more cumbersome for riders to use than for station keepers and stock tenders. Three rifles frequently identified with the Pony Express were the Spencer carbine, the "Mississippi" rifle, and Sharp's carbine. During the Paiute War Finney asked the residents of Sacramento for "20 Sharpe's rifles, and as many dragoon pistols."(4:19) Records indicate the Army provided the Pony with about twenty five Sharp's carbines and sixty Model

1841.54 caliber "Mississippi" rifles. The Sharp's carbines could have been the 1852, 1853, or 1859 models. According to some firearm historians, the Spencer carbine was not available until after the express ended. While most riders soon left their rifle because of the added weight, Andrew Anderson is said to have carried his. (6:19)

Nick Wilson, a rider, recounted, "If he had no revolver, and had to get one from the company, that would add another heavy expense to be deducted from his wages." (76:141) The types mentioned carried were the .36 caliber Navy Colt model 1851 six-shoot percussion; Wells Fargo Colt .31 caliber five-shoot percussion; and the .44 caliber, Dragoon Colt. Burton recounted that one of the express riders carried two colts and that he preferred, "the dragoon or large size, considering all others too small." (9:518) One hundred twenty-five of the Dragoon Colts were supplied by the Army and some citizens during the Paiute War.

However, the best protection the rider had in case of attack was his horse. Root noted, "In a race for life on the plains, the pony riders, mounted on their fleet animals, could soon leave the redskins far in the rear. It took the Indians only a short time to learn that they were not in it in such a race." (57:124) Alex Carlyle recalled how his grain-fed horse Wintle was able to outrun the Indians chasing them. However, upon arrival at the next station Wintle dropped dead. (61:110) It was easier for one person to outrun a party of Indians than to outfight them. If he had the fastest horse, he could escape from all of them, but it would be more difficult to out shoot all of them. The riders probably realized that fact rather quickly because it seems that many riders didn't carry their rifles, some left one of the guns and began carrying a one or two extra loaded cylinders, and some, at times, even went without a gun on their runs.

Billy Campbell commented about another item provided, "Each rider at the outset was given a horn to blow as he approached the station. This was to warn the station keepers to have fresh mounts ready. Usually, however, they could hear the hoof-beats of our ponies about as far as they could the horn." (19:177) That may explain why the riders didn't carry the horns as time went on. But there were other uses for the horn. Billy Campbell also recalled using his horn for something else. During one bad snow storm, Billy ran by a pack of wolves who soon gave chase. He had loaned his pistol to another

Ft. Kearny display of pistol carried by Richard Cleve who rode the section between the fort and Cottonwood Springs. - *Hill photo*

rider earlier that day and now had a situation where it would have been useful. As he rode in the heavy snow the pack of wolves came closer. Fearing for his mount and himself, and having no weapons, he resorted to blowing his horn at the wolves to frighten them whenever they got too close. It worked, and he made it to the next station safely with the mail. (19:180)

Pony Express rider in the snow. - *Jackson, Harold Warp Pioneer Village*

Pony Express riders. - *Pony Express National Museum*

The picture above shows two men who probably were Pony riders. The man on the left may be Johnson William Richardson, the rider identified as Billy Richardson, the first rider out of St. Joseph. The man on the right has been identified as Johnny Fry. But his features do not seem to match those in a portrait of Johnny Fry earlier in this chapter.

The announcements had been made. The preparations were complete. The riders and ponies were equipped and ready. The time was near. On April 3, 1860 the Pony was to start its historic run.

private letters and other sources, the reports are premature. I understand that Col. Hays intends to return with his command, disband, and reorganize with a smaller force.

To the Bulletin Exclusively.

Efforts to Re-establish the Pony Express—The Army in Washoe—The Volunteers—The Indians.

CARSON CITY, U. T., June 0 P. M.

A company of 20 picked men, well armed and mounted, have just left with the Pony Express and Salt Lake mail. They will proceed till they meet the Express or mail coming this way—re-establishing the route by leaving men and animals at the stations destroyed, as they go along. It is thought they will not have to go further than Ruby Valley. If necessary, however, they will go to Camp Floyd.

The Indians having fled from Pyramid Lake without giving fight, all but about 150 volunteers are to be disbanded. Of the latter, 15 arrived here yesterday ; many more are expected to-day. The remains of Ormsby, Meredith, Snowden and Story will also reach here to-night. Their funeral will take place to-morrow.

The weather is warm and showery. The grass is growing rapidly. The miners are returning to their work. No further apprehensions is entertained of Indians in the mining districts.

The Indians are peaceably disposed on Walker river.

Gossip from Napa.

NAPA CITY, June 4, 1860.

Restocking after the Indian war. - *Daily Evening Bulletin, June 9, 1860*

Chapter Two

MAPS AND ITINERARY

By the time the Pony Express was organized. the territory that lay between St. Joseph, Missouri and San Francisco, California was known and mapped. The task of laying out the specific route was focused on finding the fastest and safest route for the delivery of news and mail across the western portion of the United States with its varied topography. The Pony Express ponies would have to cross the western prairie, the Great Plains, climb the Rocky Mountains, cross the Great Basin, climb the Sierra Nevada, and finally reach the Pacific coast.

Conditions and characteristics varied greatly in the area traversed. The area in the eastern half was generally more populated than the western portion. The eastern portions of Kansas and Nebraska were settled and being farmed. The earlier California Gold Rush had resulted in the settlement of the Pacific coast to the Sierras. There were some major population centers, such as Independence/Kansas City, St. Joseph, and Omaha on the Missouri, Salt Lake City at the edge of the Great Basin and, Los Angeles, Sacramento, and San Francisco on the west coast. Smaller population centers tended to be found at either end, such as Seneca and Marysville in the East, and Placerville, Folsom and Genoa in the west. Large military forts, such as Fort Leavenworth, Fort Kearny, Fort Laramie, Camp Floyd, and Fort Churchill existed by the time of the Pony Express.

Indians still lived in the area along major segments of the route and the pressure on them was growing. In the far eastern sections of Kansas and Nebraska the Indians had been subdued and some lived on reservations. West of the Sierras they had generally been forced out. From the Great Basin to the Great Plains the Indians still tended to move and live about freely, but as new gold and silver strikes brought more miners and as emigrants began to settle the prairies, tensions increased. At that time the Great Basin, especially the Utah Territory, which included much of western Wyoming, Utah, and much of Nevada, was the most difficult and dangerous region.

Severe weather conditions were common occurrences in the Great Plains and the Rocky Mountains and Sierra Nevada, but in the Great Basin conditions were just as bad. Both were hot, but the Great Basin was dry. Finding water was a major problem. Winters were stormy and cold. Deep snows were common in the mountains and parts of the Great Plains. In the Great Basin, even nighttime in the summer could be cold.

By the late 1850s only the Great Basin was still relatively unmapped and little traveled. Frémont had explored and mapped the route of the Oregon Trail in the 1840s, and it was also used by travelers. Routes to California were opened during the Mexican War and again during the gold rush. In the mid 1840s and 1850s guidebooks were written and published about the various routes and cutoffs. Emigrant wagons, traders, commercial wagons, the military and now stagecoaches followed well defined roads. The traditional routes of the old Oregon, California, and Santa Fe trails and the Ox-bow Route all skirted or bypassed the central portion of the Great Basin. They made loops either to the north or to the south. The route of the Oregon, California, and Mormon trails through the South Pass and Salt Lake City were well developed and sufficient. However, from there all the established routes, including the Salt Lake Cutoff, the Hastings Cutoff and the new Lander Road, made loops to the north before rejoining the established California Trail to follow the Humboldt, which itself then made another small loop north following the river before turning southwest to Genoa. A straighter route through the central region from Fort Bridger and Salt Lake City cutting west southwest was the most logical. It would be much shorter and, therefore, save needed time. It was the finding of that feasible route across the Great Basin that enabled the Pony Express to become a reality.

That task was finally placed on the shoulders of the Army and the experienced Captain James Hervey Simpson. He had graduated from West Point in 1832. Commissioned in the artillery he was transferred to the topographical engineers in 1838 when it was established. In 1849 the then Lieutenant Simpson surveyed a route from Fort Smith, Arkansas, to Santa Fe, New Mexico. He also participated in some of the army's actions against the Navajo. He served briefly as the chief of the topographical engineers in the southwest area. His reports were published in 1850 and 1852. He was promoted to captain and served in Minnesota in late 1851 and then in Florida. By mid-1857 concern about a Utah War resulted in Simpson being assigned to General Albert S. Johnston's command for the Utah expedition. In August Simpson arrived at Camp Floyd which Johnston had set up after arriving earlier in June. By September 1858 he had surveyed a new route between Fort Bridger and Camp Floyd. That fall General Johnston ordered him to make a short exploration of the desert to the west from Camp Floyd. Then in the April of 1859 he was ordered to survey a wagon route to Genoa, Nevada. The command left Camp Floyd on May 2, 1859, and arrived in Genoa on June 12. He started his return trip on June 24 and returned to Camp Floyd on August 3. His work opened the central route from Salt Lake City to Genoa that the Pony Express Trail adopted. It was up to the Pony Express venture to prove that the route was feasible for the whole year.

While most of the route was over or alongside these established roads, a single horse and rider could travel places a wagon or coach could not, so in some specific areas the Pony Express could veer off the established road for short distances, and could go over, around, or through areas where wagons could not pass.

Four maps are included in this section. Three were the culmination of Simpson's expeditions, and the fourth is a political map of the United States and territories by Samuel Augustus Mitchell, a well-known map maker of the period.

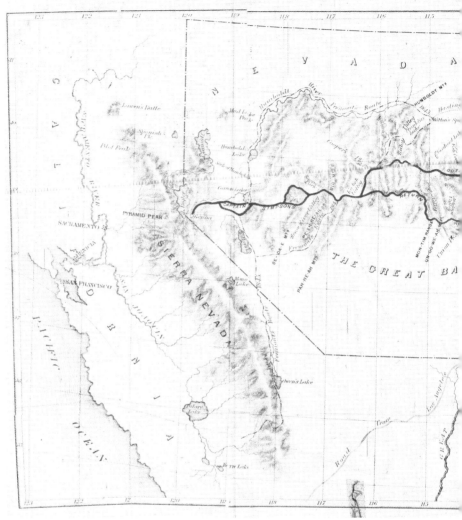

Map I. "Explorations of Capt. J.H. Simpson Corps of Top' Engrs, U.S.A. in 1859 Across the Great Basin of Utah." Simpson's Expedition – 1859

This is the map that showed the route that finally opened up the Great Basin and generally defined the Central Route that the Pony Express was to use as it traversed the Great Basin. While Simpson used or paralleled parts of the earlier Egan Trail and Chorpenning's stage route to the Ruby Mountains, his survey expedition passed there opened a new route to near Genoa, Nevada, where it intersected with

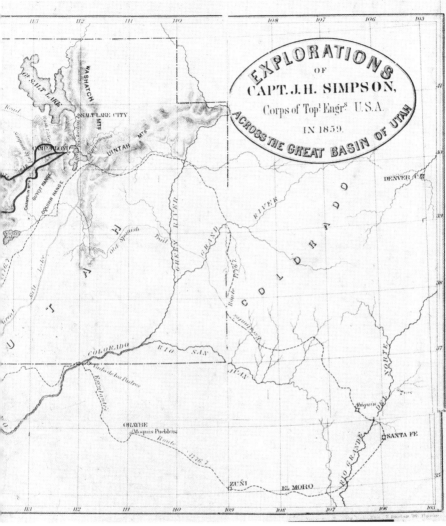

Utah State Historical Society

the established old California Trail coming down from the Humboldt. Simpson wrote in his journal "Camp Floyd, May 2, 1859.— The topographical party under my command left this post at a quarter of 8 A.M., to explore the country intervening this locality and Carson River; at the east foot of the Sierra Nevada, for a new and direct route to California." (66:44)

35

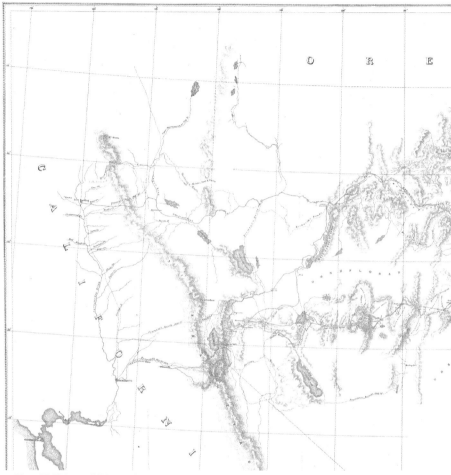

Map II."Map of Wagon Routes in Utah Territory Explored & Opened by Capt.
J.H. Simpson Tpl Engrs, U.S.A. Assisted by Lieuts. J. L. K. Smith and H. S.
Putnam Topl Engrs. U.S.A. and Mr. Henry Engelman, in 1858-59." Simpson's
Expedition – 1859.

This new route to Genoa was about 565 miles long while the
established route along the Humboldt was 853 miles. It cut off 288
miles which was just the type of savings that the Pony needed. It is
interesting to note that Simpson also realized the future significance of
his new route when compared to the older established Humboldt route
for the telegraph. Noting in his report that not only was it shorter,
but that also there were more trees near or on the route. There were

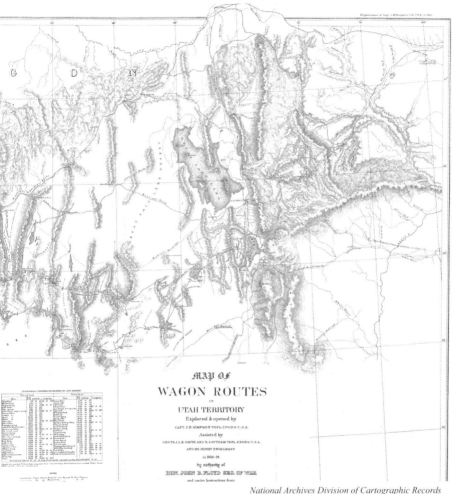

National Archives Division of Cartographic Records

over 300 treeless miles on the Humboldt route, but only two sections totaling 142 miles without trees on the new route. (66:92)

The second Simpson's map shows the different wagon routes in Utah. It includes a little more detail than the other map. The upper right corner of the map is about the corner of present Wyoming showing the road from Ft. Bridger coming down through Echo Canyon and over to

37

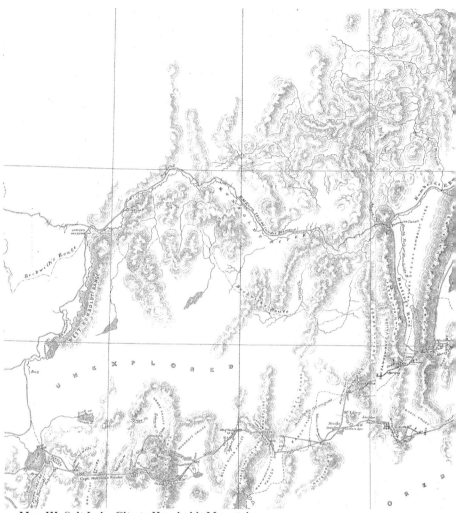

Map III. Salt Lake City to Humboldt Mountains

Great Salt Lake City. It also indicates the route surveyed by Simpson from Fort Bridger to Camp Floyd that by-passed Salt Lake City. The route to the west from Salt Lake City is the Hastings Road which was used by the Donner Party in 1846 cutting across the Great Salt Lake Desert to Pilot Peak. The road south from Salt Lake City to Camp Floyd and then southwest is Simpson's wagon road.

The third map is a detailed section of Simpson's large map. It shows the area west of Salt Lake City to the Ruby or Humboldt Mountains

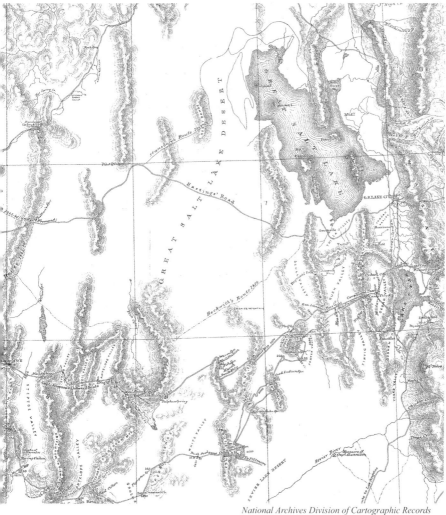

National Archives Division of Cartographic Records

in present-day Utah and Nevada. It also includes other routes and roads including part of Simpson's return route. Hastings Road is also clearly shown. The main route south out of Salt Lake City through Camp Floyd and then west is Simpson's Wagon Road. It generally corresponds to the route traveled by Burton and followed by the Pony Express. This section is described in detail by Burton in the itinerary portion as the second itinerary. It can also be referenced with both the trail map and the pictorial journey.

Map IV. The 1860 map by Agustus Mitchell is one of the few that includes the Pony Express route.

Augustus Mitchell was a well-known map maker. His "Map of the United States and Canada" published in 1860, prior to the Civil War, was one of the few that included the route of the Pony Express along with the routes of the other major wagon and stagecoach trails/roads. As is evident, most of the territory west to the Sierra Nevada had not been organized into the states as we know them today. The Utah Territory had been reduced, Nevada Territory had just been created out of it and its eastern border changed. More changes would come quickly to the map of the United States within a few years.

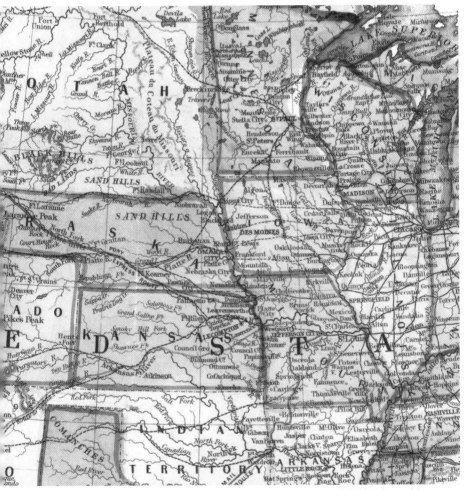

Mitchell, The Library of Congress

ITINERARY – RIDING ALONG THE TRAIL

Since much of the coach route taken by Richard Burton and the Pony Express route were overlapping, portions of his summary itinerary of the trip are included. He started in St. Joseph, Missouri, and mostly followed the route used by the Pony Express. Since the coaches carried passengers and regular mail and were run by the Central Overland California and Pike's Peak Express Company, they tended to use many of the same stations. Thus, his descriptions are good representations from the Pony Express era. The coaches

41

and mail wagons traveled more slowly. Since speed was of primary importance, the Pony Express required additional stations for relay mounts, and there were usually at least one or two stations between the stage stations. Therefore, Burton would not have stopped at all of the Pony Express stations. However, many of the Pony Express home stations were used by the stages for layovers. Stage passengers were expected to pay for their keep, while express riders did not have to. More detailed descriptions are paired with the site or station illustrations. They do impart a good sense of what life and conditions were like along the Pony Express Trail.

The itineraries for two segments of the trail are included. The first one is from Marysville, Kansas, to past Fort Laramie, Wyoming, to Horseshoe Creek, the end of Division Two.(8:610-12) Here the route followed most of the old established routes of the Oregon-California trails. The second itinerary covers the route from Salt Lake City to Deep Creek Station, near present-day Ibapah, Utah, to Ruby Valley, Nevada. (8_616-18) They are from Burton's book. For the first itinerary, modern roads can be used to closely follow the route. For the second one, except for the road from Salt Lake City to Camp Floyd which is paved, most of the route in Utah is on dirt roads, the Pony Express Byway. It follows or closely approximates the Pony Express Trail or its alternates, and in Nevada, it continues west along Whiskey Road, the old Lincoln Highway, in eastern Nevada to where it meets U.S. Highway 93. The last part, from "Shell Station" to Ruby Valley Station, is very rough. As you read along in this section you may want to refer back to Map III.

When reading the itineraries, the number in the first column represents the contract mail station number. The larger column briefly describes the section. Then comes the miles between stations, the starting time when they left, their arrival time, and the date.

No. of Mail.		Miles.	Start.	Arrival.	Date.
	Good camping-ground. Ten miles beyond lies Richland, deserted site. Thence to Seneca, capital of Nemehaw Co. A few shanties on N. bank of Big Nemehaw Creek, a tributary of the Missouri River, which affords water, wood, and grass.	18	A. M. 3	A. M. 6	Aug. 8
5.	Cross Wildcat Creek and other nullahs. Seven miles beyond Seneca lies Ashpoint, a few wooden huts, thence to "Uncle John's Grocery," where liquor and stores are procurable. Eleven miles from Big Nemehaw water, wood, and grass are found at certain seasons near the head of a ravine. Thence to Vermilion Creek, which heads to the N.-E. and enters the Big Blue 20 miles above its mouth. The ford is miry after rain, and the banks are thickly wooded. Water is found in wells 40—43 feet deep. Guittard's Station.	20	A. M. 8	NOON. 12	Aug. 8
6.	Fourteen miles from Guittards, Marysville, capital of Washington Co. affords supplies and a blacksmith. Then ford the Big Blue, tributary to Kansas River, clear and swift stream. Twelve miles W. of Marysville is frontier line between Kansas and Nebraska. Thence to Cottonwood Creek, fields in hollow near the stream.	25	P. M. 1	P. M. 6	Aug. 8
7.	Store at the crossing very dirty and disorderly. Good water in spring 400 yards N. of the road, wood and grass abundant. Seventeen and a half miles from the Big Blue is Walnut Creek, where emigrants encamp. Thence to West Turkey or Rock Creek in Nebraska T. a branch of the Big Blue: its approximate altitude is 1485 feet.	26	P. M. 6	P. M. 11	Aug. 8
8.	After 19 miles of rough road and mosquitos, cross Little Sandy, 5 miles E. of Big Sandy, water and trees plentiful. There Big Sandy deep and heavy bed. Big Sandy Station.	23	P. M. 12	A. M. 4	Aug. 9
9.	Cross hills forming divide of Little Blue River ascending valley 60 miles long. Little Blue fine stream of clear water falling into Kansas River, everywhere good supplies and good camping-ground. Along left bank to Kiowa.	19	A. M. 6	A. M. 10	Aug. 9
10.	Rough road of spurs and gullies runs up valley 2 miles wide. Well wooded chiefly with cottonwood and grass abundant. Ranch at Liberty Farm on the Little Blue.	25	A. M. 11	P. M. 3	Aug. 9
11.	Cross divide between Little Blue and Platte River, rough road, mosquitos troublesome. Approximate altitude of dividing ridge 2025 feet. Station at Thirty-two Mile-Creek, a small wooded and winding stream flowing into the Little Blue.	24	P. M. 4	P. M. 9	Aug. 9

43

APPENDIX I. 611

No. of Mail.		Miles.	Start.	Arrival.	Date.
12.	After 27 miles strike valley of the Platte, along southern bank of river, over level ground, good for camping, fodder abundant. After 7 miles Fort Kearny in N. lat. 40° 38' 45", and W. long. 98° 58' 11": approximate altitude 2500 feet above sea level. Grocery, cloths, provisions, and supplies of all kinds are to be procured from the sutler's store. Beyond Kearny a rough and bad road leads to "Seventeen-Mile-Station."	34	P. M. 10·30	A. M. 8	Aug. 10
13.	Along south bank of Platte. Buffalo chips used for fuel. Sign of buffalo appears. Plum Creek Station on a stream where there is a bad crossing in wet weather.	21	A. M. 0·00	P. M. 1·15	Aug. 10
14.	Beyond Plum Creek, Willow Island Ranch, where supplies are procurable. Road along Platte, wood scarce, grass plentiful, buffalo abounds; after 20 miles "Cold Water Ranch." Halt and change at Midway Station.	25	P. M. 2·30	P. M. 8	Aug. 10
15.	Along Valley of Platte, road muddy after rain, fuel scarce, grass abundant, camp traces everywhere. Ranch at Cottonwood Station, at this season the western limit of buffalo.	27	P. M. 9	A. M. 1·45	Aug. 11
16.	Up Valley of Platte. No wood, buffalo chips for fuel. Good camping-ground, grass on small branch of Platte. To Junction House Ranch and thence to station at Frémont Springs.	30	A. M. 6·15	A. M. 11	Aug. 11
17.	Road passes O'Fallon's Bluffs. "Half-way House" a store and ranch, distant 120 miles from Fort Kearny, 400 from St. Joseph, 40 from the lower crossing, and 68 from the Upper crossing of the South Fork (Platte River). The station is called Alkali Lake.	25	NOON. 12	P. M. 5	Aug. 11
18.	Road along river, no timber, grass, buffalo chips, and mosquitos. Station at Diamond Springs near Lower Crossing.	25	P. M. 6	P. M. 10·15	Aug. 11
19.	Road along river. Last 4 miles very heavy sand, avoided by Lower Crossing. Poor accommodation at Upper Ford or Crossing on the eastern bank, where the mail passes the stream en route to Gt. S. L. city, and the road branches to Denver City and Pike's Peak.	25	P. M. 11	A. M. 3·15	Aug. 12
20.	Ford Platte 600 yards wide, 2·50 ft. deep, bed gravelly and solid, easy ford in dry season. Cross divide between North and South Forks along bank of Lodge Pole Creek. Land arid, wild sage for fuel. Lodge Pole Station.	35	A. M. 6·30	P. M. 12·45	Aug. 12
21.	Up Lodge Pole Creek over spur of table-land, then striking over the prairie finishes the high divide between the Forks. Approximate altitude 3500				

R R 2

No. of Mail		Miles.	Start.	Arrival.	Date.
	feet. On the right is Ash-Hollow, where there is plenty of wood and a small spring. Station is Mud Springs, a poor ranch.	25	P. M. 3	P. M. 5·45	Aug. 12
22.	Route lies over rolling divide between the Forks, crossing Omaha, Lawrence, and other creeks where water and grass are procurable. Cedar is still found in hill-gullies. About half a mile north of Chimney Rock is a ranch where the cattle are changed.	25	A. M. 8	P. M. 12·30	Aug. 13
23.	Road along south bank of North Ford of Platte River. Wild sage only fuel in valley: small spring on top of first hill. Rugged labyrinth of paths abreast of Scott's Bluffs, which lie 5 miles S. of river in N. lat. 41° 48′ 26″, and W. long. 103° 45′ 02″. Water found in first ravine of Scott's Bluffs 200 yards below the road, cedars on heights. To Station.	24	P. M. 1·30	P. M. 5·30	Aug. 13
24.	Road along river, crosses Little Kiowa Creek, a tributary to Horse Creek, which flows into the Platte. Ford Horse Creek, a clear shallow stream with a sandy bottom. No wood below the hills.	16	P. M. 6·30	P. M. 8·30	Aug. 13
25.	Route over sandy and heavy rolling ground, leaving the Platte on the right: cottonwood and willows on the banks. Ranch at Laramie City kept by M. Badeau, a Canadian, who sells spirits, Indian goods, and outfit.	26	A. M. 6	P. M. 10·20	Aug. 14
26.	After 9 miles of rough road cross Laramie Fork and enter Fort Laramie, N. lat. 42° 12′ 38″, and W. long. 104° 31′ 26″. Alt. 4519 feet. Military post with post-office, sutler's stores, and other conveniences. Thence to Ward's Station on the Central Star, small ranch and store.	18	P. M. 12·15	P. M. 4	Aug. 14
27.	Rough and bad road. After 14 miles, cross Bitter Cottonwood Creek, water rarely flows, after rain 10 ft. wide and 6 inches deep, grass and fuel abundant. Pass Indian shop and store. At Bitter Creek branch of Cottonwood the road to Salt Lake City forks. Emigrants follow Upper or South road over spurs of Black Hills, some way south of river to avoid kanyons and to find grass. The station is called Horseshoe Creek. Residence of road-agent, Mr. Slade, and one of the worst places on the line.	25	P. M. 5	P. M. 9·30	Aug. 14
28.	Road forks, one line follows Platte, the other turns to left, over "cut off;" highly undulating ridges crooked and deeply dented with dry beds of rivers; land desolate and desert. No wood nor water till end of stage. La Bonté River and Station, unfinished ranch in Valley, water and grass.	25	A. M. 10·45	A. M. 2·45	Aug. 15
29.	Road runs 6 miles (wheels often locked) on rugged				

45

Here is the itinerary from Salt Lake City to Deep Creek Station to Ruby Valley: See map II.

Altitude 4300 feet.

The variation of compass at Temple Block in 1849 was 15° 47' 23'', and in 1860 it was 15° 54', a slow progress towards the east. (In the Wind River Mts. as laid down by Col. Frémont in 1842 was E. 18°.) In Fillmore Valley it is now 18° 15', and three years ago was about 17° east, the rapid progression to the east is accompanied with extreme irregularity, which the people attribute to the metallic constituents of the soil.

Total of days between St. Jo. and Gt. S. L. City	19
Total stages	45
Distance in statute miles	1136
From Fort Leavenworth to Gt. S. L. City	1168

ITINERARY OF THE MAIL ROUTE FROM GREAT SALT LAKE CITY TO SAN FRANCISCO.

No. of Mail.		Miles.	Start.	Arrival.	Date.
1 and 2.	Road through south of City, due south along right bank of Jordan. Cross many creeks, viz. Kanyon Creek, 4¼ miles, Mill Creek, 2½, First or Great Cottonwood Creek 2. Second ditto 4. Fork of road 1¼. Dry Creek 3½. Willow Creek 2¾. After 22—23 miles, hot and cold springs, and halfway house, the brewery under Point of the Mountain. Road across Ash Hollow or Jordan Kanyon, 2 miles. Fords river, knee deep, ascends a rough divide between Utah Valley and Cedar Valley 10 miles from camp, and finally reaches Cedar Creek and Camp Floyd.	44	10·30	9·30	Sept. 20
3.	Leaves Camp Floyd, 7 miles to divide of Cedar Valley. Crosses divide into Rush Valley, after total of 18·2 miles reaches Meadow Creek, good grass and water. Rush Valley Mail Station 1 mile beyond, food and accommodation.	20	10·30	9·30	Sept. 27
4.	Crosses remains of Rush Valley 7 miles. Up rough divide called Genl. Johnston's Pass. Spring often dry, 200 yards on right of road. At Point				

No. of Mail.		Miles.	Start.	Arrival.	Date.
	Look Out leaves Simpson's Road, which runs south. Cross Skull Valley, bad road. To bench on eastern flank of desert. Station called Egan's Springs, Simpson's Springs, or Lost Springs, grass plentiful, water good.	27	A. M. 9·30	4·30	Sept. 28
5.	New station, road forks to S.-E. and leads after 5 miles to grass and water. After 8 miles River Bottom, 1 mile broad. Long line over desert to Express Station, called Dugway, no grass, and no water.	20	12	P. M. 5·30	Sept. 29
6.	Steep road 2½ miles to summit of Dugway Pass. Descend by rough incline, 8 miles beyond road forks to Devil's Hole, 90 miles from Camp Floyd on Simpson's route, and 6 miles S. of Fish Springs. Eight miles beyond fork is Mountain Point, road winds S. and W. and then N. to avoid swamp, and crosses three sloughs. Beyond last is Fish Spring Station on bench, poor place, water plentiful but bad. Cattle here drink for first time after Lost Springs, distant 48 miles.	28	P. M. 6·30	A. M. 3·30	Sept. 29
7.	Road passes many pools. Halfway forks S. to Pleasant Valley (Simpson's line). Road again rounds swamp, crossing S. end of Salt Plain. After 21 miles, "Willow Creek," water rather brackish. Station "Willow Springs" on bench below hills at W. end of Desert, grass and hay plentiful.	22	A. M. 10	3·30	Sept. 30
8.	Road ascending bench turns N. to find Pass. After 6 miles Mountain Springs, good water, grass, and fuel. Six miles beyond is Deep Creek Kanyon, dangerous ravine 9 miles long. Then descends into fertile and well watered valley, and after 7 miles enters Deep Creek Mail Station. Indian farm.	28	A. M. 8	P. M. 4	Oct. 1
9.	Along W. Creek. After 8 miles, "Eight Miles Springs," water, grass, and sage fuel. Kanyon after 2½ miles, 500 yards long and easy. Then 19 miles through Antelope Valley to station of same name, burnt in June 1860 by Indians. Simpson's route from Pleasant Valley, distant 12·5 miles, falls into E. end of Antelope Valley, from Camp Floyd 151 miles.	30	A. M. 8	P. M. 4	Oct. 3, 4
10.	Road over valley for 2 miles to mouth of Shell Creek Kanyon, 6 miles long. Rough road, fuel plentiful. Descends into Spring Valley, and then passes over other divides into Shell Creek, where there is a mail station; water, grass, and fuel abundant.	18	A. M. 6	P. M. 11	Oct. 5
11.	Descends rough road. Crosses Steptoe Valley and bridged creek. Road heavy, sand or mud. After 16 miles Egan's Kanyon, dangerous for Indians.				

47

618   THE CITY OF THE SAINTS.

No. of Mail.		Miles	Start.	Arrival.	Date.
	Station at W. mouth, burned by Indians in Oct. 1860.	18	P. M. 2	P. M. 6	Oct. 5
12.	Pass divide, fall into Butte Valley, and cross its N. end. Bottom very cold. Mail Station half way up hill, very small spring, grass on N. side of hill. Butte Station.	18	P. M. 8	A. M. 3	Oct. 6
13.	Ascend long divide, 2 steep hills and falls. Cross N. end of Long Valley, all barren. Ascend divide and descend into Ruby Valley, road excellent, water, grass, and bottom, fuel distant. Good Mail Station.	22	A. M. 8	P. M. 1·45	Oct. 7
14.	Long divide, fuel plenty, no grass nor water. After 10 miles road branches, right hand to Gravelly Ford of Humboldt River. Cross dry bottom. Cross Smith's Fork of Humboldt River in Huntingdon Valley, little stream, bunch-grass and sage fuel on W. end. Ascend Chokop's Pass, Dugway and hard hill, descend into Moonshine Valley. Station at Diamond Springs; warm water but good.	23	A. M. 8	P. M. 1·45	Oct. 8, 9
15.	Cross Moonshine Valley. After 7 miles sulphurous spring and grass. Twelve miles beyond, ascend divide, no water, fuel and bunch-grass plentiful. Then long divide. After 9 miles, station on Roberts' Creek at E. end of Sheawit, or Roberts' Springs Valley.	28	A. M. 8	P. M. 1·45	Oct. 10
16.	Down Valley to west, good road, sage small, no fuel. After 12 miles, willows and water-holes, 3 miles beyond are alkaline wells. Station on bench, water below in dry creek, grass must be brought from 15 miles.	35	A. M. 6·30	P. M. 12·30	Oct. 11
17.	Cross long rough divide to Smokey Valley. At northern end creek called "Wanahonop," or "Netwood," i. e. trap. Thence long rough kanyon to Simpson's Park, grass plentiful, water in wells 10 feet deep. Simpson's Park in Shoshone country, and, according to Simpson's Itinerary, 348 miles from camp Floyd.	25	A. M. 8·15	P. M. 2·25	Oct. 12
18.	Cross Simpson's Park. Ascend Simpson's Pass, a long kanyon, with sweet, "Sage Springs," on summit, bunch-grass plentiful. Descend to fork of road, right hand to lower, left hand to upper, ford of Reese's River. Water perennial and good, food poor.	15	A. M. 10	P. M. 2	Oct. 13
19.	Through remainder of Reese's River Valley. After long divide Valley of Smith's Creek, saleratus, no water nor grass. At last, station near kanyon, and hidden from view. Land belongs to Pa Yutas.	28	A. M. 7·20	P. M. 2·45	Oct. 14

48

Chapter Three

HISTORY

Τ he history of the Pony Express Trail entails more than just the development of the physical route. It is the product of a number of events and issues: Manifest Destiny, the gold rush and silver rushes, and slavery. Each of these became interwoven with the others and had a significant impact on our history. The massive migration of people west to Oregon, California, and Utah, the lure of the riches and wealth found in the Sierra Nevada and Rocky Mountains, and the growing tensions over the abolitionist movement and slavery, all had their powerful political, social and economic implications and ramifications. One of these effects was the need for improved and faster transportation and communications across the expanding nation. Another was the resulting competition for the control of them.

It is also important to remember that while the focus here is on the Pony Express, it was only one of the business ventures of Russell, Majors and Waddell. Once it was formed they still had to spend much time and energy overseeing their other businesses. They were often away for days or weeks looking after some other concerns.

HISTORY OF THE PONY EXPRESS TRAIL

There were a number of events between the early 1800s and the late 1830s that set the stage for later developments that impacted the development of the Pony Express. Mexico became independent from Spain. The Adams-Onis Treaty set the northern American-Mexican border at the 42° parallel to the Continental Divide. American commercial interests began to increase in the resources of the Pacific coast and in the West. The era of the mountain men, including Joseph Walker, Jim Bridger, Kit Carson, the Robidoux and Sublette families, and fur trading resulted in increased knowledge and interest in the

West as they explored the Great Basin and Sierra Nevada. The South Pass became known. Fur trading posts such as Fort Bridger and Fort John (Laramie) were established. American presidents starting with Andrew Jackson negotiated with Mexico to buy California.

1836 –

The first Californian independence revolution was led by Juan Bautista Alvarado and Jose Castro. They felt isolated and that their concerns were not being adequately addressed by the government in Mexico City nor by its local officials. It was supported by some of the local Americans. It ended when Alvarado was appointed the governor. The movement subsided, but it was not forgotten.

1837 –

Samuel Morse developed an improved telegraph. He soon developed his dot-dash code. He patented his invention in 1840, but interest in it was slow to develop.

1839 –

John Sutter immigrated to California. His colony, known as "New Helvetia," was established at the junction of the Sacramento and American Rivers. Sutter's Fort was its center and became the future site of the city of Sacramento. He encouraged settlement there, and it became one of the ends of the California Trail. It would also be the location of the discovery of gold that drew tens of thousands of people to California.

1841 –

The American migration to California began. Three groups arrived. One party of about sixty-nine people left from Independence, Missouri. West of Soda Spring the party split. While thirty-four continued to Oregon, the Bartleson-Bidwell party of thirty-five people decided to head for California. Some parts of the route they opened to California were incorporated into the route that came to be known as the California Trail. A second group of emigrants came from Oregon, and the third from New Mexico.

1842 –

John C. Fremont, known as the "pathfinder," began leading a number of mapping and exploring expeditions into the West for the military. On his first trip he started west from Westport with Kit Carson as his guide and Charles Pruess as his cartographer. They traveled west along the Santa Fe Trail through part of Kansas and then north to pick up the Platte River. They followed along it to where they crossed over to the North Platte and continued to follow it until the river turned south. They turned up the Sweetwater and followed it and then crossed the great South Pass into the Oregon Territory. They had mapped their route. This established the main Oregon Trail along the Platte River, the North Platte and Sweetwater River to the South Pass. With minor modifications that route became part of the later Pony Express Trail. President Tyler tried to obtain California through negotiations with Mexico. However, his efforts failed after Commodore Jones captured Monterey thinking war had broken out. Mexico became increasingly suspicious of the American intentions.

Dr. Elijah White led a wagon company comprised of 112 people to present-day Oregon. Landsford Hasting was one of its members. He later wrote one of the earliest guidebooks to Oregon and California. No Americans migrated to California over the trail, but as more people went to Oregon, some left there and traveled to California.

Horace Greeley of the *Tribune* began writing about the West. He soon becomes a proponent of the American movement west. "Manifest Destiny" became the cry. Control of the lands to the Pacific coast became the goal.

1843 –

St. Joseph, Missouri, was formally laid out. It was established on the site of Joseph Robidoux's old 1826 trading post. St. Joseph was destined to become a major jumping off point for emigrant wagon companies, freight wagons, stage lines, and the Pony Express. For those emigrants who came by riverboat up the Missouri River, St. Joseph was farther north and west, thus shortening the length of the overland route and saving them time.

Emigration over the Oregon Trail continued. The "Great Emigration" piloted by Dr. Marcus Whitman and John Gantt, a fur trader, brought nearly one thousand people over the Oregon Trail. The trail became a well beaten path.

Fremont continued to explore and map the West. He completed mapping the route from the South Pass, where he had left off in 1842, to Oregon. While parts changed during the ensuing years, the basic route to Oregon was now mapped. Copies of his maps soon became available to the public.

Migration to California by Americans resumed. Joseph Chiles and Joseph Walker led emigrants into California. The general route Walker blazed from Fort Hall on the Snake River southwest to the Humboldt River and down to the Humboldt Sink became part of the main California Trail used by later emigrants.

Congress authorized $30,000 for the construction of a telegraph line between Washington, D.C. and Baltimore, Maryland. Morse was awarded a contract.

1844 -

Fremont returned from Oregon by way of California. His presence at Sutter's Fort with his U.S. Army troops made Mexico even more nervous. He finally left, and continued to map his way east across the Great Basin.

On May 24, the telegraph line between Washington, D.C. and Baltimore, Maryland was completed. Morse sent the Biblical phrase, "What hath God wrought!" from the Supreme Court chamber of the Capitol to his assistant Alfred Vale in Baltimore. Vale sent the same message back. Interest in the device increased. Newspapers soon began posting news columns with "Telegraph News." By 1846 Washington was connected to New York City. The following year St. Louis, Missouri was connected. Over the next five years over fifty telegraph companies had formed.

The Stephens-Townsend-Murphy Party, led by Elisha Stephens, successfully brought their wagons over the trail into California.

1845 –

American migration to California continued. William B. Ide and his family were part of the migration.

Fremont started on his third mapping expedition. His forces were greater than in prior years. By the end of the year he was again in California.

1846 –

Relations between Mexico and the United States continued to deteriorate. The increased American migration to California caused more problems. The desire to fulfill America's "Manifest Destiny" which was becoming a rallying cry, was a major irritation. The old question of Texas and its border still festered. Fremont's recent arrival intensified concerns. He was forced to leave and headed for Oregon. A military courier, Lieutenant Archibald Gillispe, intercepted Fremont. After discussions Fremont turned around. On April 25, on the Rio Grande, an incident resulted with Mexican troops firing on General Zachary Taylor's troops. Fremont, it is believed, had been ordered back to California. He made it in time for the revolt.

On May 11, President Polk sent a War Message to Congress. The Mexican War was declared. Back in Sonoma, California, William B. Ide continued the agitation and led some Americans to proclaim California an independent republic, the Bear Flag Republic, on June 14, 1846. On July 7, American Commodore Sloat landed in Monterey, the Bear Flag revolt ended as local Americans joined forces with the Army. On July 9, American forces under Captain Montgomery landed in San Francisco and raised the American flag. Fighting continued there and elsewhere for some time, but an agreement was signed January 13, 1847, to end the fighting. The formal treaty would be signed later.

Part of the migration west included the Donner Party. They were persuaded to use the Hasting's Cutoff to California. In doing so they actually blazed the road west from Fort Bridger to the future site of Salt Lake City. This section to Salt Lake was used the following year by the Mormons. From Salt Lake, the Donners struck out west across the Great Salt Lake Desert to Pilot's Peak. Then heading west they came to the Ruby Valley and mountains. They traveled south down the valley to a pass in the mountains. They crossed the mountains and then headed back north along the South Humboldt to where they rejoined the established California Trail along the Humboldt. Most of the route from Fort Bridger to Salt Lake and the pass in the Ruby Mountains that the Donners used later became part of the Pony Express Trail.

1847 -

Under the leadership of Brigham Young, the Mormons left their Winter Quarters in Nebraska and followed the Oregon-California trail to Fort Bridger. Then they followed the route cut by the Donner Party and entered the Salt Lake Valley. There they established Salt Lake City, and they soon spread out throughout the Great Basin. Many of the Mormons later played important roles in the Pony Express. Salt Lake City served as the central point on the trail.

Congress authorized the construction of five mail steamships to deliver mail between the East and West Coasts. Two ten-year contracts were awarded. One company delivered the mail from coast to coast. Once the mail arrived in San Francisco, the other company delivered it to its destinations in the west. Annual government payment was to be $199,000.00. Mail still took months to get to California.

By December telegraph lines had been laid to St. Louis, Missouri.

1848 -

On January 24, James Marshall, an employee of John Sutter, discovered gold while working on Sutter's sawmill on the American River. Sutter tried to keep the discovery quiet until a decision was made on how to best handle the discovery. It did not remain quiet very long.

On February 2, the Treaty of Guadalupe Hildago formally ended the Mexican War. California & the Southwest including later parts of Utah, Nevada, Arizona, New Mexico, and Colorado were ceded to the United States.

On May 8, on Montgomery Street in San Francisco, Sam Brannan reportedly shouted, "Gold, Gold! Gold on the American River!" The history of California and the United State was forever changed.

On October 6, the *S.S. California*, the first mail steamship, left New York for San Francisco by way of Cape Horn. News of the California gold strike had not yet reached the East coast when it departed. When it arrived in California its crew abandoned the ship for the gold fields. Other ships suffered the same fate.

Alexander Majors entered the Santa Fe freighting business. He continued to prosper and soon became one the major freighting companies in the West.

1849 -

Americans rushed to California. An estimated 25,000 Forty-Niners or Argonauts followed the California Trail intent on striking it rich. Nearly as many came by sea from the east coast and other parts of the world.

1850 -

The Gold Rush was still on. 44,000 people took the overland trails to California. About 6,000 went to Oregon and between 3,000-6,000 went to Utah.

Samuel Woodson was granted a government contract to open a monthly mail service between Independence, Missouri and Salt Lake City. He was unable to keep to the schedule.

On September 9, California entered the Union as a free state. It was part of the Compromise of 1850 which tried to balance the interest of the proslavery and anti-slavery factions. With its status as a state, the need for fast communication between it and federal governments and its citizens increased.

The government began examining its postal contracts. The cost for the ocean mail service was rising. It was estimated that it cost the government a half million dollars a year. People in the West were unsatisfied with the slow service that still took months.

1851 –

George Chorpenning and Absalom Woodward were granted a government contract for mail delivery between Salt Lake City and Sacramento. It was supposed to be for monthly service. They used mule packs, or what was commonly called "Jackass Mail." They started in May from Sacramento. Woodward was killed by Indians. Chorpenning was wounded and unable to make the return trip. Chorpenning still hoped he would be able to succeed.

The Mississippi Valley Printing Telegraph Company was formed. It began merging with other companies. Five years later on April 4, 1856, it became the Western Union Telegraph Company. Its major rival was the American Telegraph Company.

1852 –

In February, five Chorpenning employees attempted another delivery. All their mules died, and they were forced to travel the last

200 miles by foot. They arrived with the mail, nearly starving, almost two months later. Chorpenning now found it very difficult to hire employees to deliver the mail. However, he was able to renew the contract but decided to shift his route through the southwest and then back north through California.

The firm of Russell & Waddell was formed in Lexington, Missouri. It became one of the major freighting firms in the West.

The Johnson's Cutoff on the Carson Route of the California Trail was opened. It headed off west to the south shore of Lake Bigler (Tahoe) and then to Placerville. It became the main route for the next decade and was generally followed by the Pony Express.

1853 -

Howard Egan began the exploration of the area west of the future site of Camp Floyd for about 300 miles towards the Ruby Mountains in what is now Utah and central Nevada.

On September 13, the California Telegraph Company completed the connection of San Francisco to San Jose, Stockton, Sacramento and Marysville. James Gamble had led the crews that completed the 200-mile line.

1854 –

The Army changed its contract policy regarding shipping goods and supplies to its military post. Instead of using many smaller individual contracts, it decided to have one overall contract for all its freighting needs.

In California the Alta Telegraph Company was formed. It connected Sacramento with numerous gold towns in the Sierra Nevada. In the future it became agents for the C.O.C.&P.P. and the office in Sacramento.

1855 -

On January 1, the agreement made December 24, 1854, establishing the partnership generally known as Russell, Majors, & Waddell, became effective. The three men had pooled their capital and assets of $60,000.00.(62:12) They felt that in doing so they could more easily take advantage of the government's new contracting system. Their firm soon became the major outfitting company in the West. Initially headquartered at Lexington, Missouri, it was then relocated to

Leavenworth, Kansas. They spent about $15,000 constructing offices, warehouses, blacksmith and wagon shops, and a store. They even had their own sawmill, lumberyard and meat packing operation. (62:14)

Responsibilities were divided. William Russell served as president and was known to many as "the Napoleon of the West." (14:249) On March 27, they contracted with the War Department to haul all military supplies west of the Missouri. They soon employed 1,700 people as wagon masters, assistants, stock tenders, cooks, office workers, and messengers. One of those messengers hired later was a young boy, William Cody. It was reported that they owned 500 wagons and 7,500 oxen. They had enough wagons for more than twenty trains of twenty-six wagons. The estimated investment for the wagons alone was nearly $20,000 for each train. (62:15)

To raise necessary capital, the company borrowed heavily. However, their records indicated that they showed a total profit of $300,000 during 1855-6. (44:156) Later at their peak, it was estimated that they had 7,000 employees and owned about 75,000 oxen. (55:32) Majors stated that in 1858 they needed 3,500 wagons and sufficient men and teams just for the military freighting operation to Utah. (44:77)

Congress appropriated funds to introduce the use of camels. They were to be used by the Army to carry freight and mail in the western deserts, but by the next year the experiment had failed. Horses and mules didn't work well with camels. The camel's feet became sore and were cut by the rocky nature of the western deserts, and shoeing them only slowed the animal's speed. The use of horse, mule and wagon was superior.

Egan again traveled the route used in 1853 on his way to Sacramento in ten days to win a bet. (61:139) The route became known as "Egan's Trail." It later became the basic route followed by Chorpenning's stage line and then Simpson's exploration.

1856 –

Over 165,000 people had emigrated to California by the land route since 1841. An estimated 75,000 people signed a petition asking the federal government for a U.S. Mail service to California.

1857 -

On February 25, Russell, Majors, and Waddell signed a one-year contract with the War Department to transport its regular supplies to the posts out West. They made preparations for their normal schedule of shipments to start in early May.

Congress finally responded to the demand for faster mail service to California. In March, Congress passed and President Buchanan signed the Overland Mail Bill. It called for bids to provide for the establishment of mail service from a point on the Mississippi River to San Francisco taking no more than thirty days. The Postmaster General favored the southern route. Winters on the central route tended to be more severe causing the route to be closed. Bids were accepted for the government subsidized program.

John Butterfield and his Overland Mail Company was awarded a six-year mail contract by U.S. Postmaster General Aaron Brown. It was to use the southern route favored by Brown. The route was about 2,800 miles. It was referred to as the "oxbow" route because of its big loop to the south. Commencing from St. Louis, it went south through Springfield, Missouri; Fort Smith, Arkansas; Fort Belknap and Abilene, Texas; west to Las Cruces, New Mexico; Tucson Arizona; Yuma, Arizona and then north to Los Angeles and San Francisco, California. The contract called for delivery in thirty days or less. The route and time for delivery was still long but much quicker than the sea route around South America.

Relations between the Mormons and non-Mormons that had been simmering for some time, were brought to the boiling point. Complaints were being sent back East and to Washington questioning the Mormons' loyalty to the nation and their treatment of non-Mormons. One of the federal judges who had earlier been sent to Utah testified before Congress that federal officials were regularly insulted, federal records destroyed, some officials killed and that Brigham Young was a dictator.

President James Buchanan ordered the army to move to Utah in response and to restore order.(50:148-9) On May 28, a force of 2,500 soldiers was ordered to assemble at Fort Leavenworth. It is first placed under the command of General S.W. Harney and later that fall under Colonel A. S. Johnston. The Utah or Mormon "War" was on.

The military expected its need for additional supplies, about 60 percent more than contracted, to be met by Russell, Majors and Waddell. Based on verbal assurances that the firm would not suffer any losses, additional wagons, stock and men were hired. As word got out, prices for the wagons, mules, oxen and beef cattle increased. Wages for bullwhackers increased fifty percent. (62:17-8) Russell, Majors and Waddell were forced to increase their borrowing and debt to honor their word to haul the additional supplies.

The Army moved out in July and August. Word of the Army's march reached Brigham Young in September. On September 15 Young placed the Utah Territory under martial law and threatened to burn everything in the valley if army soldiers set foot in Salt Lake. In October the Mormon militia was ordered to hamper the army's advance, but not to take any lives.(62:19)

Three supply wagon trains along the Big Sandy River, two in Simpson's Hollow and one farther back were burned and most of the stock taken with no casualties. However, the military's food supplies for three months were lost. (62:19-20) It was now difficult for the Army to stay on its planned advance. Plans were changed, but even those were thwarted. More losses occurred as the oxen that were left were forced to work harder. Another Mormon raid took over nine hundred cattle and mules. Winter set in and more of the weakened remaining oxen died. The army was content to spend the winter at Fort Bridger, now called Camp Scott. The Mormons had earlier strengthened the fort with stone wall, but had burned the structures when they retreated to Salt Lake. Total freighting losses for Russell, Majors and Waddell amounted to almost $500,000 for that year. (62:23) Over the next two years they were forced to borrow more.

During this time Russell entered into a separate contract with Waddell and A.B. Miller of Leavenworth. It was called Miller, Russell & Company. It also took supplies west and established a store at Camp Scott. When the army finally moved into Salt Lake in 1858, the company also opened stores in Millersville and Camp Floyd. By the end of that year it had incurred a debt of $200,000.00 to Russell, Majors and Waddell. (62:25) That served to increase the firm's problems even more.

At the December meeting of the North American Telegraph Association, Hiram Sibley promoted the idea of a cross country telegraph line. The discussions seemed to focus on the problems of Indian hostilities, buffalo, insufficient wood, the dryness of the county and the problem and expenses of upkeep over long distances. The American Telegraph Company favored a southern line running west from New Orleans to California. (16:191) Sibley's interest was not dampened.

1858 –

A new two-year contact with the War Department was signed by Russell, Majors and Waddell on January 16th with higher rates. Relations with Congress were mixed at best, as a bill regarding the incurred losses were discussed. The new contract called for an additional center for shipping, and Nebraska City was selected. Work began on building the necessary facilities there. As a method of meeting its freighting responsibilities while decreasing its financial ones, Majors began to subcontract with other private freighters.

The Hannibal and St. Joseph Railroad was completed to St. Joseph. Service opened in February.

Congress questioned the value of the loss and the conduct of both the military and the freighting firm. Congress had not allocated funds for payment or to the War Department. Russell worked out a deal with the Secretary of War, John Floyd. Russell received signed drafts or acceptances based on the firm's anticipation of funds. There were no guaranteed payment dates and there was some concern whether Floyd had the authority to grant them. The drafts were to be considered the obligation of the firm, not the War Department. (62:24) Even with those, Russell had a difficult time raising needed funds. Many banks would not accept them as backing.

Gold was discovered in the Pikes Peak area of Colorado. Traffic along the Platte River portion of the Oregon Trail increased. "Pike's Peak or Bust" was seen on many a wagon. As more people went, there was a corresponding need for supplies and mail service. New routes to the area opened and new companies were formed to provide those services. The Smoky Hill route cut more than one hundred miles off the old established Platte route, but it was considered more dangerous. Some sought out an even more direct route. Silver was discovered in the

Washoe Mountains in Nevada/California. Any route to the "diggin's" that was shorter would be used to beat the other fellow. Pressure was felt by the Indians along the whole route as the emigrants passed through. As more and more settlers and miners arrived, relations with the local Indians, especially the Paiutes, in the Sierras and Great Basin deteriorated. The Indian subsistence way of life was being disrupted. Trees were cut, animals killed, water diverted, their lands occupied and the Indians, especially the women, were often mistreated.

The Placerville, Humboldt & Salt Lake City Telegraph Company was formed. It hoped to build a line to Salt Lake City. Progress is slow. It took two years to get over the Sierra Nevada, and then they stopped.

George Chorpenning opened a mail line west from Salt Lake City through the Great Basin over the Egan Trail. He had five stage stations built. Egan was placed in charge of them.

On September 15, the Butterfield Overland Stage Company fulfilled its mail contract and opened its stage service over the southern or ox-bow route to San Francisco. Postage for a letter was to be ten cents per half ounce and one hundred dollars per passenger. The scheduled time was twenty-five days.

In October, Captain James H. Simpson started an exploratory trip west from Camp Floyd. He was forced to return due to the onset of winter. Earlier in the year he had surveyed a new route for the military from Fort Bridger to Camp Floyd by passing Salt Lake City.

1859 -

In February, Russell formed a partnership with John S. Jones. It was known as The Leavenworth & Pikes Peak Express Company. They hoped to capitalize on the recent discovery of gold in Colorado. Benjamin F. Ficklin was a major stockholder. Russell hoped that Majors and Waddell would join, but they were opposed to it. (44:164) The firm purchased fifty Concord coaches, one thousand Kentucky mules and other equipment. By March, men were sent out to build and establish stations along the new route. The route to Denver through Kansas they selected was south of the main trail along the Platte. It was also a more direct route than the Smoky Hill Trail which lay to its south. It was about fifty miles shorter and about 200 miles shorter than the route from Leavenworth along the Platte. They hoped that would bring them more traffic. However, the cost of building and equipping the new stations was high. They borrowed extensively from Russell, Majors, and Waddell.

In April, Simpson resumed his expedition west to develop a new route through central Nevada. He followed much of Egan's and Chorpenning's route west from Camp Floyd to Ruby Valley, but before reaching Hastings Pass had decided not to follow their route, but cut southwest to Genoa. (66:58) Simpson's expedition opened the new route and made it to Genoa and then returned. The Central Route across Nevada was now mapped and shown to be feasible. It was used almost immediately by some emigrant trains, and Chorpenning altered his route west of Ruby Valley.

On May 11, Jones, Russell and Company, The Leavenworth & Pike's Peak Express Company, took over Hockaday and Liggett. It was the stage line that had the government mail contract between St. Joseph and Salt Lake. However, that required them to switch from their newly establish route through Kansas to the one in the mail contract along the Platte, which also included a cutoff to Denver. (57:487) That purchase, the rerouting, the longer route, and the refurbishing of the purchase line added more expenses and debts mounted. They used many of the former company's employees and stations.

On October 28, Russell, Majors, & Waddell took over the bankrupt Leavenworth & Pikes Peak Express Company with its reported debt of over one half million dollars. (62:57) Russell's reputation was saved, and also, indirectly, Majors' and Russell's reputation and investments. (44:165)

The Central Overland California & Pike's Peak Express Company (C.O.C. & P.P.) was organized on November 23, with William H. Russell as president. Its Kansas charter authorized it ". . .to operate express, stage, passenger, and transportation routes...for the conveyance of persons, mail, or property in Kansas or beyond its limits." (62:62) Benjamin Ficklin was retained and put in charge of operations as route superintendent and was expected to handle problems. One involved financial records and expenses, and the other was the trouble with stock thieves in the Julesburg region. Jules Reni had a trading post in the area and had been put in charge of the station. Ficklin believed that Jules was associated with, if not the leader of the thieves. Ficklin had hired Joseph Slade who then fired Jules, and Slade took over that section. The famous feud between Jules and Slade developed.

The C.O.C. & P.P. ran daily stages that made the 1,200 mile trip in ten days. They used Concord coaches and about 1000 Kentucky mules, except in the mountain area where 300 smaller mules were used. (44:166)

Sometime, probably in December or perhaps early January, Russell met in Washington with Senator Gwin of California. They discussed the need for faster communications with California and how it could best be accomplished. After some discussion Russell committed the firm to establishing a Pony Express to California. He left Washington and returned to Leavenworth to tell his partners of the meeting. Both Majors and Waddell were initially opposed to the idea. They feared that it would be a financial disaster for them. Russell told his partners he had given his word that the firm would do it and that Gwin would work for a government subsidy for them if they proved the viability of the Central Route. Once again in order to save their reputation, Majors and Waddell agreed. (44:184) They also hoped to attract the public's attention and support from Congress for the Central overland route, and thus more government contracts and money.

1860 –

On January 27, Russell sent a dispatch to his son, John W. Russell, the secretary for the C.O.C. & P.P., announcing his decision, "Have determined to establish a Pony Express to Sacramento, California, commencing 3rd of April. Time ten days." Two days earlier in New York an incorrect dispatch reported that the government was to institute a horse express from St. Joseph to Placerville. (58:42)

On February 3, the Central Overland California and Pikes Peak Express was chartered in Kansas. Its concerns were coaches, freighting and the Pony Express. The organization of the Pony Express was established. It had one general manager and five districts, each with its own superintendent.

In February, ads appeared for purchasing horses. Ads for riders appeared in March. Arrangements were made to obtain or build stations along the selected route. Men and equipment moved out along the route from Sacramento, Salt Lake City and St. Joseph.

Even though Leavenworth was the central office for the C.O.C. & P.P., St. Joseph was selected as the eastern terminus of the Pony Express. It was kept a secret until March 31, when announced in the St. Joseph *Weekly West*. Leavenworth was shocked. St. Joseph was already served by both the railroad, the Hannibal & St. Joseph Railroad, and the telegraph. It was the natural starting point. In addition, St. Joseph businessmen and the C.O.C. & P.P. had been negotiating and finally signed a confidential agreement on March 20. The C.O.C. & P.P. agreed that St. Joseph would be the starting point for its express and stage service in return for certain concessions including land in Missouri and across the river, a building, office space, free passage across the Missouri and other items and concessions related to future railroads. (62:76-77

Severe winter weather and continued disruptions resulted in near starvation for many of the Indians in the Great Basin. Discontent was high.

On April 3, the Pony began its first run west from St. Joseph, Missouri. In San Francisco, California, the eastbound mail also started its run. The mail was delivered in St. Joseph on April 13 and in San Francisco shortly after midnight on April 14. Russell's promise was fulfilled. Celebrations were held far and wide. The event was even covered in Europe. This column appeared in *St. Joseph Daily Gazette*'s April 3, 1860 *Pony Express Edition*. Because of a delay in the arrival of the train with the mail, it was 7:15 when the rider left St. Joseph.

The Army delayed its normal May and June shipments for the Southwest to August and September. Russell, Majors and Waddell had already organized their wagons, men and stock for May shipping, but now had to hold back. However, they still had to pay their men while they waited and also had to pay for the purchases. It also delayed government compensation until later in the year. This put further financial strain on the firm because their loans would be due before income was received.

In early May, a council was held among the different Paiutes to discuss what actions should be taken to combat their deteriorating situation. Many blamed the white man for the loss of food supplies and supported war. Just as old Chief Winnemucca had supported peace, so did Chief Numaga.

On May 7, an incident occurred at Williams Station, Nevada, which ignited the Paiute or Pyramid War. Three men, James Fleming, Dutch Phil and Samuel Sullivan, had arrived at Williams Station east of Buckland's. James O. Williams, the stationkeeper, was away and had left his two younger brothers, David and Oscar, in charge of the station. At some time the three men took some Paiute women captive. One of the captives escaped and got word to her husband who was attending the council meeting. He and others decided to free the other captives. They attacked the station and killed the Williams brothers and the other three men.

On May 8, James Williams returned to the station and found the bodies of all the men killed. He hurried back to Carson City warning of an Indian uprising along the way, not knowing the actual circumstances leading to the "massacre/killings." Reported accounts varied but all described the results of the attack and the conditions of the bodies as horrific. An expeditionary force of volunteers with Major Ormsby as their leader was formed, intent on revenge. By then some of the raiding party had returned to the council meeting and told their story, demanding further attacks. The Paiute War was on. (The exact location of Williams Station is not known. It has been put at ten miles northeast of Buckland's on the bend of the Carson to near the Carson sink station or at Smith/ Honey Lake Smith's station. A *Daily Evening Bulletin* article put it about two miles from the Big Meadows on the Carson.)

On May 11, the Postmaster General annulled Chorpenning's mail contract for failure to fulfill it. The contract was given to the C.O.C. & P.P. It was hoped that this would provide some financial relief and possibly more contracts once they could prove the success of their Central Route. However, the government still owed them money for their earlier losses.

On May 12, the Battle of Pyramid Lake occurred between 105 volunteers and a group of Paiutes. It was a disaster for the volunteers who suffered at least seventy-six dead and others wounded. Ormsby was one of those killed. Actual Paiute casualties were three wounded. (14:69) Local newspapers followed the fighting. A column in the San Francisco *Daily Evening Bulletin,* "The Army in Washoe" kept readers informed about the actions by both the Indians and the army. A reporter with the forces noted that the men in the field at the end of

May numbered 822, 610 volunteers and 212 regular army. His reports which commenced shortly after the Battle of Pyramid Lake were sent by telegraph.

Fighting along the Central Route in Nevada and Utah broke out. While reports don't all agree, other stations including Miller's, Cold Spring, Smith's Creek, Cold Springs, Jacob's Spring, Simpson's Park, Dry Creek, Roberts Creek Station, Butte Station, Schell Creek, Antelope Springs Station, and Egan's Station were also reportedly attacked, burned or destroyed. Some of these were attacked more than once. The mail runs were soon brought to a halt. Station keepers and the stock-hands suffered the most. Damage to property was placed at about $75,000 by July. This only added to the deteriorating finances of the C.O.C. & P.P.. Indian attacks did not end, but continued off and on throughout the next year, but they were never as intense, nor did they halt the mail. Some of the stations that were non-existent or spared during the Paiute War, such as Edwards Creek, Eight Mile and Spring Valley were later raided.

On May 31, an article in the San Francisco *Daily Evening Bulletin* reported that, "W. W. Finney, agent for the Pony Express, conveys the unwelcome intelligence that no express will depart from this city to-morrow, and that whether the enterprise will be renewed at an early day, will depend on the suspension of Indian hostilities on the route to Salt Lake."

In June, the internal conflicts, both personal and organizational, between Russell and Ficklin came to a head. By July 1, Ficklin had resigned. At this same time, Russell had hoped to secure government mail contracts for the C.O.C. & P.P. stage service, yet by July, none were awarded. Creditors were becoming worried.

On June 16, Congress passed a bill authorizing bids to establish a telegraph to be completed no later than July 1, 1862. It also provided for the end of the Pony Express once the telegraph was completed. Hiram Sibley, president of Western Union Telegraph Company, submitted a bid. The contract was awarded to Western Union in October after the two other bidders withdrew. (16:191) The plan was to build from the east and west and meet in Salt Lake City.

By early June, hostilities had quickly dropped off as military strength, patrols and actions increased. Efforts were underway to resupply and open the express stations across the Great Basin. A wagon train arrived without trouble with the Indians.

On June 24, the *Daily Evening Bulletin*'s *Extra Bulletin*'s column "By Magnetic Telegraph" led with "HURRAH! THE PONY EXPRESS AGAIN!" Mail delivery west from Salt Lake City resumed and arrived in Carson City. The mail arrived safely in San Francisco on June 25th. Attacks on the Pony Express stations & riders decreased dramatically as military patrols and action increased. Incidents still occurred, but the mail was never stopped again because of Indian problems. On July 8th the mail from California arrived safely in St. Joseph.

In July Russell traveled to New York and Washington. There he tried to secure loans on the government acceptances and to receive payment from the government for funds due. The needed funds were more difficult to obtain.

On July 20, construction on Fort Churchill began under the direction of Captain George Stewart. The fort was located on the Carson River adjacent to Buckland's Station. It was built in response to the Paiute War. It was completed that fall after the fighting had subsided. It replaced Buckland's as the Pony Express station

In July, the railroad was completed to Folsom, California. It then became the western terminus for the mail & Pony Express. Mail could then be taken by train.

The financial state became so poor that the employees of the Central Overland California and Pike's Peak Express were complaining about their not being paid in a timely manner. At one point, Bill Trotter, a stage driver for the C.O.C. & P.P. said it now stood for "Clean Out of Cash and Poor Pay." (56:584)

By October, Majors realized the financial mess the company was in. Estimates for the daily costs for the Pony Express alone were placed at one thousand dollars a day. The income from the mail did not come close to paying for it. Majors' and Waddell's initial fears were correct- the Pony Express would not make money, and it had not brought new contracts as they had hoped. Majors began to sell some of his and the company's land, equipment and stock in Kansas in order to pay off some of the creditors and hold others off. Concern about the firm's possible bankruptcy spread to investors.

On November 6, Abraham Lincoln was elected President. By the time he was sworn in on March 4, 1861, the Confederate States of

America had been formed. Fears increased that California, with its vast resources, might also join.

In December, reports were published about the possible theft of some Indian bonds from the Department of the Interior. On December 24, William Russell was arrested and charged with accepting the bonds against the "acceptances" based on those received earlier from Secretary of War John Floyd. Godard Baily, a clerk in the Department of Interior, was also arrested. He was the one who, during the prior months, had offered the bonds to Russell. Russell used those bonds as collateral with some banks, but even then the loans obtained were not equal to their face values. Russell was held on $200,000 bail and Baily on $3,000. Both men were eventually released on bail. Suspicions of possible intrigue developed. Russell had both his supporters and his enemies. Unfavorable reports continued, and Congress soon began hearings and an investigation. On December 24, the House called for a Select Committee to investigate the charges. It commenced hearings on December 27 and held its last one on February 8, 1861. Russell's reputation was severely questioned by some while others stood firmly with him. Secretary Floyd had resigned and came under more suspicion. Even today there is speculation over the exact role Bailey played in the event and the political intrigue behind it. Some people think that Bailey offered the bonds, which he had no right to do, in order to entrap Russell. Perhaps it was part of a plot by his competitors or southern sympathizers to discredit his company and also the Central Route.

1861 -

On January 11, the Pacific Telegraph Company was chartered as a division of Western Union. Its function was to build a telegraph line from Omaha to Salt Lake City. The year before, Edward Creighton was assigned the task of surveying the whole route to the Carson River. After he returned he was put in charge of building the line west to Salt Lake. The fact that Creighton had completed the survey during the winter was considered more proof of the Central Route's advantages. The route was nearly identical to the Pony Express Trail.

By the end of January, the financial indebtedness of the firm of Russell, Majors, and Waddell was enormous. They had practically no more credit and their earlier notes were past due. Short term loans had been made using their land, facilities, equipment, and future income as collateral. The value of their assets and liabilities based on their records and those of the government were open to debate. This was true of both the firm's and the respective individual's data. There seemed to be no question that the firm and partners were in debt and there was little hope they could overcome it. They claimed that the government owed them $1,349.548. Two years later the firm's liabilities were placed at $1,731.00. (62:114-5) According to some, Ben Holladay had become one of their largest creditors over the ensuing year. He was later given a mortgage on the company. In spite of all this, the Pony Express kept running.

Secretary of the Interior, Jacob Thompson, who had been criticized for his carelessness, resigned. As the Indian bond scandal continued, a grand jury handed down indictments on January 29 against all three- Floyd, Russell, and Bailey- for conspiracy to defraud the government and also against Russell for accepting stolen bonds. Ultimately, none of the men were convicted or served time. The cases dragged on and were finally dropped. Perhaps the Civil War became more important or interest subsided.

By February, five states including Texas had seceded from the Union. Mail delivery over the Southern route by the Overland Mail Company came to a sudden halt. Some of their stations and equipment had been destroyed and stock taken. The central route with the Pony Express and stage line became the main overland system for communications between the East and the West coast. Russell and company now had another opportunity to secure the government mail contract, but they needed the support of Congress.

Jefferson Davis became president of the Confederate States of America on February 18. The secessionist movement in California was still a concern even though the state legislature had passed a resolution of loyalty to the Union. General Albert S. Johnston, commander of the Department of the Pacific in San Francisco, resigned his post to join the Confederacy. He was replaced by General Edwin A. Sumner, an ardent supporter of the Union. He sent troops to Los Angeles in response to secessionist activities. In July, after the Rebel flag was raised in Virginia City, additional troops were sent to Fort Churchill with orders to disarm and disperse those responsible. Both actions were successful.

In March, the Pony made its fastest run, carrying a copy of President Lincoln's March 4th Inaugural Address. Special preparations were taken to ensure the quickest possible delivery. Riders were reminded of the importance of the mission. Extra relays were used. The address was delivered in seven days and seventeen hours.

On March 2, the southern route was formally abandoned. News of the attack in Texas reached Congress. The postal appropriations bill was introduced and quickly amended. Congress switched mail delivery to the central route without opening it for bids. That was a blow to the hopes of Russell, Majors and Waddell. The Overland Mail Company was allowed to retain its contract as amended by the new bill. It was awarded a $1,000,000 subsidy and even was reimbursed for losses along its former route. The arrangement required continued service from either St. Joseph or Atchison to Placerville.

The Overland Mail Company had its own financial and management problems. Three of largest investors in the Overland Mail Company were directors of Wells Fargo & Company, its major competitor. Even though the Overland Mail Company was given control of the whole route, it took control over only the section west of Salt Lake, while the C.O.C. & P.P. was allowed to continue operating the eastern section. It was not covered by the government contract but under a subcontract with the Overland Mail Company. The subsidy was split and $470,000 was given to the C.O.C. & P.P.. However, the amount was still not enough to pay its mounting debts. The new service was to commence July 1 and rates were to be cut in half. The agreement was supported by William Russell and William Dinsmore, presidents of their respective companies. As called for by the bill, an investigation began into the feasibility of moving the stage and Pony Express route through Denver and then over the Cherokee Trail to Salt Lake City. Russell's spirits were revived. By April, it was confirmed the estimated cost was too high. The C.O.C. & P.P. had no money.

In some areas the employees were not being paid in a timely manner. The anonymous poem, "On or about the first of May, The Boys would like to have their pay; If not paid by that day, The stock along the road may stray" made its appearance. Someone found the funds. (56:584) The coaches and the Pony kept running.

The Overland Telegraph Company was chartered on April 10. It soon began the task of completing the building of the transcontinental telegraph line. Lines had already been laid to Fort Churchill in the West and to Fort Kearny in Nebraska.

On April 12, Fort Sumter was attacked. The Civil War began.

On April 26, Russell was asked to resign, and Bela M. Hughes became the President of the C.O.C. & P.P. Hughes was Benjamin Holladay's cousin.

In May, telegraph construction crews were organized, and in June they began to move east from Fort Churchill at about five miles a day. James Gamble was in charge of the construction.

The Central Pacific Railroad was incorporated on June 28. Within a few years it played a major role in the construction of the transcontinental railroad and speeding the delivery of the regular mail. However, its final route did not make use of the central route through the great basin.

On July 1, Placerville became the western terminus for the Pony Express.

On July 4, the telegraph construction crews moved west from Fort Kearny. Creighton was said to require no less than twenty-five poles per mile and hoped to complete five to six miles per day. By August, they approached the forks of the Platte. Construction also occurred about the same time in Salt Lake City. The first pole was put up on July 11 as crews also worked east.

On July 5, Hughes was authorized to grant Holladay a deed of trust covering all the C.O.C. & P.P. property to cover Holladay's loans. It is generally held that the deed covered much more than the value of any of his loans to the company. It was not recorded until November.

Concern over riots and strong Southern sympathies in St. Joseph as well as with the new ownership and management, Atchison became the eastern terminus of the Pony Express. It was about fifteen miles farther west, and by then, it was also served by the railroad and telegraph.

On October 24, the western telegraph line was completed to Salt Lake City. The eastern line had been completed on October 17. The nation was successfully crossed by the telegraph. Based on Creighton's requirements, no less than 31,500 telegraph poles had probably been used to connect the points between Fort Kearny to Fort Churchill.

On October 25, the announcement was placed that the Pony Express had ended. Many newspapers soon lamented the passing of the faithful "Pony."

"Our little friend, the Pony is to run no more. . . .Farewell and forever, thou staunch, wilderness-overcoming, swift-footed messenger! For the good thou hast done we praise thee...Rest, then, in peace; for thou hast run thy race, thou hast followed thy course, thou hast done the work that was given thee to do."
—*Sacramento Bee*

"A fast and faithful friend has the Pony been to our far-off state. Summer and winter, storms and shine, day and night, he has traveled like the weaver's shuttle back and forth til now his work is done. Goodbye, Pony! No proud and star-caparisoned charger in the war field has ever done so great, so true and so good a work as thine. No pampered and world famous racer of the turf will ever win from you the proud fame of the fleet courser of the continent. . . .We have looked to you as those who wait for the morning, and how seldom did you fail us!... You have served us well." —California *Pacific*

In early November, the last eastbound mail was delivered in Atchison, and later that month the last run west was completed to Sacramento on November 18, and the mail arrived in San Francisco. The Pony ran no more.

On November 22, C.O.C. & P.P. president Ben Hughes and secretary John Russell gave Holladay a bond and a mortgage on the whole company. Holladay called it shortly thereafter, but it could not be paid.

1862 –

After two earlier attempts, the final sale of the C.O.C. & P.P. was held on March 21. Ben Holladay was the sole bidder for $100,000 and became the official owner.

1863 -

It was reported that mail which had been lost during an earlier Indian attack was found and delivered.

On October 6, Johnny Fry, the first rider out of St. Joe, was killed during the Battle at Baxter Springs by Quantrill's Raiders during a surprise attack on the Union forces. (43:65) William Tough, another former rider lived through the battle.

1872 -

On April 1, William Waddell died. He had returned to his old home in Lexington, Missouri. Before the company failed, he had sold his home to his son and put away $100,000 for his wife. Later that year on September 10, William Russell died. He had tried to recover his resources. Still the "risk taker," he invested in road building companies that soon failed. He then moved to New York City were he invested in mining stocks. Nothing seemed to work for him. Neither of these men had been able to overcome their financial loses.

1883-

Buffalo Bill's Wild West show opened in Colville, Nebraska. He had had his "Old Glory Blowout" on July 4 the year before in North Platte, Nebraska. It was more like a rodeo, but his Wild West Shows included many more events and acts. Over the years its acts and participants changed some. His acts included authentic or real people. Indians, buffalo, horses, cattle, cowboys, sharpshooters, soldiers, stagecoaches were all there, but it was the Pony Express and its now famous rider, Buffalo Bill Cody that drew the shouts of praise. It was the part of the show that he had created. He brought the West, as he portrayed it, to all the people. The show operated into the turn of the century and even performed in Europe before kings and queens.

1900 -

On January 14, Alexander Majors passed away. He was the last of the founders to die. After the Pony Express he had become involved in some freighting projects. He even tried investing in mining interests. Nothing seemed to work out well. He had moved to Denver where he came in contact with Buffalo Bill. He assisted Majors in writing his memoirs *Seventy Years on the Frontier* and arranged for its editing and publishing.

1917 –

William "Buffalo Bill" Cody, the great promoter of the Pony Express, died on January 10.

1934 –

William Campbell the last of the authenticated Pony Express riders died on May 23. In one of his last interviews he stated, "Greatest of all the inventions to me, because it affected me directly, is the telegraph. In the two minutes we used to be allowed to change a horse at a station, Western Union now sends a message to New York or even to London. The telegraph does in a second what it took eighty young men and hundreds of horses eight days to do when I was a rider in the Pony Express." The Pony's passage into history was now complete.

1992 –

The Pony Express Trail was designated a National Historic Trail.

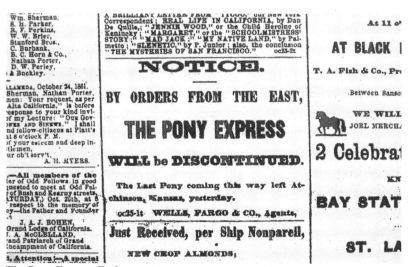

The Pony Express Ends. - *Daily Evening Bulletin, October 25, 1861*

Chapter Four

Artists and Recorders

In my research and writings about many of the historic trails, I noticed that certain artists are associated with specific historic trails. Some of these were emigrants, such as J. Goldsborough Bruff and Jonas Hittle, who wanted to record their journey and the wonders seen as they traveled west. Some, such as James F. Wilkins and J. Wesley Jones recorded scenes with the plan to profit from their sketches and paintings by producing pantoscopes to show to the general public. And others, such as William H. Tappan, as part of a military expedition recorded the journey as they followed the Oregon Trail. Frederick Piercy was engaged to record the Mormon trek to Salt Lake City. Some of the emigrants, such as J. Goldsborough Bruff, were skilled and created accurate portrayals, while others such as Jonas Hittle made very basic or crude drawings.

At times, individuals such as William Henry Jackson, who originally recorded his journey for individual reasons and later became a skilled photographer and artist, were employed to record government sponsored expeditions. Bruff, Hittle, Wilkins and Jones followed the California Trail; Piercy, the Mormon Trail; Tappan, the Oregon Trail; and Jackson parts of the Oregon, California, and Mormon trails.

Unfortunately, there seems to be no single artist whose known intention was to record the Pony Express Trail. Fortunately, however, there were artists that did intend to record scenes along the route they took that happened to correspond to segments of the Pony Express route. Six of these illustrators will be highlighted, but the works of others are also used in this section.

Captain James Hervey Simpson was assigned to survey a new route across the Great Basin from Camp Floyd, Utah, to Genoa, Nevada. As with most military exploratory expeditions, Simpson brought some people specifically assigned to make illustrations of plants, animals and the topography. One was a sketch artist, H. V. A. Von Bechk. He was given "the duty of sketching the country in a manner to illustrate its common as well as peculiar characteristics." (66:44) John J. Young, a Washington, D.C. artist, used the Von Bechk sketches to make watercolors that accompanied the official report to Congress. They provide a vivid view of the Great Basin area.

Simpson's initial budget included a request for $200 to $400 for photographic equipment, and he also received authorization to hire a photographer at $40 per month and an assistant for $25. In the spring of 1858 Samuel C. Mills was hired as the photographer with Edward Jagiello as his assistant. (17:4) Mills joined the expedition at Fort Leavenworth. He took a number of photos of sites along the trail as they traveled west to Camp Floyd. Once at Camp Floyd he took a number of photos of the fort. Many of these old photos have recently been identified as the product of Mills and some are used in the pictorial section. However, no photos of the journey west of Camp Floyd have been identified or are known to exist, but this does not mean none were ever taken. After the expedition Mills returned to Washington in the fall of 1859. He continued his career as a photographer for a few years. He began to study law, was admitted to the bar in 1872 and was soon appointed as a judge. He died in 1911.

Sir Richard F. Burton, an Englishman, was a world traveler and explorer-writer and is perhaps best known for his work and translation of *Arabian Nights* published in 1885. He began his world travels early in his military career when he was stationed in India. Returning to England he was later sponsored by the Royal Geographical Society. In all, his journeys and explorations took him to Arabia, eastern and central Africa. Then in 1860 he decided to come to the United States and write about it. He came to St. Joseph, Missouri and took passage on a C.O.C. & P.P. Overland Stage. His journey from St. Joseph, Missouri began on Tuesday, August 7, 1860. He arrived in Salt Lake City on August 25. He remained there until September 20 while he explored the area and the beliefs and practices of the Mormon Church. Leaving Salt Lake City, he reached Carson City, Nevada, October 19, 1860. He stayed there for a short time and then continued on to San Francisco. He was already writing his draft for his book in November

1860. It is important to mention that while the stage did not stop at every Pony Express station, the Overland Stage line and Pony Express did share a great many of the stations. Thus, his route west to California coincided with much of the route and stations that the Pony Express used. He traveled after the Paiute War had "ended", but he could see the results of it on the stations in the area west of Camp Floyd to Carson City. He rode in a Concord coach during the journey to Salt Lake City and then in an Ambulance, or lighter coach. He returned to England by way of Mexico and Panama. His book, *The City of the Saints and Across the Rocky Mountains to California*, printed in 1861 was about his journey, observations and experiences. He did not mince his words. His book was used as an important source for a number of the early illustrations and extensively for the quotes to describe life at the stations and conditions along the Pony Express Trail. He made other sketches along the route which were not published in his book.

William Henry Jackson first went west by way of Salt Lake City to California and back in 1866-7 five years after the Pony Express had ended. His journey began in Nebraska City, Nebraska, and continued to Salt Lake City. Then he turned off southwest to meet the Old Spanish Trail to California making sketches and paintings along the way. After he returned to Omaha, he opened up a photographic studio in 1867. He began photographing the westward movement of the railroad and then became one of the official recorders for the Hayden Expeditions during the 1870s. By the 1930s he began turning many of his earlier sketches and photographs into paintings. He died at the age of 99 in 1943. Today, he is one the best well-known trail artists and his works are featured in the Oregon Trail Museum in Scotts Bluff National Monument. Although his jumping-off place was different, the routes converged east of Fort Kearny and were nearly identical or closely paralleled the earlier route of the Pony Express, all the way to Salt Lake City and south towards Camp Floyd. The single largest holding of his works is with the National Park Service located in Scotts Bluff National Monument, Gering, Nebraska.

Charles Moellman was a soldier in the U.S.Army. He was stationed in the Idaho/Nebraska Territory which included part of modern Wyoming. He served as a bugler in the Eleventh Ohio Volunteers. He kept a journal and sketch book and made a number of sketches of the posts he served at or passed through in the early 1860s. Since his service was after the Pony Express's run, his drawings show how a number of the old Pony Express station sites looked like two years later when the military increased its presence and expanded its outposts. Based on limited sources, it seems that many stations were expanded or replaced or perhaps new ones were built nearby. Many of his works are at the University of Wyoming. Most of his sketches and those drawn by Caspar Collins are very similar and also similar to ones painted later by Jackson.

Edward Vischer was an artist-photograper-historian. He had earlier emigrated to Mexico from Germany when he was nineteen and worked for some commercial establishments. In 1842 he came to California when he was about thirty-three. He became interested in sketching and painting when he was fifty years old. He started sketching the landscapes of California, its mountains and forests. He expanded his subjects to include the California missions, rural scenes, mining, and homes and inns. A number of the places he sketched in 1860 and 1861 were associated with the Pony Express. They were along the old emigrant trail or Bonanza Road in California that was used by the Pony Express. His sketches were quite accurate. He often added water color or crayon. He also reproduced his sketches as lithographs and later photographed them and published them as portfolios. The largest holdings of his works are in Claremont University.

The comments of a number of individuals, in addition to those of Burton, are relied upon to provide much of the information quoted that is paired with the illustrations and used in other sections of the book. Frank Root had served as the assistant postmaster and postal clerk at Atchison, Kansas which was the eastern terminus of the Pony Express during the last few months of its operation. He then became a stagecoach driver and drove over much of the Pony Express route. He personally knew many of the individuals with the Pony Express. He co-authored a book about the history of the overland route. Billy Campbell was a Pony Express rider. Although he rode during the last twelve months, he was an employee of Russell, Majors and Waddell prior to that. He had first-hand knowledge of the route and employees. His ride took him through most of Division II along the Platte River. He continued to live in the area. He was one of a few riders interviewed later by many writers and historians. He died in 1932. Superintendent Major Howard Egan's sons, Howard and

Richard "Ras," rode for the Pony Express. They were all stationed at and rode in Division IV. Howard also served as the station keeper at Deep Creek. Some of their experiences, along with their father's ,were recorded in a book about their father's life. Nick Wilson was another Pony Express rider. His routes were in Divisions IV and V. He wrote about his experiences and was also interviewed by later writers and historians. I. J. Benjamin was a German traveler who traveled by stagecoach across the western United States to California. He also spent time in Salt Lake City, as did Burton, to learn about the Mormon religion. He spent three years in the United States and wrote about his experiences upon his return to Germany. His account of his stagecoach trip is not as detailed as Burton's, but it was helpful in corroborating information. For information about their books, see the bibliography. Doctor Charles Clark traveled by wagon from St. Joseph to Denver. His diary over the eastern portion of the route was also helpful, with general information about conditions along the trail. He did not need to stop at the stations, but does comment about some of them.

Scout's Rest Ranch. Home of Buffalo Bill Cody—the most famous promoter of the Pony Express. - *Hill photo*

79

Scotts Bluff National Monument

Chapter Five

The Mail Goes Through
A Pictorial Journey Across the Continent

L et us now ride along with the Pony through the sketches, paintings, and photos and the words of those who long ago made similar journeys. While the Pony ran both east and west, the journey taken here will be from the east to the west.

Jumping off from St. Joseph, Missouri, across the Kansas prairies, up the valley of the Little Blue, then across to and along the valleys of the Platte, the South Platte and the North Platte rivers, over to and up the Sweetwater River Valley to the great South Pass went the Pony. Thence, cutting southwest to cross the Wasatch into Salt Lake City in the valley of the Great Salt Lake, skirting south and west around the Great Salt Lake Desert, then west across the Great Basin, over the Sierra Nevada to Sacramento, and finally, down to San Francisco. Sit back and read along as the sights go by as we cross the continent, and experience what the Pony did in ten days of hard riding. Along with the sketches, prints and photos, there are quotes and comments about the riders, events and sites by some of those who experienced them firsthand. It is hoped that these will provide a clearer understanding of the circumstances surrounding the Pony Express and the conditions faced by its riders.

By comparing the yesterday and today illustrations, the reader will notice a number of things. In some areas it will seem that little has changed, while in others, the sites are barely recognizable. With the growth of settlement, the expansion of agriculture and the use of irrigation, some areas have been greatly altered. Some sites were in cultivated areas which made finding the exact spot difficult. Some areas have had only slight changes in vegetation while others more. Most notably is the growth of trees in many parts. They also made photographing sites very difficult. In some areas they all but obscured the whole view. In others it was necessary to move slightly away from the actual site because trees have grown up and now block the view. Rivers have changed course. Many have been dammed to control flows, provide for irrigation and end seasonal flooding which has enabled trees to take hold along the river bottom. Local inhabitants have also planted trees along fence rows or to act as wind breaks. Other changes have occurred that are not readily observable. The native wildlife has changed. Most noticeable is the absence of the buffalo, but other animals, such as the elk, the wolf, and the prairie dog are also greatly reduced or gone, especially in the Great Plains. As America's population growth has increased, these changes seem to be happening even faster.

Railroad steam locomotive *Missouri.*

- De Golyer Library, Southern Methodist University ag 1982.0232

A train pulled by the locomotive *Missouri* brought the mail on the last portion of its journey to St. Joseph before being placed in the mochila's cantinas. The mail had been collected from as far east as New York City and Washington, D.C. A special courier who collected the mail was to deliver it to Hannibal, Missouri. It was then to be transported by the Hannibal & St. Joseph Railroad to St. Joseph, Missouri, in time for the opening ceremonies and the scheduled departure of the Pony at 5 p.m.

Due to an unfortunate mishap, the courier missed the scheduled train in Detroit. He had to take another which resulted in the mail arriving two and a half hours late in Hannibal. J. T. K. Haywood, the superintendent of the Hannibal & St. Joseph Railroad, was informed by telegraph of the courier's pending late arrival. Orders were then sent to Hannibal to make special arrangements to ensure that the late mail would arrive in St. Joseph as quickly as possible. Addison Clark, the most experienced engineer, was selected to make the run, and the *Missouri* was the engine selected for the special task. The tracks were cleared, and he was told to make a record that would stand for fifty years. (61:54) Clark and the *Missouri* made the 206-mile run in a record four hours and fifty-one minutes, arriving about 7 p.m. From the station, the mail was delivered to the Pony Express.

Patee House - *Patee House Museum, St. Joseph, Missouri*

PATEE HOUSE

The Patee House, a 140-room hotel, was one of the most luxurious hotels west of the Mississippi. It was built by John Patee in 1858. It was constructed a little uphill which afforded it a good view of the area and river below. Burton referred to the Patee House as "the Fifth Avenue Hotel of St. Jo." Burton began his trip from there as did the Pony Express. The offices of the Central Overland California & Pikes Peak Express and the Pony Express were on the first floor. The hotel also served as the home station, and riders stayed there.

Today the area surrounding the old hotel has been built up, and the view is somewhat obscured. The building is now a national historic landmark. Inside it is an area devoted to the Pony Express and a reconstructed office shown here. It also houses many other worthwhile attractions. The hotel is located at the corner of 12th and Penn Street.

Today there is less disagreement about the location from where the first mail actually left. Most report it was from the headquarters in the Patee House, but others maintain it was from the stables. Today it is believed it started from the hotel. The mail train was late. Some reports noted how onlookers pulled the horse's tail hairs out as souvenirs. The

84

Patee House today - *Hill photo*

horse and rider went back to the stable to wait for the mail's arrival. Both Majors and Russell were in attendance. Newspaper reports about the send-off indicate a crowd had gathered in the area, speeches were given, Rosenbladt's five piece band played *Skip to My Lou* and *What was Your Name in the States*. The mail was laid out on a table for all to see, and then it was packed in the cantinas, and the mochila was

Express Office Display - *Hill photo*

placed on the horse, and the rider was off. That seems to indicate that the Patee House was where the send-off happened. If so, the rider returned from the stables to the Patee House upon the arrival of the train. This account of the mail being laid out in the express office and then packed and placed on the horse was substantiated by John A. Young who recorded the event in his journal. (14:50-1) The train station, stables and hotel were all within a few blocks of each other. Today the hotel and the stable still stand, and a marker identifies the old station site.

An exhibit in the Patee House depicts the office of the Pony Express. The mail would have been laid out there. Even though Waddell, Majors, and Russell's main office had been in Leavenworth, Kansas, St. Joseph, Missouri was selected as the starting point for the Pony Express because it was served by both the railroad and most importantly, the telegraph.

PEAK'S LIVERY STABLES

A sketch shows the old Pike's Peak Livery Stables as it looked in the 1860s when it housed the horses used for the Pony Express. The stable was originally built by Ben Holladay in 1858 for his stagecoach line which served Colorado. It was a wooden pine-clad building about 60' x 120'. It could house 200 horses. Other businesses also used the stables. It was located only a few blocks from the Patee House. This is where the first rider and pony waited for the mail to arrive after the earlier ceremony at the Patee House.

Around 1888, a fire damaged the old wooden stables. The front façade was redesigned and rebuilt with brick. The roof line, however, was kept the same. It retains that appearance today. By the mid-1900's the building had been abandoned. It had deteriorated and was threatened to be demolished. Fortunately, it was saved and restored. Today it is the home for the National Pony Express Museum. Inside are terrific displays relating to the Pony Express, including special display areas showing original parts of the Pony Express stables. It is located at 914 Penn Street.

One of the displays in the museum depicts Johnny Fry getting ready to leave the stables.

Some of the stables have also been reconstructed .

Old Stable Sketch - *St. Joseph Daily Herald, January 27, 1889*

Visitors can see the original well that was dug inside the stables. It was uncovered during the building's renovation. A hand pump has been added, and it is part of a hands-on activity for kids. The museum has other interesting historical exhibits besides those that highlight the archaeological work that occurred during the stable's restoration.

Pony Express Stables Today - *Hill photo*

One is the diorama that depicts the trail with its varied geography and some of the stations.

On April 3, 1860, just after sundown at about 7:15 p.m., the historic journey began. The cannon boomed and the express rider rode down to the river. He boarded the paddle wheel steamer *Ebenezer* that was waiting at the wharf near Jules Street to take the horse and rider across the Missouri River to start his historic run.

While a number of riders have also been credited with being the first rider out of St. Joseph, the two most frequently cited are Johnny Fry and Johnson William "Billy"

Ready to Leave - *Hill photo*

Richardson. Today it seems that most historians believe that the first rider to take the mail west out of St. Joe was Johnny Fry.

The April 7, 1860 edition of St. Joseph's *Weekly West* described the ceremonies and events of the send off. It noted that "At a quarter past seven o'clock last evening, the mail was placed by (Mayor) M. Jeff Thompson on the back of the animal, a fine bay mare, who is to run the first stage of the great express from St. Joseph to her sister cities of the Pacific shore. Horse and rider started off amid the loud and continuous cheers of the assembled multitude, all anxious to witness every particular of the inauguration of this, the greatest enterprise it has yet become our pleasant duty, as a journalist, to chronicle."

"The rider is a Mr. Richardson, formerly a sailor, having sailed for years amid the snow and icebergs of the Northern ocean." (12:107) However, it should be noted, according to later records, that Billy Richardson, who claimed to be the first rider, was born in 1851. He would have been only nine years old. If he had been a sailor, he must have been a cabin boy. He certainly would not have been sailing the oceans for years. In October 1931, Billy was reportedly interviewed and gave an account. He stated that he was only a kid at the time, and that his half brother, Paul Coburn, worked at the express. During all the excitement, Paul accidentally put the mochila on Billy's horse, not Fry's, for the short ride to the river. Waiting at the ferry was Johnny Fry where the mail was handed off and Fry took the mail across the river and rode the first leg west from Elwood through the eastern part of Kansas. Ten days later the mail was delivered in San Francisco, California.

It should be noted, however, that there are no known existing records of an interview with Johnny Fry concerning the issue. After the Civil war broke out he resigned his position in May, 1861, and joined the Union forces. While reports differed, it is believed he was killed October 6, 1863, at Baxter Springs, Kansas, during a raid by Quantrill's guerillas. (43:65) Perhaps that should clear it up. However, there is another photo of four young men. One is sometimes identified as Johnson Billy Richardson, a Pony Express rider. He is surely older than nine and is pictured with three others who appear to be about the same age and are thought to be riders. Another is sometimes identified as Johnny Fry. Some question the identity of the other three young men. Even if the person is Richardson, he certainly doesn't look old enough to have "sailed for years" before becoming a rider as in the reported claims. That would not be the first time a reporter had the incorrect information or exaggerated the account of it. Perhaps the identities of the individuals in the photo are incorrect.

Today, Hustan Wyeth Park, the riverfront park, and monuments mark related sites near where the riders departed. The ferries docked near either Jules or Francis Streets. From the Patee House the rider rode about one mile to where he boarded the ferry. Jackson's view looks up river towards the old landing near Jules Street. While Jackson's painting shows a steamboat in the distance appearing to come around a bend, in 1860 the bend in the river was to the west in the opposite direction. By the time Jackson made his painting, the river's course had changed.

Approaching the Ferry at St. Joseph - *Harold Warp's Pioneer Village, Minden, Nebraska/ SCNM.*

Today the Interstate highway dominates the Missouri side of the shoreline of the Missouri River where the Pony Express rider and horse boarded the steamer to cross the river. The modern railroad tracks are also near the riverbank. The bluffs to the left in the old lithograph are now blocked by trees and a high bank made to protect the railroad from the river. The river is not as wide and its course has changed. At the time of the Pony Express the river made a horseshoe loop to the west. Elwood was located west across the river just south where the loop to the west began. At the westward end of the loop was the small town of Wathena. Elwood was not considered to be a regular station, nor was it listed on the 1861 U. S. Mail Contract. However, the *Elwood Free Press* of April 21, 1860, indicated Elwood was a station. Because the Pony had to take the ferry across the river, it was necessary to have some place to stay or wait for the ferry, especially if the rider arrived in Elwood during the night. The horse was stabled and the rider rowed across the river with the mail and returned the next day for his mount. The logs and sawyers in the river in a lithograph suggest nighttime crossings would have been dangerous for steamboats.

Although Elwood is still across the river from St. Joseph, later flooding and changes in the river's course forced the little town to move a bit to the south. The old rock road which the riders would have taken after arriving on the Kansas bank is now in the fields or old

St. Joseph 1861 - *Illustrated London News, 1861*

flood plain. Most of the buildings were destroyed or have deteriorated over time, but some later ones were moved to slightly higher ground. The town of Wathena still hugs the west side of the Missouri River Valley, but the river no longer runs west next to it. There are early newspaper reports that seem to indicate that riders may have departed from Wathena. They may have also had stables here.

There are a number of stories that have made their way into the history and lore of the Pony Express. While the details sometimes differ, the general storylines are the same. The following two relate to Johnny Fry and the section of the trail near Troy, Kansas:

Johnny Fry was a local boy from the area and an excellent rider. He was well known for his interest in horse racing and skill as a jockey. He was considered to be one of the most handsome young riders and

St. Joseph today - *Hill photo*

91

was very popular with the young girls along his run. It seemed that Johnny may have also had a sweet tooth and enjoyed eating pastries. The Dooley Sisters often made sweets for Johnny. They gave them to him as he rode by, but they were always hard to grab and hold. One of the sisters came up with the idea of putting a hole in the center so they would be easier for him to grab and hold, and thus, the doughnut was born. (43:8)

Another story is about a "log cabin" quilt. It seems that one young lady was making a quilt. She was intent on getting Johnny Fry's red neckerchief and incorporating it as a log into her quilt. She asked Johnny for it, but he refused. She, however, would not take 'no' for an answer. She then devised a plan to get it. The next time Johnny rode by she went out to meet him and rode along next to him. She again asked for the neckerchief. He refused again, and then rode on ahead. Not to be outdone, she spurred her horse on and caught up. She grabbed for the red neckerchief, but missed. She did, however, get a hold of his shirt. Tugging on it she succeeded in ripping off part of it as Johnny rode away. She then incorporated the piece of the shirt into her quilt. (61:94)

Troy Station marker today, Troy Kansas - *Hill photo*

TROY STATION

In 1858, Leonard Smith moved to Troy where he purchased the old Troy Hotel. In 1860, he contacted with the C.O.C. & P.P. and was asked to build a barn large enough to stable five horses. The barn and Smith's hotel, not to be confused with the Smith's Hotel in Seneca farther to the west, served as the Troy relay station. Dr. Charles Clark wrote, "Troy is a small town. . .comprising a blacksmith shop, some whiskey shops, denominated groceries, etc. It is perfectly located on the summit of a hill. . . ." (13:10) Burton noted on August 7, "Passing through a few wretched shanties called Troy. . . ." (9:23)

After leaving Troy, the Pony exchanged horses at the Lewis, Kennekuk, Kickapoo, and Log Chain relay stations before reaching Seneca. No remains of the Lewis, Kennekuk and Kickapoo stations exist on their sites.

Today a marker for the Troy Station stands at the northwest corner of Courthouse Square near the site of the relay station. The hotel and station was located at the northeast corner of First and Myrtle. (29:99)

ROGERS HOUSE

The Rogers House was one of the "shanties" that Burton noted. It would also have been seen by the riders and perhaps even visited by them. The house was built in 1856-7 by Nelson Rogers. He was the first blacksmith in the village of Troy. His shop may have been the one that was noted by Dr. Charles M. Clark. His smithing skills could

The Rogers House, today - *Hill photo*

93

have been used by the Pony Express. His house still stands across the street and less than one block east of the site of the Pony Express monument. The house has recently been restored. It is believed that Abraham Lincoln may have stayed there when he visited Troy before he became president.

The Nelson Rogers House is down the block to the east of the monument. The house is opened on a limited basis.

LOG CHAIN/LOCHANNE STATION

The building on the site is believed by some to include parts of the old Log Chain or Lochnane Station.

According to some historians, Log Chain Station was located near Locklane, Locknane, Locknan, or Muddy Creek as it was known by the various names. The station's name is believed to have originated either from a corruption of the name of the nearby creek or because of the number of large chains or links that accumulated there as chains snapped when wagons were driven over the rough ford. In 1857 Noble H. Rising had brought his family from New York to Kansas and established his ranch at a creek crossing. According to some, the station may have served both as a stage station and as a Pony Express relay station. Log Chain Station was reported to include a log structure about twenty-four by forty feet, a fireplace and a seventy foot log barn nearby. Noble Rising served as the station keeper, and his son, Don C., was hired as an express rider in Division One. Don rode in the area,

The Old Log Chain Station site today - *Hill photo*

94

but was soon assigned to ride the section a little farther west between Big Sandy and Fort Kearny. Theodore "Little Yank" Rand had been hired by Lewis before April 1860. He was small in stature and hailed from New York State, hence his nickname. Yank's first job was to take a herd of ponies from St. Joseph and to deliver them west along the line at the different stations. (61:105) Log Chain would have been one of those stations. Afterwards Yank was assigned to ride in Division Two.

Burton's entry for the early morning of August 8 was "Arriving about 1 A.M. at Locknan's Station, a few log and timber huts near a creek well feathered with white oak and American elm, hickory and black walnut, we found beds and snatched an hourful of sleep." Later that morning he noted that he was "refreshed by breakfast and the intoxicating air. . ." (9:26) The streambed is still "feathered" with trees.

There seems to be a good case to support those historians who today believe Log Chain and Locknane were two separate stations. Locknane was the stage station visited by Burton, but Log Chain, the Pony Express Station, supported by local history, was over a mile away to the southwest on a branch of the Muddy that became known as Log Chain. Originally, the stage route used the old military and established trail. After leaving the Kickapoo Station, also maintained by Noble Rising and a W. W. Letson, the old trail continued up along the divide between Craig and Muddy creeks through the village of Granada. From Granada it still followed the high ground north and then cut west winding north at times along the ridges for almost four miles before crossing the Muddy or Lockane Creek. This route is verified by the early Capioma Township survey map.

However, the Pony did not have to stick to the high ground. In the vicinity of Granada its route cut northwest, like the hypotenuse of a right triangle. It forded the Muddy, followed the western ridge to use the station at Log Chain, thereby saving valuable time and a few miles. It rejoined the old route a couple of miles west of the Locknane Stage Station. By 1862 the stage route had switched to use the new route and station at Log Chain. It is believed that over time the old Log Chain station was modified, expanded and remodeled, including the renovation of its old fireplace, into a more modern looking house. The large barn no longer stands. An area believed to be the old buffalo wallow is still evident, but the Pony Express marker, placed there years ago based on local history, is no longer on the house. The house and other non-historic structures have deteriorated and are presently abandoned, but it may be renovated again. Based on an examination of its foundation, some local historians feel that parts of it date to the time of the Pony Express.

Smith's Hotel Station. Seneca

Most sources seem to agree that the station in Seneca was an early Pony Express home station. The Smith's Hotel served as that station. John E. Smith built the two-story house and hotel in 1858. Frank Root drove a stagecoach and also used the station. He noted, "as it came in view, looked like a mammoth concern. It was a well-built structure, painted white, and everything about the premises was kept in the best order. His wife was a model landlady, and no one ever stopped there and partook of a meal without hoping he might some day come again." Another traveler noted "Mrs. Smith kept the kitchen floor of her house clean enough to eat off it." (56:196-7) The station was also the site of many social events that employees of the Pony Express would have attended. Johnny Fry would have ended his first ride here ,handing off the mochila to the next rider, thought to be Don Rising. (16:55) Because of its outstanding accommodations, the express riders assigned here were some of the lucky ones. The riders stationed in Utah and Nevada served under far different conditions as will soon be seen.

The excitement associated with the Pony Express had a strong draw for men. William Boulton was one of the oldest riders. He was married with children and was in his mid-thirties. In order to be hired to ride, he lied about his age and claimed to be single. His section was usually east out of Seneca. On one run when he was five miles from Guittard's, his horse collapsed and died. Boulton removed the mochila, walked to the station, got on a fresh horse and continued his run. (6:54-5) After the Pony Express ended, he brought his family to Seneca to live.

At the other end of the age spectrum was David Jay. He may have been the youngest rider of the Pony Express. He must have been big for his age because he was really only thirteen when hired. His parents had settled near Manhattan, but his desire to be a Pony Express rider was so strong that he walked all the way to Marysville. There he was hired and was assigned the section between Seneca and the Big Sandy. Later, he was assigned to ride between the Big Sandy and Fort Kearny. (43:77)

Jack H. Keetley was also assigned the section from Seneca to Big Sandy. During one run from the Big Sandy Station to Seneca, there was no other east bound rider so Jack had to continue east to St. Joseph. There he picked up the mail and headed back to Seneca for a ride of 340 miles in 31 hours. When he arrived at Seneca he was found asleep in the saddle and had to be woken up. (43:83) James Beatley was another to ride west out of Seneca. (43:127).

Tom Willson is the only rider known by name to ride the segment from Seneca to Atchison during the last months of the Pony Express. Perhaps he was the last rider for the Pony when the final eastbound mail was delivered in November 1861.

It was here at the Smith's Hotel that Johnny Fry arrived at 1:40 a.m. after riding the first eighty-mile section from St. Joseph. His time out was about 6 hours, twenty-five minutes, less than the time allowed. Don Rising is thought to have been the next rider west, but some think it was Jim Beatley. (50:42).

This is the Smith's Hotel and station the decade after the Pony Express. Part of the large barn can be seen on the left. The Smith's

Smith's Hotel—Pony Express Station, Seneca, Kansas

- From Root & Connelley's The Overland Stage to California

97

Site marker today - *Hill photo*

Hotel was moved a few blocks away around 1900 and then razed in 1970. Today, only a stone monument marks the corner where the hotel first stood. Not even the large old barn is standing. Now railroad tracks occupy the area of the barn and corral.

Today the Pony Express Museum is located from where the old photo was taken diagonally across from the Smith's Hotel site. Not all riders led upstanding lives. The museum tells the story of Mel Baughn ,who turned horse thief after the Pony ended. He mortally wounded a member of the posse chasing him. Mel was finally caught, tried for murder, found guilty, and hanged on the Seneca Court House lawn. Read another incident involving Mel on the page discussing Thirty-two Mile Station.

After the Pony left Seneca, mounts were changed at Ash Point and again at Guittard Station. On August 8, Burton wrote, "At Guittard's I saw, for the first time, the Pony Express rider arrive." (9:32) He continued to write a little about the history of the express. He noted, "The riders are mostly youths, mounted upon active and lithe Indian nags. They ride 100 miles at a time—about eight miles per hour—with four changes of horses, and return to their stations the next day—of their hardships and perils we shall hear more anon. The letters are carried in leathern bags, which are thrown about carelessly enough when the saddle is changed. . . . ." (9:34)

There is some debate as to whether Marysville served as a home station or only a relay station. It would not have made sense to have both Seneca and Marysville as a home station at the same time since they were so close to each other. Marysville was laid out by General Frank J. Marshall in 1854. He named it after his wife Mary. Marshall had come to the area in 1849 and opened the first ferry crossing of the Big Blue. In 1851 he moved his ferry a little to the north to the future site of Marysville.

MARYSVILLE

Albert Richardson came through Marysville in mid-May 1860 and noted, "Marysville is improving rapidly, and now claims some fifty houses. . .For shootings and stabbing affrays, whiskey drinking and horse-racing Marysville can bear away the palm from all other towns in Kansas." When Burton came through later that summer, he concurred and wrote, "Passing by Marysville. . .which thrives by selling whiskey to ruffians of all descriptions, we forded before sunset the "Big Blue," a well-known tributary of the Kansas River. It is a pretty little stream, brisk and clear as crystal, about forty or fifty yards wide by 2.50 feet deep at the ford." (9:34) Russell, Majors, & Waddell had contracted to have a stone livery stable built in Marysville and leased as part of a home station. The stone structure was divided into a blacksmith shop

Barrett Hotel - From Root & Connelley's *The Overland Stage to California.*

Marysville 1860. – *Marysville Post Office*

on the north end and stables on the south. Riders stayed at a nearby Barrett Hotel two blocks north, as did other travelers. It had been built in 1859 and then expanded. It was used for celebrations and dances. Marysville could then have replaced Seneca as the home station once the structure was completed.

A fire burned the roof in 1876, and the original structure was expanded and a hip roof added for larger storage. The inside has been restored as a stable and a blacksmith shop with bunks, and the attached structure now houses a fine museum. It is reported that the barn's original well is now under the entrance to the attached museum. About a block west is a statue of the Pony Express. Also in the town was the crossing of the Big Blue. Today there is a park west of the railroad tracks near the site. The river is not as wide and has moved closer to the west side of the valley. A reproduction of the ferry run by

Marysville barn today – *Hill photo*

Robert Shibley that was used by wagons and riders during periods of high water is located in the park. (14:249)

Barrett had the lumber cut for his hotel from his own lumber mill and hauled the twenty miles to Marysville. Construction on the house began in 1859. The hotel changed names over the years. In 1899 it was razed to make room for a commercial building. (56:528-9)

Today, an extension at the rear of the barn houses the museum. If you look closely at the differences in the stones and joints in the stable's walls, you can see the modifications made to the building over time.

HOLLENBERG/COTTONWOOD RANCH STATION

After crossing the Big Blue in Marysville, the trail angled northwest up the valley of the Little Blue River. It was headed for the Platte River. The next station was Cottonwood Station located near the crossing of Cottonwood Creek. Gerat Hollenberg started construction of his ranch in 1857. He hoped to profit from the emigrant traffic. His ranch was strategically located just west of the junction of the trails from Independence, Fort Leavenworth and St. Joseph. Russell, Majors and Waddell contracted with him to serve as a stage stop for the Central Overland California & Pikes Peak Express and then as a Pony Express relay station. In addition to the ranch house and small outbuildings, a large pole barn that had room for 100 animals was built. Company employees, stage passengers and other visitors slept in the attic. The main floor served as the Hollenberg's living quarters and store. It was the last station before riders entered the Nebraska Territory. Part of

Hollenberg Pony Express Ranch / Cottonwood Station Today, Hanover, Kansas
- *Hill photo*

101

Preservation opening today - *Hill photo*

Burton's entry for August 8 was "At 6 P.M. we changed our fagged animals for fresh, and the land of Kansas for Nebraska, at Cottonwood Creek, a bottom where trees flourished, where the ground had been cleared for corn, and we detected the prairie wolf watching for the poultry." (9:35) Jimmy Clark rode between Hollenberg and Big Sandy. (56:128) William Jones is thought to have been another of the riders who would have ridden this segment and changed mounts here.

Today only the house remains standing. In the early 1990s during preservation work on the station, much was learned about the building's architectural construction and history. The site was uphill from where the Oregon Trail crossed Cottonwood Creek. The earliest part of the structure was built about 1857-8 as a log cabin. In 1860 the cabin was expanded with a post and beam addition at one end and a plank addition to the other. The eastern plank addition was a lean-to shed used as a kitchen. More lean-to sheds were added to the rear and the rest of the attic opened up. Additional changes were made in the mid 1870s to give it its present look. Although its appearance today is a little different, the Pony riders would still be able to recognize it. Even the cornfield can be found along the creek bottom.

Attic today - *Hill photo*

Some of the original structure was uncovered during the preservation work. The inside of the original log structures was covered with laths and then plastered to give it a smooth white wall.

Pony Express and stage employees slept in the attic. Today, some of the original log structure can be seen sticking above the floor.

The trail swales are evident as the trail approaches the crossing and as it leaves the creek. The station can be seen in the middle in the distance near the top of the hill. It is one of the few stations still in its original location that is open to the public.

Trail approaching Hollenberg Ranch - *Hill photo*

103

Jackson's sketch of the rider and horn - *Scotts Bluff National Monument.*

During the first few months riders often carried a horn which they were supposed to blow when they were approaching the station. This would give the stock tenders and station keeper time to finish preparations for the horse exchange. Lizzie Mohrbacher was a fourteen year old girl in Marysville when the Pony Express came through. She later recalled, "Just before they came in sight at the top of the hill they blew a horn. It was a shiny tin horn and the rider carried it in the back of his saddle bag. When he blew the horn it was a signal. . ." (14:249)

A horn on display is believed by some to be one of those horns used by the express riders. It was previously in the holdings of a descendent of the Hollenberg family. It is now on display at the Washington County Museum.

Horn today - *Hill photo*

104

ROCK CREEK STATION

The Pony passed Rock House relay station a few miles inside Nebraska on its way to Turkey or Rock Creek Station located about seven miles southeast of present-day Fairbury. In 1859 David McCanles purchased the ranch from S. C. Glenn who had settled the site in 1857. McCanles expanded the ranch and built the west ranch house and a toll bridge over the steep banked creek near the old Oregon Trail crossing. A toll house was added as well as another ranch house and barn and corral on the east side. The east side ranch was first rented and then sold to Russell, Majors and Waddell for use as both a stage and Pony station. Describing their late arrival and two-hour stop on August 8, Burton noted the inhabitants bedded on the floor "in a seemingly promiscuous heap, men, women, children, lambs, and puppies." Their supper was "cold scraps of mutton and a kind of bread" and "tea and some found milk which was not more than one quarter flies." And the price for the food was high. (9:35)

On July 12, 1861, the infamous shooting between James Butler "Wild Bill" Hickok and David McCanles occurred. It seems that McCanles was trying to collect the payment owed him by the C.O.C. & P.P. from the station keeper Horace Wellman. Wellman and his wife and Hickok, a stock hand or tender for the express, were inside the house. After McCanles entered and spoke with Mrs. Wellman, Hickok stepped from behind a curtain and shot and killed McCanles. Hearing the shot, James Woods, James Gordon, and McCanles's twelve-year-old son Monroe who were with McCanles, came running. Hickok then shot Woods and Gordon. Both were subsequently killed. Monroe escaped by hiding in a nearby ravine. Hickok, Wellman, and "Doc" Brink were arrested and tried for murder. They pleaded self-defense and were acquitted. Thus was born the legend of the shootout between Wild Bill and the murderous McCanles gang. which later became the story told in the dime novels of the time. In February 1867, *Harper's* monthly magazine published the first story describing how Wild Bill successfully defended the station. In the attack, Hickok single-handedly fought off and killed ten men of the notorious "M'Kandlas Gang" while suffering numerous gun and knife wounds.

Pony rider Frank Helvey, a substitute rider, helped to participate in the burial of the three men killed. (43:75) Harry Lamont was making his run. He arrived shortly after the shooting. Finding his mount not prepared and no food, he had to get his own mount and continue on. (43:91). James "Doc" Brink, another substitute rider and stock tender who was assigned there at the time.(56:129) The actual reason for the shooting is unknown, but some stories have pointed to earlier romantic feelings between some of the individuals, personal animosity involving comments about Hickok's looks, to differing political views.

Another incident involved Frank Helvey during one of his runs between Marysville and Big Sandy. As he rode along, Helvey's horse fell and broke its leg. Fortunately, Helvey was unhurt. He took the mochila off his horse and walked to the station to complete his run. (43:75)

Rock Creek Station, Nebraska, 1859 - *California State Library*

The horseman in the 1859 photo is thought to be David B. McCanles. The old photo has often been published in reverse. The famous shootout with Hickok started in the building behind the coach. The building on the far right is the toll house for the bridge.

Rock Creek Station Reconstruction today - *Hill photo*

There is an excellent reconstruction of Rock Creek Station. It is run by the Nebraska Parks and Recreation Department. Riders would easily recognize the station and feel right at home. The park includes camping and a hiking area. The visitor center has reproductions of the saddle and mochilla along with other displays and information about the history of the ranch and station. The swales left by all the wagons, stagecoaches, and Pony riders passing through are extensive and something worthwhile to experience. It is one of this author's favorite sites.

The Pony now headed for his next home station, the Big Sandy. Continuing up the valley, the Pony riders passed a number of relay and home stations before they finally reached Kearny Station, a home station and end of Division One. Some of those stations included: Big Sandy, a home station; Millers or Thompson's; Oak; Liberty Farms, another home station; Spring Ranch; Thirty-Two-Mile Creek Station; and Sand Hill or Summit Station on the low sandy divide or watershed between the Little Blue and the Platte rivers. That was the last stop before Kearny Station. Most of these stations later fell victim to the Indian Wars of 1864 along the Platte and were burned. Little evidence of them exists.

THIRTY-TWO MILE STATION

Burton noted that at Liberty Farms they stopped and had eggs and bacon, and upon reaching Thirty-Two-Mile Creek, "we were pleasantly surprised to find an utter absence of the Irishry. The station-master was the head of a neathanded and thrifty family from Vermont; the rooms, such as they were, looked cosy and clean, and the chickens and peaches were plump and well "fixed." Soldiers from Fort Kearny loitered about the adjoining store, and from them we heard past fights and rumours of future wars which were confirmed on the morrow." (9:44) George A. Comstock was the station keeper of the long log one story building. The site has been designated as a historic archaeological site by the National Register of Historic Places.

Burton understood the significance of the Platte River for travel and communications such as the Pony Express, and the railroad. He noted, "the Platte is doubtless the most important western influent of the Mississippi. Its valley offers a route scarcely to be surpassed for natural gradients, requiring little beyond the superstructure for light trains; and by following up its tributary—the Sweetwater—the engineer finds a line laid down by nature to the foot of the South Pass of the Rocky Mountains. At present the traveler can cross. . .by its broad highway, with never-failing supplies of water, and in places, fuel. Its banks will shortly supply coal to take the place of the timber that has thinned out." (9:45)

One of the first express riders in this area was Mel Baughn (Vaugh), a twenty-year-old, who rode between Thirty-Two-Mile Station and Fort Kearny. Once while Mel was resting between rides, a thief made off with the rider's favorite horse. When Mel found out, he took after the thief. He was finally able to catch up to him after several miles near the Loup. The thief, in order not to be caught, let the stolen horse go. Mel went after his horse and caught it. By the time he returned to his station, the mail had come and he had to make his normal run. (6:55) Another rider in this section between the Big Sandy to Kearny Station was William Campbell. He recalled his trouble with snow. During the winter of 1860-1 on one of his rides, the trail was covered with snow two and a half feet deep. It took him twenty-four hours to make his run.

The swales still are visible where the trail approaches Thirty-Two- Mile Creek and the station monument and site today. The trail is coming in from the right towards the creek. Cultivation has obliterated

Thirty-Two-Mile swales today - *Hill photo*

Thirty-Two-Mile Station Monument and site today - *Hill photo*

the trail on the flatter land. The photo was taken from the raised country road. The station was about a quarter of a mile farther.

The log station was in the field with the creek behind it in the trees. The trail had crossed the creek nearby. The station was destroyed during the Indian raids in the mid 1860s.

Ft. Kearny

Fort Kearny Station was the end of Division One. The exact location of the Kearny Station is still debated. It is generally held that since Fort Kearny was a major military reservation and post the Pony Express would not have been allowed to have its own station on the grounds. However, for several months the fort was the terminus of the telegraph, and it is logical that there would have been some accommodation to enable the riders to stop there. Perhaps the fort's post office or telegraph office was used. Many believe the first Division Two station was located a couple of miles west of the fort, just off the military reservation boundary.

On August 10, Burton recorded, "at 4 A.M. reached Kearny station, in the valley of La Grande Platte, seven miles from the fort of that name."(9:45) His statement supports those historians who place the station near present-day Lowell, Nebraska east of the fort. Burton wrote, "After satisfying hunger with the vile bread and viler coffee . . .for which we paid $.75, we left Kearny Station without delay. Hugging the right bank of our strange river, at 8 A.M. we found

Officers Quarters, Ft. Kearny - 1858 - *Mills, Library of Congress, LCMS-65612-6.*

ourselves at Fort Kearny, so called, as is custom, after the gallant officer, now deceased, of that name." (9:47)

Burton continued to comment upon the general layout of a military post which it seems Fort Kearny followed closely. "The position usually chosen is a river bottom, where fuel, grass, and water are readily procurable. The quarters are of various styles: some, with their low verandahs, resemble Anglo-Indian bungalows or comfortable farmhouses, others are the storied houses with the "stoop" or porch of the Eastern States in front, and low, long, peat-roofed tenements are used for magazines or outhouses. The best material is brown adobe or unburnt brick; others are of timber, white-washed and clean-looking, with shingle roofs, glass windows, and gay green frames.... The habitations surround a cleared central space for parade and drill; the grounds is denoted by the tall flagstaff, which does not, as in English camps, distinguish the quarters of the commanding officer. One side is occupied by the officers' bungalows, the other, generally that opposite, by the adjutant's and quartermaster's offices, and the square is completed by low ranges of barracks and commissariat stores, whilst various little shops, stables, corrals for cattle, a chapel, perhaps an artillery park, and surely an ice-house. . .complete the settlement. Had these cantonments a few more trees. . . ."(9:47-8)

The photos show the fort a little prior to the Pony Express period and the fort grounds today. It is a state historic park well worth the

Fort Kearny today - *Hill photo*

stop at the visitor center, the blacksmith shop and a walk around the grounds. The parade ground is evident with its tall flagpole. Only a few trees originally planted when the fort was constructed are still alive. A Pony rider would not recognize the area today as it is all green and irrigated. Then it was dry and sandy.

This old photo was taken by Samuel C. Mills, Simpson's official photographer, on his way to Camp Floyd. It shows the Officers' Quarters at Fort Kearny as it appeared two years before the Pony Express.

Small posts about one foot tall mark the outline of the officers' quarters shown in the old photo. The position of the flagpole remains the same. Lying on the ground to the right of the flagpole on the other side of the parade grounds is a fallen tree that was one of the original trees planted and appears in the old photo.

The main emigrant trail was to the north of the fort between it and the river which is on the horizon.

After the Pony entered Division Two, the riders would generally parallel the Platte River, changing mounts at as many as thirty-three more stations until they reached the last one in Division Two, Horseshoe Creek Station twenty-five miles northwest of Fort Laramie in present day Wyoming.

BUFFALO BILL'S SCOUT'S REST RANCH

Historians have differed as to whether or not Buffalo Bill was a Pony Express rider or that he was the youngest, but everyone agrees that he brought back the interest in the Pony Express and truly made it part of the history and lore of the American West. His 4,000-acre Scout's Rest Ranch was located in North Platte, Nebraska. He had an eighteen-room mansion built in 1878. At the time, it was a treeless prairie. The third floor room or widow's walk had a commanding view of the surrounding area for miles. He could easily see north to the North Platte River and south to the trains approaching the town of North Platte on the South Platte River. It was here that he started his Wild West Show.

William Cody was born in 1846 in Iowa. In 1854 his parents moved the family to Kansas. A few years later after his father died he started working for Russell, Majors, and Waddell. He became a messenger in the Leavenworth area. He wrote that in 1860 he was hired and rode for the Pony Express. In his *Seventy Years on the Frontier*, Majors substantiates Cody's reported run on the Red Buttes to Three Crossings section. He described it as ". . .a most dangerous, long, and lonely trail, including the perilous crossing of the North Platte River. . . ." (44:176) Once Cody made his run to Three Crossing, but finding the next rider had been killed the day before, he took the mail as requested to Rocky Ridge. He then returned all the way back to Red Buttes having ridden 384 miles, making it the longest run in Pony history and all on time. (44:177)

The idea of his Wild West Show began to develop by 1882 at North Platte with his first show called "Old Glory Blowout," and in 1883 the tours began. His shows became more elaborate including famous western personalities such as Annie Oakley and Sitting Bull, wagons, stagecoaches, Indians, buffalo, the U.S. Calvary, and, of course, the Pony Express. His show was even taken to Europe and performed for Queen Victoria. By the mid 1890s he had moved to Wyoming. He died in 1917.

WILLOW ISLAND

Willow Island or Willow Bend Station was a relay station and mail station located about six miles southeast of Cozad on the south side of the Platte. Burton noted "we watered at "Willow Island Ranch," and then at "Cold Water Ranch,"—drinking shops all—five miles from Midway Station. . ." (9:56) It must have been quite hot and dry when he was traveling to require all that refreshment. In the mid-1860s the

Willow Island Station was described as including an adobe house, stables, and a long store. (46:273)

The Pony ran all year long, but the scheduled time was nearly doubled to eighteen days during winter months. Winters all along the trail were severe. Nebraska winters were no exception.

Billy Campbell rode this section between Kearny and Cottonwood Springs. During one storm the snow was three feet deep with drifts over his head. He kept to the trail during the day by watching for the tops of tall weeds that lined the trail and at night by trusting his horse. He arrived at his home station, but there was no rider waiting so he continued on to the next relay station where he found a rider. He had been in the saddle for twenty-four hours. (19:178)

Joseph Barney Wintle was another rider who rode this segment and used this station. He carried the news of Lincoln's Presidential address over this 110- mile segment in five hours changing horses ten times. He rode for the Pony Express from its start in April 1860 until early 1861, or perhaps to its end. During this time he also rode a segment of the trail in Nevada and had some exciting adventures there. (11:29)

Willow Island Pony Express Station, Cozad, Nebraska, today - *Hill photo*

113

Today the station resides in the Cozad's Veterans Park at 9th and E Street. It was moved there by the American Legion to provide use by the Boy Scouts. It is open during the summer on a limited basis.

MIDWAY STATION

According to Frank Root, a driver for the stage line, Midway Station's name was based on the fact that it was the half way point on the Denver to Atchison line. (56:128) Burton wrote that Midway was five miles west of Cold Water Station, but some historians have indicated the two stations were one and the same. Most agree that Midway was a stage stop and many say that it was a home station. Burton's coach changed their mules there. The passengers tried to get the landlady to make supper, but she refused. However, Burton noted that the employees were given bread and buttermilk. (9:56)

Rider James Moore's section was between Midway and Julesburg. On June 8· the westbound rider came in carrying important government dispatches. Moore took the mochila and was off in less than a minute. He rode the 140-mile distance to Julesburg. The eastbound mail had arrived also with an important government dispatch, but there was no rider, so with little or nothing to eat and no rest, Moore took the mail and rode back to Midway. He reportedly covered the 280 miles in fourteen hours, forty-six minutes. The ride was one of the fastest, averaging over eighteen miles per hour. (56:128)

Midway Pony Express Home Station - *Nebraska State Historical Society*

Midway Station, today - *Author's photo*

It was on Richard Cleve's segment between Fort Kearny and Cottonwood Springs near Midway that he ran into a terrible blizzard. He remembered, "I got about seven miles from the last station and found it impossible to find the road. I would git off the horse and look for the road. I would find it and mount the horse but in five yards I would lose it. I tried several times but gave up. So I dismounted and led the horse back and forth until day light. It seemed a long while but at last day light came. It was a terrible night. I got to the station about nine o'clock hungry as a wolfe, 40 below." (43:39) He finally completed his run, but it had taken him thirty-six hours. The station site is located south of Gothenburg. It is thought that the original structure was built about 1855. It is still on its original foundation. Today a steeper roof protects the original structure, the corral has been replaced with a ranch house, and it sits in the middle of the ranch complex and large grain bins.

MACHETTE STATION

In Gothenburg's Ehmen Park is the small log cabin now known as Machette's Station. There is still some debate about it among Pony Express enthusiasts and historians. Local history places the Machette Station on the Gilman's Ranch, [and later part of William's Ranch]. A two story structure, believed to be the station with the stables below was moved to Gothenburg from William's Upper 96 Ranch in 1931, but either only the top was moved or it was rebuilt as the one story cabin as exists in the park today. Depending on the historians, it may or may not have served as a station there.

At the location from which it was moved, there was a smaller, but similarly constructed cedar log structure, 12'11" x 16'8", believed to have been the blacksmith shop. That structure is now at the Lincoln County Historical Museum in North Platte. If it was a structure moved there from MacDonalds Ranch- Cottonwood Station, it could actually be part of the Cottonwood Springs station. Or as others hold, it was part of Gilman's or Machette's station. Here is the old station before its move and the station today. Today the station has small exhibits and displays about the Pony Express inside. It is located in Gothenburg's city park at 15th and E Street.

Machette's Pony Express Station today. - *Author's photo*

COTTONWOOD SPRINGS

By the 1860s the buffalo had disappeared from much of the western part of the plains to the Rockies, but central Nebraska was still its home. Burton noted that and wrote about the buffalo: their numbers and herds, their habits, methods of hunting buffalo, and their importance to the Indians. As the Pony was approaching Cottonwood Springs they were moving out of buffalo country. Rider Billy Campbell, who rode in this area, recalled that "The greatest danger I faced on the trail were the buffalo." Perhaps that was because one night his pony, Ragged Jim, stumbled in a buffalo wallow throwing Billy and the mochila off. Ragged Jim ran back to the station, and Billy took the mochila and started to walk to the next station. Luckily a stage came along and gave him a lift to the station. (62:79) Herds were large and could block the trail, and riding through one was very dangerous.

Cottonwood Springs was sometimes called McDonald's Ranch or Station. This station was located near the junction of the North Platte and the South Platte. The station, on the south side of the South Platte, was less than a mile east of the mouth of Cottonwood Canyon. The canyon was the route used by Indians to enter the Platte Valley and to ford the Platte rivers. Lieutenant Eugene Ware noted that water "seeped out at a place down the bank where there had grown a large cottonwood tree. The spring had been dug out, and was the only spring as far as then known along the Platte for two hundred miles…" (28:68) From there until Julesburg, the trail now paralleled the South Platte on the south bank. Describing the station Burton wrote, "we entered the foul tenement, threw ourselves upon the mattresses, averaging three to each, and ten in a small room, every door, window, and cranny being shut,—after the fashion of these western folk. . . The morning brought with it no joy."(9:56) "We proceeded by means of an "eye-opener,… for a breakfast composed of various abominations, especially cakes of flour and grease, molasses and dirt, disposed in pretty equal parts. After paying the usual $0.50, we started. . ." (9:59)

An early photo matches very well with Ware's October 11, 1863,description. "Charles McDonald had built a cedar ranch at the mouth of Cottonwood Canyon. . .a year or so before our arrival. . .The

Cottonwood Springs Station, Nebraska. -*SJM-p39, Nebraska State Historical Society*

main building was about twenty feet front and forty feet deep, and was two stories high. A wing 50 feet extended to the west. The latter was, at the eaves about eight feet high and fifteen feet deep in the clear. Around it in the rear was a large and defensible corral, which had been extended to the arroyo coming out of the canyon. There was a stage station there, and a blacksmith shop kept by a man named Hindman. In the stage station was a telegraph office." (28:59)

Ware also noted, "McDonald had dug, in front of his store, and cribbed up, an inexhaustible well, which was said to be forty-six feet deep; it was rigged with pulley, chain, and heavy oaken buckets. . ." (28:69) If Ware was correct that McDonald's ranch was only a couple of years old in October of 1863, then Machette's or Gilman's could have been used as a station in 1860 when the Pony began. Then once McDonald's Ranch was built it could have replaced Gilman's. The two sites are about five miles apart. It would not have made sense to have them both in service as a relay station at the same time.

Rider William E. Gates was one of those who rode the next segment west from Cottonwood Springs into modern Wyoming. The next station was Fremont Springs. Another rider stationed here was known as "Little Yank." He originally rode in Division One, but was sent west and rode the section east between Cottonwood Springs and Julesburg. (6:56)

As Indian hostilities increased in 1863, it was evident that a fort was needed between forts Kearny and Laramie. Cottonwood Springs was a natural site. A fort was established there during the fall of 1863. It was first called Cantonment McKean, then Post Cottonwood, then Fort Cottonwood, and in 1866, Fort McPherson.

The photos show Cottonwood Springs Station in the early 1860s and the area today. The monument and site of MacDonald's Station are located about a mile south and east of Fort McPherson's National Cemetery. The station was in the field. Note the hill in the background in both photos. Next riders changed mounts at Cold Spring and then again as Frémont Springs about thirty miles west. Frémont Springs may also have served as a home station.

Monument area today.- *Author's photo*

Fremont Springs

Burton wrote "we halted for "dinner," about 11:00 A.M., at Frémont Springs, so called from an excellent little water behind the station. The building is of a style peculiar to the south. . .two huts connected by a roof-work of thatched timber which acts as the coolest verandahs. The station-keeper, who receives from the proprietors of the line $30 per month. . .and his wife, a comely young person, uncommonly civil and smiling for a "lady," supplied us with the luxuries of pigeons, onions, and light bread, and declared her intention of establishing a poultry-yard."(9:60) Patrick McEneany rode the section between Frémont Springs and Julesburg to the west. He rode from April to August 1860. Riders faced a variety of problems along their route. Weather proved to be one of his worst. He noted, "here I was a sicloon(cyclone) coming off to my right…the poney knew what coming so I gave him his head and he galloped to the left for about a mile." He escaped safely, but notice when he returned to the trail it was covered with teacup sized hailstones and broken trees. (43:97)

The view in the photo taken near the spring is looking west towards the distant O'Fallon's Bluff. The site is on private property, but evidence of structures and a large corral are visible. The trail's depression is evident. The photo was taken from the trail's depression. On the horizon to the right of center is the bluff. The trail headed straight towards it. Nearby is evidence of a small military outpost

119

setup to protect the station during the Indian troubles that started in 1863.

O'FALLONS BLUFF

After the ranch at Fremont's Springs, Clark noted, ". . .just beyond which the road ascends and crosses the bluffs, and finally transverses a high ridge, that presents a hard, even surface, covered with a short, stunted grass, and in some places with large field of "Prickley Pear."" (13:50)

These are the swales where the Pony rode as "the road ascends" up the bluff. Circular iron hoops represent the wagon wheels. Today rest stops are on the bluff. Only the I-80 east bound stop has the physical

View from Fremont Springs to O'Fallons Bluff, today - *Author's photo*

evidence of the trail. A path leads the traveler over to the trail. As you walk, close your eyes and imagine the sound of the ponies' hooves beating on the ground as they come around the curve and up the hill. Much of the bluff and its face were removed in order to make room for the modern highways. When the Interstate was built, more of the bluff was removed for the construction of the divided highway and the two rest areas.

Charles R. Savage, a famous photographer of the west, took photos of the trail scenes as he traveled west in 1866. The recently uncovered photo is of the famous O'Fallon's Bluff. The Platte River cut over to the edge of the Bluffs. The trail split. One rough narrow fork stayed on the bottom hugging the base of the bluff. This was quite dangerous and was rarely used. Frank Root recalled that the area was considered

Trail going up O'Fallons Bluff - *Author's photo.*

a natural area for Indian ambushes and attacks. (56:211) The main trail was forced to climb the bluff where the trail was smoother and in the open. It descended from the high ground about two miles west.

An old photo indicates the absence of trees along the river. However, if a closer look is taken there are some trees in the distance to the right of center on the left bank. That is the area where the present bridge from Sutherland crosses the South Platte. The river is not as wide and has moved some. Much of the steep bluff shown was cut during the construction of the modern highways. Interstate 80 runs parallel to the trail usually from only a few hundred feet to a mile or so.

Today trees obscure the view of the bluffs from where Savage took his photo. A recent photo was taken north of the site across the river where the tops of the bluffs become visible. The bluff to the right of center in Savage's photo can be seen in the present photo. The curving fence row is on an old river bank.

O'Fallon's Bluff Station listed as a contract mail station was located about five miles west of where the trail went up the bluff and a few miles west of where it came down off the bluffs near the Williams Ranch. The station keeper's name may have been Dorsey. The station was known as Dansey's in 1861. It may also have been the same as Elkhorn or Halfway House Station. It was a stage stop and Pony Express relay station.(26:128) Burton wrote "We halted at Half-way House, near O'Fallon's Bluffs, the headquarters of Mr. M—. . .the contents of the store. . . everything from a needle to a bottle of champagne. A sign-board informed us that we were now distant

O'Fallons Bluff - *Savage, Nebraska State Historical Society, RG 2154:8-27*

400 miles from St. Jo , 120 from Fort Kearny, 68 from the upper, and 40 from the lower crossing of the Platte. As we advanced the valley narrowed, the stream shrank, the vegetation dwindled" He had lived there twenty years and there were signs listing mileages to other sites. (9:60). This area from Cottonwood to Alklai Station was a favorite camping area for the Sioux.

Low somewhat flat mounds remain as possible evidence of adobe structure sites and corrals on the private property west of the present marker. Like the Frémont Springs site, there is also evidence of a military post nearby established during the later Indian conflict. The

Area view today - *Author's photo*

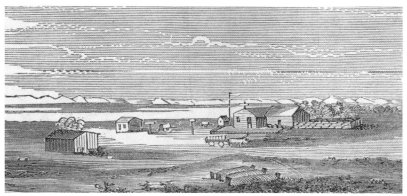

O'Fallon's Mail Station - *Colorado Historical Society CHSJ1186*

old lithograph shows the mail station at O'Fallon's Bluff. The next station was Alkali Lake Station, a few miles west of present Paxton. It is also believed to have served as a home station. (46:278) There Burton ate antelope and had "the unusual luxury of ice."(9:61)

A modern view shows the trail just after it has entered Colorado heading towards Julesburg. Note the white trail markers as it descends to the dry streambed and comes up the opposite cut bank near the trees.

JULESBURG

In 1859, Jules Reni built a trading post at the crossing of the South Platte. Jules served as the station keeper for the stage and then in 1860 for the Pony Express. The station was also referred to as the Upper, Morrell's or South Platte Crossing. Frank Root drove the stage along the Platte shortly after the Pony Express ended. He recalled that "Both the station and the stable were long, one story, hewed cedar-log buildings; there was also a store and blacksmith shop; and here was the fifth and last telegraph office on the Pacific line between Atchison and the Colorado metropolis. It was at this place that the stages for Salt Lake and California crossed the (South) Platte. The Pacific telegraph line at this point also crossed the south fork of the Platte, having been completed through to San Francisco *via* Fort Bridger and Salt Lake, the shortest and best route overland known in the early '60's." (56:219)

Trail in dry streambed - *Hill Photo*

Pony Express statue at Colorado Welcome Center - *Hill photo*

The present tri-state area of Nebraska-Colorado-Wyoming was the center of thievery and horse stealing. Many thought that Jules Reni was responsible for much of it and that included Benjamin Flickin and Joseph (Jack) Slade who was assigned the position as Division Superintendent replacing Reni. Relations between the two went from bad to worse. Reni and Slade got into a fight which almost cost Slade his life. Slade finally recovered and, according to some, ultimately

The raid on Julesburg- *Colorado Historical Socirty CHSJ1186*

killed Reni. Much has been written about the feud and accounts differ widely. Both Burton and Twain wrote about the feud in their respective books about their journey west. (See Dan Rottenber's book for a detailed review of the subject.)

Twain wrote, "It did seem strange enough to see a town again. . .We tumbled out into the busy street. . . .For an hour we took as much interest in Overland City as if we had never seen a town before." (72:43) Aside from the stations, the last populated area would have been back near Fort Kearny or back in Marysville, Kansas. As is evident from the sketch, it was made after the completion of the telegraph and the end of the Pony Express. George Chrisman was the station keeper. (73:44) Israel Benjamin passed Julesburg on July 26 noting, "We then crossed the Platte River at a place where it is about half a mile wide but only two to three feet deep. There is an island here in the middle of the river. The telegraph-poles have already been set upon it." (1:262)

Today a monument and banner mark the spot in the field where the station is believed to have stood in old Julesburg. Old Julesburg was raided by the Indians in January 1865 and then burned in February. A new Julesburg was built about four miles to the east. Then in 1867 it was moved again, but to the north side of the river with the name

Weir. Then in 1881 the town again moved about six miles under a new name, but in 1886 it was renamed Julesburg.

Julesburg Monument site, today. - *Hill photo*

FORDING THE PLATTE

Jackson's depiction of the fording of the South Platte.shows a wide expanse, the absence of trees and the wide river. Flowing almost due east from present-day Wyoming, Lodgepole Creek, depicted as a thin dark line on the left, turns south and enters the South Platte. After the fording, the trail continued paralleling the creek west. Twain wrote, "We came to the shallow, yellow, muddy South Platte, with its low banks and its scattering flat sand-bars and pigmy islands—a melancholy stream straggling through the center of the enormous flat plain. . . . it was a dangerous stream to cross, now, because its quick-sands were liable to swallow up horses, coach, and passengers. . ." (72:43)

There is a report of a near drowning at the Platte ford. The river was swollen from recent storms making the fording difficult. It seems that the pony lost its footing, knocking the rider off as they were being swept downstream. The rider grabbed the mochila and swam ashore. He got another horse and completed his run. His first horse was rescued and returned. (77:72)

Once again trees dominate the present river area and block the view of the opposite bank. The two trees in the foreground denote an

Jackson's Fording of the South Platte - *Scotts Bluff National Monument*

early bank of the river. The crossing was made in the center angling a little to the left.

MUD SPRINGS

After following Lodge Pole Creek for about thirty-five miles to a point east of present-day Sydney, Nebraska the trail turned north to cross over the plateau to the valley of the North Platte. It was headed for its home station, a sod house structure at Mud Springs. Burton

South Platte ford today - *Hill photo*

127

described the station on August 12, "Descending into the bed of a broad "arroyo," at this season bone dry, we reached, at 5:45 P.M., Mud Spring Station, which takes its name from a little run of clear water in a black miry hollow. A kind of cress grows in it abundantly, and the banks are bright with the "morning glory" or convolvulus. The station-house. . . .material was sod, half peat with vegetable matter; it is taken up in large flakes after being furrowed with a plough, and is cut proper lengths with a short-handled spade. Cedar timber, brought from the neighboring hills, formed the roof. The only accommodation was an open shed, with sort of a doorless dormitory by its side. We dined in the shed, and amused ourselves with feeding the little brown-speckled swamp blackbirds that hopped about us tame and "peert" as wrens. . . .The host, who was a kind, intelligent, and civil man, lent me a "buffalo" by way of bedding."(9:78-9) Breakfast that morning was an antelope-steak.

Lieutenant Caspar Collins made a sketch of the layout of the station in 1864. An archaeological study of the grounds confirmed the accuracy of Collins's sketch. The station was used by both the Pony Express and the stage. The clear spring was a welcome relief after a long dusty ride. From here the Pony Express continued northwest towards Court House Rock.

Hiram L. Kelley was stationed at Mud Springs and rode the segment west to Fort Laramie. (43:85) William Sloan Tough rode the

Looking across the broad arroyo at Mud Springs today. - *Hill photo*

section west out of Julesburg to Mud Springs. During the winter of 1860-61, a blizzard hit hard and slowed the express down. Tough was two days late so another rider was sent out to find him. Fortunately he was found, but he was nearly frozen to death. He was brought back to Mud Springs. His feet were in the worst condition, and it was feared he might loose his feet and never walk. After some time and good care he recovered and was able to walk. He fought in the Civil War, became a marshall, operated a stockyard in Kansas City, and died in 1904. (43:133) James McArdle served as the station keeper. (DiCerto-p.118)

Travelers crossing the plains were captivated by the sight of the Pony Express. It was in western Nebraska, somewhere between Mud Springs and Flickin's that Mark Twain finally saw the Pony Express rider from a mudwagon during the day time. He noted that ". . .all that met us managed to streak by in the night, so we heard only a whiz and a hail, and the swift phantom of the desert was gone before we could get our heads out of the windows. But now we were expecting one along every moment, and would see him in broad daylight. Presently the driver exclaims:

"HERE HE COMES!"

Every neck is stretched further, and every eye strained wider. Away across the endless dead level of the prairie a black speck appears against the sky, and it is plain that it moves. Well, I should think so! In a second or two it becomes a horse and rider, rising and falling, rising and falling—sweeping towards us nearer and nearer—growing more and more distinct, more and more sharply defined—nearer and still nearer, and the flutter of the hoofs comes faintly to the ear—another instant a whoop and a hurrah from our upper deck, a wave of the rider's hand, but no reply, and man and horse burst past our excited faces, and go swinging away like a belated fragment of a storm!

So sudden is it all, and so like a flash of unreal fancy, that but for the flake of white foam left quivering and perishing on the mail-sack after the vision had flashed by and disappeared, we might have doubted whether we had seen any actual horse and man at all, maybe." (72:54)

The express station was located across the arroyo on the low bench visible in the center of the photo. The monument is barely visible between the trees. The present approach still crosses the arroyo. The

"Here he comes!" - *Scotts Bluff National Monument*

"little run" has been dammed and a small pond encompasses part of the area in the more densely treed area behind the bench.

Today's view of the monument site shows part of the pond visible at the left, and you can still feed the birds as Burton did. It is thought the name originated because of the muddy buffalo wallows nearby. (43:133) The area surrounding the site is private property and should be respected.

Mud Springs Monument today. - *Hill photo*

Court House Rock Station

After leaving Mud Springs on August 13, Burton's route followed the valley of the North Platte heading to Chimney Rock Station. Burton expressed what most travelers thought of the area, "After twelve miles' drive we fronted the Court-house, the remarkable portal of a new region, and this new region teeming with wonders will now extend about 100 miles."(9:80)

"The Court-House, which had lately suffered from heavy rain, resembled anything more than a court-house; that it did so in former days we may gather from the tales of many travellers. . ."(9:81) The stage route continued north and passed Courthouse on the east side while the Pony Express, ever mindful of time, had struck out more to the northwest. It forded Pumpkin Creek and passed the Courthouse just to its southwest. (47:109) James More was another of the pony-riders who passed through this section.

Burton's coach followed the main route. Burton's sketch shows Court House Rock and the area near the former site of Court House Station, about six miles south of Bridgeport and three quarters of a mile east at the crossing of Pumpkin Creek. Most of the emigrant travelers on the older route who had forded the South Platte farther east and passed through Ash Hollow viewed Courthouse Rock from the northeast.

Burton noted, "At 12:30 P.M. we nooned for an hour at a little hovel called a ranch, with a corral; and I took occasion to sketch the far-famed Chimney Rock. The name is not, as is that of the Court-house, a misnomer: one might almost expect to see smoke or steam jetting from the summit." (9:82) "After a frugal dinner of bisquit and cheese we remounted and pursued our way. . . ." (9:84)

Piercy also sketched the formation from nearly the same place in 1853. Assuming the sketch was made while at the station as stated, it would support the position that Chimney Rock Station was located on the north side off Highway 92 about a mile west of Bayard north of the historical marker, not at Facus Springs about four miles to its east. The next station, Flickin's Springs Station was about 12 miles west, a little past present-day Melba. On July 24, 1861 Israel Benjamin noted, "The telegraph from Salt Lake to this point was already completed, and here lay much material to carry it forward." (1:263)

Court House Rock, Jail Rock and Pumpkin Creek. - *Hill photo*

Pumpkin Creek Station. - *Hill Photo*

SCOTTS BLUFF

"Scotts Bluff,. . .was the last of the great marl formations which we saw on this line, and was of all by far the most curious. . . .it is a striking and attractive object. . . .As you approach within four or five miles, a massive medieval city gradually defines itself, clustering, with a wonderful fullness of detail, round a colossal fortress, and crowned with a royal castle. Buttress and barbican, bastion, demilune and guardhouse, tower, turret, and donjon-keep, all are there: in one place parapets and battlements still stand upon the crumbling wall of a fortalice. . ."(9:86-7)

The pass between the formations was called Mitchell Pass. In his sketch, Burton described the trail through the pass: "The route lay between the right-hand fortress and the outwork, through a degraded

Chimney Rock. - *Burton, The City of the Saints - Hill Collection*

Chimney Rock today. - *Hill Photo*

bed of softer marl, once doubtless part of the range…cut up the ground into a labyrinth of jagged gulches steeply walled in."(9:88)

The "labyrinth" has "degraded" more during the past 150 years, but you can still walk through it and hear and feel the wind blowing. Just imagine the ponies twisting and turning as they rush through the pass to the next relay station. Burton noted it was twelve miles from the earlier station or about two miles from the pass. The 1859 mail contract for the stage places the stop at about the same place, twelve miles west of Flickin's and fifteen miles east of Horse Creek Station. That would place it at or near the post of Fort Mitchell. Burton wrote, "I had intended to sketch the Bluffs more carefully from the station, but the western view proved to be disappointingly inferior to the eastern." (9:88) Today nothing is left of either the station, about 1857, nor the fort which was established in 1863 and used till 1868.

The lithograph is based on Burton's sketch made during a windstorm. He implies that the sketch was made quickly from near the station. It also appears to show the Dome formation in the center, but there is no place along or near the trail as it approaches or departs Scotts Bluff that matches unless the lithographer misinterpreted part of the sketch or left something out, or Burton did. below is the approach from the west. If the center formation was connected to that on the far left by a "saddle", the sketch and photo would match better. On cloudy days as it was when the photo was taken, the connecting "saddle" formation almost disappears

Moellman also sketched the scene. Burton's sketch was made closer to the actual pass. There is still some question about whether the Pony Express Station and the later military post were located at the same site. Some local inhabitants believe so. Most agree if they weren't, they were very close to each other. Burton's sketch of Scotts Bluff would indicate they were.

Once again trees, buildings, cultivation and road construction have altered the site. The present view is from the edge of the field north of the site.

Scotts Bluff . - *From Burton's The City of the Saints - Hill Collection*

The Pony was headed towards Fort Laramie. It was also Indian territory. The Sioux, the Arapahoe, the Cheyenne were all nearby. After leaving Scotts Bluff Station, the riders would next stop at Horse Creek Station. In 1851 the Horse Creek area had been the site of the

Scotts Bluff today. - *Hill photo*

large peace conference and signing of the Horse Creek Treaty with the Plains Indians. The station was about eleven miles east of Fort Laramie. It served as a station for both the stage and Pony Express. The station keeper, a French-Canadian named Reynal, his Indian wife, daughter and son-in-law ran the station. (9:89) Burton spent the night on the floor on a buffalo robe. He spoke at length with Reynal about his life, but noted, "M. Reynal's history had to be received with many grains of salt." Breakfast "was prepared in the usual prairie style. First, the coffee-three parts burnt beans. . .Then rusty bacon, cut into

Fort Mitchell. - *Mollman - American Heritage Center, University of Wyoming, ah002260*

Ft. Mitchell view today. - *Hill photo*

thick slices. . .Thirdly, antelope steak. . .Lastly came the bread."(9:93)
The next station was Bedeau's Ranch or Laramie City. There was a
large store and smaller huts. A little past the station was the site of the
1854 Grattan Massacre which was the result of an argument over an
emigrant's cow.

The landscape was now changing, making it harder on the Pony.
Burton noted, "As we advanced, the land became more barren; it
sadly wanted rain: it suffers from drought almost every year, and what
vegetable matter the soil will produce the grasshopper will devour.
Dead cattle cumbered the way side, the flesh had disappeared, the
bones were scattered over the ground, but the skins, mummified, as it
were, by the dry heat, lay life-like and shapeless. . .upon the ground.
This phenomenon will last till we enter the humid regions between the
Sierra Nevada and the Pacific Ocean. . . .The road was a succession of
steep ascents and jumps down sandy ground."(9:99)

He also noted, "In these lands, the horse thief is the greatest enemy
of mankind, for him there is no pity, no mercy; Lynch-law is held
almost too good for him; to shoot him. . .entitles you to the respect
and gratitude of your species." (9:100) This seems to substantiate the
problem that Division Superintendent Slade had faced with Jules Reni
in this region west from Julesberg.

FORT LARAMIE

Burton noted "we reached Fort Laramie. . . ..it has the usual large
flag, barracks, store-houses, officers' quarters, guard-houses, sutlers'
stores, and groceries. . ." He dined at the commanding offficer's
quarters and then left. (9:100) The officers' quarters, "Old Bedlam"

136

was the two story building facing the parade ground and the flagpole in Moellman's drawing. Trees block the view today.

Mill's photo shows the remains of the old adobe Fort John. It was taken two years before the Pony Express. By the time the Pony came through, Fort John had been removed. The fort was undergoing expansion. Note the growth of trees and change in the course of the Laramie River. Moellman's drawings were made two years after the Pony Express.

There is no evidence of a station at Fort Laramie, but its location between Bedeau's and Wards or Sand Point makes it a natural location. Additionally, there was a sutler's store and post office at the

Sketch of Ft. Laramie. – *C. E. Moellman, American Heritage Center, University of Wyoming*

Ft. Laramie - *Mills, Library of Congress, LCMS 55612-8*

Fort Laramie today. – *Hill photo*

Sutler's store, Fort Laramie today. – *Hill photo*

fort. Evidence shows that the Sutler's store served as the post office during the 1850s, 70s and 80s. It would be logical that the same may have been true in the 1860s. Stops were made at other forts. This would have been especially true during the time when the telegraph had reached there. Moellman's sketch of the fort in 1863 was similar to that seen by the Pony Express riders. The one story sutler's store would be behind and to the right of the larger building dead center in his drawing.

SAND POINT

The next station Nine Mile, also known as Sand Point, Central Star or Ward's Station was about nine miles west. The station was large enough that the stagecoaches changed mules there. (9:101) It

138

was located about a quarter of a mile west of Register Cliff, another landmark on the old Oregon-California Trail. Here is the station site looking east at the famous Register Cliff near Guernsey, Wyoming. About one mile to the west is the famous Guernsey Ruts where the wheels of the wagons and coaches and animal hooves cut deeply into the sandstone hills. The trail was a maze of tracks, like a woven strand rope, as the trail climbed over the hills next to the river allowing riders and wagons to pass one another.

HORSESHOE STATION

After another twenty-five miles, passing Cottonwood Station, the Pony Express rider arrived at Horseshoe Station. It was the home of Joseph (Jack) Slade, the Division Two superintendent and his wife, Maria Virginia. Burton noted the "buildings, which were on the extensive scale-in fact, got up regardless of expense. . .(the) house with the Floridian style verandah. . ." (9:101) Benjamin commented about the station noting, ". . .there is a very deep well of cold water. The station is splendidly built and the chief agent of this mail service. . .lives here." (1:26) After Ben Holladay took over the line, the station included: a blacksmith shop, coach shops, harness shops, warehouses, lodging houses, offices, and corrals. (59:170)

Slade had been hired to bring order to his division to stop the loss

Sand Point/Register Cliff. – *Hill photo*

of company property. Mark Twain noted, "He made short work of all offenders. The result was that delays ceased, the companies property was let alone. . . .in order to bring about this wholesome change, Slade had to kill several men –some say three, others say four, and others

Trail Ruts today. – *Hill photo*

six." (72:64) There seems to be general agreement that Slade brought order to his division.

After the express period, Moellman made a sketch of Horseshoe Creek Station with Sibley Peak behind it. Some think there may be some evidence of the station on a hill near the alfalfa field. The photo below shows a similar view. The construction of the earlier road and present Interstate has altered the area a little. A monument by the barn and ranch are nearby. A few years ago a tunnel was reported to have been unearthed by the house, and some speculated it was associated with Slade. Perhaps it was dug by the military. When the Army built their post at Gilman's Station in 1865, they constructed a tunnel between the post and the corral. Perhaps it was also done at Horseshoe. (25:140)

After Horseshoe, five more stations were used before reaching Deer Creek Station. Indian encounters were now becoming a concern to the riders. Twain had stopped at Horseshoe station and enjoyed breakfast there. He noted that they had not yet reached "hostile Indian country", but wrote, "During the preceding night an ambushed savage had sent a bullet through the pony-riders jacket, but he had ridden on, just the same, because pony-riders were not allowed to stop and inquire into such things except when killed. As long as they had life enough left in them they had to stick to the horse and ride even if the Indians had been waiting for them a week. . ." (72:57) Twain also noted that in an

Horseshoe Station. – *C. E. Moellman, American Heritage, University of Wyoming, ah002262*

earlier trip, the coach he was riding in had been shot at and the driver wounded in nearby "Laparelle Station," and that the station-keeper had shot at Indians shortly before Twain arrived.(72:58)

DEER CREEK

Henry Avis's normal run was between Mud Springs and Horseshoe Creek. Once, after completing his run to Horseshoe Creek, a stage arrived and the driver reported that a Sioux war party was near Deer Creek. Hearing that, the scheduled rider refused to leave. Avis was asked to continue on to Deer Creek. He did and arrived safely, but the Indians had raided and driven off the stock. The regular eastbound rider also refused to leave, so Avis took the eastbound mail back to

Sibley Peak & Horse Shoe Creek area today. – *Hill photo*

Horseshoe Creek. He rode 220 miles and reportedly was given a bonus of $300.00 (61:77).

A sketch of Deer Creek was made before the military post was constructed in 1862 and similar to what the express riders saw. The view is to the east. It was probably sketched from the lower portion of "the rock in the glen." The trail crossing of Deer Creek was about a mile east of the rock in the tree line. The station was a little west of the crossing. The station was located south of the old Indian and emigrant crossing area of the North Platte. The Pony Express stayed on the south side and crossed farther up the river by present-day Casper, as did most of the emigrants.

For August 16 Burton wrote, "we reached at 10 A.M. Deer Creek, a stream about thirty feet wide, said to abound in fish. The station boasts of an Indian agent, Major Twiss, a post office, a store, and grog-shop. M. Bissonette, the owner of the two latter and an old Indian trader. . . A delay of fifteen minutes and then we hurried forwards. The ravines deepened; we were about entering the region of canyons. Already we began to descry bunch-grass clothing the hills." (9:154). The next station was ". . .Little Muddy Creek, after a hot drive of twenty miles. It is a wretched place, built of 'dry stones,' viz. slabs without motar, and the interior was garnished with efforts of pictorial art. . . .The furniture was composed of a box and a trunk. . ." (9:155)

Glenrock later grew up around the old station site. Deer Creek Station and Bisonette's trading post were burned by the Indians on August 18, 1866. A marker identifies their site, but it is now hidden by the town.

There is no marker for the Little Muddy or Muddy Creek Station.

Deer Creek Sketch. — *American Heritage Center, University of Wyoming, ah 101023*

Moellman made a sketch of Deer Creek Station looking west. The large rocky formation with a few trees on it in the sketch was sometimes referred to as the "rock in the glen," hence, the name for the town, Glenrock, Wyoming. The military and telegraph station are on the left. The building on the right might be Bissonette's trading post or store.

A marker notes the location in the town of Glenrock. The distance from the military station to the rock was about three quarters of a mile. Eagle Rock, the flat rock formation was another half mile farther. This view, off the old trail and Center Street, is about a quarter mile from the rock.

Charles Becker rode the section between Deer Creek and Red Buttes. He considered Indians to be a major problem on his run. In one chase he lost his horse, but fortunately recovered the mochila and made it on foot the next relay station. He was also the rider when the Pony carried the news of Lincoln's election. (43:29) Israel Benjamin stopped at the station and commented about the large number of Sioux in the area which is thought to be about 700. (1:260)

Deer Creek Station. — *C. E. Moellman, American Heritage Center, Univ. of Wyoming #ah 002261*

143

Glenrock today, looking east. *— Hill photo*

Glen Rock area today. *— Hill photo*

FORT CASPAR

Burton noted, "Our station lay near the upper crossing or second bridge, a short distance from town. It was also built of timber at an expense of $40,000, about a year ago, by Louis Guenot, a Quebecquois, who has passed the last twelve years upon the plains. . . .The usual toll is $0.50, but from trains, especially of Mormons, the owner will claim $5; in fact, as much as he can get without driving them to the opposition lower bridge, or to the ferry boat. . . .The heights behind the station were our old friends the Black Hill. . . They are covered with dark green pine; at a distance it looks black, and the woods

Ft. Caspar Platte River Bridge Station. - *C. E. Moellman, American Heritage Center, University of Wyoming., ah 101025*

shelter a variety of wild beasts." (9:156-7) While at the station Burton encountered an Arapaho war party, perhaps some of those that Charles Becker encountered during his rides. The Pony Express also crossed the North Platte here, finally turning away from the river near Red Buttes.

The present reconstruction matches the drawing, but the river has moved away and is much narrower today. Parts of the bridge have also been reconstructed and the remnants of many of the old bridge cribs can still be seen. The site of old trading post and station were the right end of the main fort structure.

Jackson's paintings are based on or similar to his earlier photos of their camp and crossing at Red Buttes. The view is to the south across the river. The mountain in the background is the famous Red Buttes. This is where the Pony Express Trail finally left the North Platte after

Ft. Caspar site today. - *Hill photo*

145

paralleling it since it had made its approach near Courthouse Rock in the Nebraska Territory.

RED BUTTES STATION

Commenting about the Red Buttes Station, Burton noted, "After ten miles of severe ups and downs, which, by-the-bye, nearly brought our consort, the official's wagon, to grief, we halted for a few minutes at an old-established trading post, called 'Red Buttes.' The feature from which it derives its name lies on the right bank of, and about five miles distant from, the river. . . .The bluffs are a fine bold formation. . . .The ranch was on the margin of a cold clear spring. . . .Having allowed the Squaws and half-breed a few minutes to gaze we resumed our way, taking off our caps in token of adieu to Father Platte, our companion for many a weary mile."(9:161-2)

The area known today as Bessemer Bend was also the last fording area on the Oregon-California trails for those emigrants who had not crossed earlier to the north side. Jackson first passed through in 1866. All remnants of the station are gone, and none were visible in Jackson's 1870 photos. The old trading post's site is believed to have been on the site of the later Goose Egg ranch house. Jackson's painting shows the station from near where he took his photo, but some believe it was on the bench to the far right under the power lines where the old Goose Egg Ranch house stood. Note the change in vegetation since 1870. Today there is a rest area with interpretive kiosks near the old fording

Red Buttes, Wyoming. — *Jackson, Fort Caspar Museum*

146

Red Buttes area today. - *Hill photo*

area. From there it is possible to drive on dirt roads which closely follow the trail over to meet the Sweetwater River where it rejoins a modern highway Wyoming 220 near Independence Rock.

Devil's Backbone/Rock Avenue

The Pony Express was now on its way to meet the Sweetwater River. This is one of the landmarks on the route in this section. Burton wrote on August 17, "After eighteen miles' drive, we descended a steep hill, and were shown the Devil's Backbone. It is a jagged, broken ridge of huge sandstone boulders, tilted up edgeways, and running in a line over the crest of a long roll of land: the *tout-ensemble* looks like the vertebrae of some great sea-serpent or other long crawling animal. . . ." (9:162)

Riders even today would recognize it. The trail, now a graded dirt road, is much smoother in this section. Emigrants and early guidebooks often called the rocky formation "Rock Avenue." The riders were now heading to Willow Springs Station.

WILLOW SPRINGS STATION

Willow Springs served briefly as a Pony Express and stage stop. Burton wrote, "We nooned at Willow Springs, a little doggery boasting of a shed [with a fireplace] and bunk, but no corral; and we soothed, with a drink of our whiskey, the excited feelings of the Rancheros. The poor fellows had been plundered of their bread and dried meat by some petty thief who had burrowed under the wall, and they sorely suspected. . .Jack the Arapaho. . . .The water was unusually good at Willow Springs: unfortunately, however, there was nothing else."(9:163) The area was also a very popular resting or camping place with the emigrants.

The grass in the area is good and the springs are still there. The remnants of an old spring house is in the area, but it is believed to be a later one. The location of the station is believed to be near the old spring house and the nearly dead cottonwood. The nearby foundation is from a later structure.

Willow Springs. - *Hill photo*

Immediately after leaving Willow Springs, the riders began their climb up Prospect Hill. At the top they got their view of the Sweetwater Valley. Depending on the time of day, Independence Rock and Devil's Gate was just visible in the distance. An interpretive site is located near the summit and is well worth the stop. The trail can be seen clearly as it goes up the hill in the photo.

Prospect Hill today. - *Hill photo*

Even as the Pony Express ran and carried the mail and telegrams, the telegraph lines were being strung. For most of the route, the telegraph line closely followed the trail and that was true in this area.

THE TELEGRAPH

There still are remnants of what is believed to be one of the original or early telegraph poles in the area. They stood about sixteen to eighteen feet tall and were placed about 150 feet apart along this section. In most sections the company allowed twenty-two to twenty-five poles per mile. (14:119) Because the line was going up a long hill, they required more. In most areas the old poles were later cut and hauled off for some other use, however, here they were cut and never hauled off. The other item shown is one of the original insulators that

The Pony Express and the telegraph. - *Harper's Weekly, November 2, 1867, Hill Collection*

Cut telegraph pole & old insulator. - *Hill photo*

held the wire. Note the wooded cap on the insulator. It was found near the trail on a different portion of the route.

SWEETWATER STATION

After climbing Prospect Hill, the trail led over the divide passing down to Horse Creek Station about halfway to the Sweetwater River. Next came Sweetwater Station on the river about twenty miles away. Sweetwater Station served as a Pony Express station for only a few months. When Burton passed in August 1860, he noted "Near the lake (a waterless, saleratus plain) is a deserted ranch, which once enjoyed the title of "Sweetwater Station." [Burton-p.164] In 1861 the station was active again. Benjamin notes, "we reached Sweetwater

Sweetwater Station, Wyoming. — *C. E. Moellman, American Heritage Center, University of Wyoming, ah002258*

150

Bridge Station." (1:259) The sketch was drawn by C. Moellman. Lieutenant Collins also made a similar sketch of the post. The valley of the Sweetwater was now the corridor that the Oregon, California, Mormon and Pony Express trails followed to reach the South Pass. This view is looking west towards the southern end of Independence Rock depicted above the telegraph poles on the right.

The modern view shows of the trail looking west towards Independence Rock. This was also the site of the first bridge across the Sweetwater. The site is marked and evidence of what appears to be parts of old structures are in the sage brush.

Sweetwater Station, view from site today. — *Hill photo*

Independence Rock

Jackson took a photo after the Pony rode by the rock. The view is looking back east. The trail split, passing the rock either on the south by the river bank or the north end as shown here. Members of the Hayden Expedition are seen standing in the well-beaten trail.

Independence Rock. - *Jackson, National Archives # 57-HS-385.*

151

Independence Rock. - *Hill photo*

Today there is a historical marker and interpretive displays in the Independence Rock rest area. As visitors walk over a small bridge over the trail, they will be in about the same spot where the men in the photo are standing. Just imagine a Pony Express rider heading straight down the trail towards you.

DEVIL'S GATE

After passing Independence Rock, the trail funneled through a narrow gap south of Devil's Gate. Jackson took numerous photos and made paintings of Devil's Gate. One is from near the river's entrance. Burton wrote, "En route we had passed by Devil's Gate, one of the great curiosities of this line of travel. It is the beau ideal of a canyon, our portal opening upon the threshold of the Rocky Mountain. . . .The height of the gorge is from 300 to 400 feet: perpendicular, and on the south side threatening to fall, it has already done so in parts, as the masses which cumber the stream-bed show. The breadth varies from a minimum of 40 to a maximum of 105 feet, where the fissure yawns out, and the total length of the cleft is about 250 yards. The material of the walls is a grey granite. . .and the rock in which the deep narrow crevasse has been made, runs right through the extreme southern shoulder of a ridge which bears, appropriately enough, the name of "Rattlesnake Hills."' (9:167)

Today there are a few more bushes along the bank and the river has meandered a little in the immediate area. The trail enters through

152

Jackson's Devils Gate looking east . - *Colorado Historical Society, 20101186*

Devil's Gate, today looking east. - *Hill photo*

Rattlesnake Pass far off to the right of the photo. The riders had no time to examine the formation.

From near the top on the south side looking west, the trail is evident as a thin light line as it heads west diagonally up the Sweetwater Valley on the south side. Some records indicate that an Overland Mail Company stage stop was located there near the site of the former Sun Ranch. Burton makes no mention of a station near there, only a blacksmith's shop in the vicinity, and places "Planté" or "Muddy Station" farther west. Burton planned to make a sketch of the Devil's Gate from the station, but once he arrived he lamented because, ". . . the station proved too distant to convey a just idea of it." Based on his itinerary chart, this comment and others about mileage, Planté or Muddy Station would be between four to six miles west of the gate. That would place it near the horizon. Coincidently, that would also place it near Muddy Creek or Muddy Draw.

There was an earlier trading post at the site of the Sun ranch, but it was destroyed and burned by the Mormons during the Mormon War. Only recently has the University of Wyoming identified the actual site and a reconstruction of it made.

The modern view shows the location of the old Sun Ranch which is now owned by the Mormon Church and has a visitor center that focuses on the Mormon Trail and the Handcart Disaster.

Jackson's painting on page 130 depicts the heavy trail traffic that might have been found along the trails in the Sweetwater Valley. Near the lower left center, a Pony Express rider is shown going east towards Devil's Gate. Dominating the background in the west is the famous landmark – Split Rock and a depiction of a station which appears to be Plant's Stage and Express Station west of Devil's Gate. This is not a depiction of Split Rock Station which was farther west. The painting may have been based on his similar photo with a closer view of Split Rock. Richard Burton stayed at Planté on August 18 but did not speak highly of its appearance, food or accommodations. He left at 7 a.m. and continued without stopping at a ranch on the right of the road which, according to the coach driver, belonged to a Canadian, "a mighty mean man." (9:170) That station might have been Split Rock Station. They did stop at another ranch. That station is not noted in other Pony Express books. It was located north across the trail from a sandstone formation noted by Burton as the "Devil's Post-office," or

Jackson. — *L. Tom Perry Collection, Harold B. Lee Library, BYU, mss1068, It#57*

Devil's Gate, today, looking west. - *Hill photo*

"Old Castle" as it is known today. The formation is a little more than four miles to the west of the Split Rock Station site. Burton continued, "We 'stayed a piece' there, but found few inducements to waste our time. Moreover, we had heard from afar of an 'ole 'ooman,' an Englishwoman, a Miss Moore. . .celebrated for cleanliness, tidiness, cuvulity, and housewifery in general, and we were anxious to get rid of the evil flavour of Canadians, squaws, and 'ladies.'" (9:171)

155

Split Rock. — *Hill photo*

SPLIT ROCK

A modern view shows the trail in the vicinity of Pante Station. The Split Rock Station, was located about fourteen miles west from Plante south of the split or cleft in the mountains. Three Crossings was eleven or twelve more miles farther west.

THREE CROSSING STATION

In this area the main trail and Sweetwater River were forced through a narrow gap in the rocky hills. Three Crossings was a stage station and also a home station for the Pony Express. Jackson's photo shows the ruins of a station believed by some to be that station. However, based on its layout and construction it appears to be the remnants of the military post. Both Moellman and Collins sketched the military post. Perhaps it was expanded or constructed on the same site. There is some question about whether the stations were different. (24:137) It seems unlikely that the C.O.C. & P.P.. would have had two stations within a mile of each other on the river. Jackson's painting of the station was probably based on his photo or the other sketches. During Burton's visit and stay on August 19, he had only high comments for Miss Moore's cooking and the cleanliness of the accommodations. He described the area noting, "Straight before us rose the Rattlesnake Hills, a nude and grim horizon, frowning over the soft and placid scene below, whilst at their feet flowed the little river—*splendidior vitro*-purling over its pebbly bed with graceful meanderings through the clover prairillons and garden spots full of wild currants,

Three Crossing Station. — *Moellman, American Heritage Center, Univ. of Wyoming, ah 002259*

strawberries, gooseberries, and rattlesnakes." (9:172) He did note both the mosquitoes and rattlesnakes in the area, and I can attest to the ferocious mosquitoes and a rattlesnake which I encountered nearby.

Today the station has deteriorated into low piles of rubble and rock hidden by tall sage brush. The 1862 grave of Bennet Tribbettes, a soldier, stands nearby on the bench on the far left. It was from those "graceful meanderings" Burton so aptly noted that the site derives its name. Within less than a mile, the river twisted and turned and had to be crossed three times in the distant gorge.

Three Crossing Station area today. — *Hill photo*

Rocky Ridge/St. Mary's Station. — *C. E. Moellman, American Heritage Center, University of Wyoming, ah002263*

From there the Pony was headed towards Rocky Ridge. Historians still debate the existence and specific station sites of Ice Slough and Warm Springs, but there is agreement about Rocky Ridge.

ROCKY RIDGE/ST. MARY'S STATION

Moellman sketched the St. Mary's or Rocky Ridge Station which served as a military post after 1862. Jackson's painting is very similar. Lieutenant Caspar Collins drew a layout of this station. Burton wrote that the "Foot of Ridge Station. . .which derives its name is a band of stone that will cross the road during to-morrow's ascent." It was near Muskrat Creek, ". . .a willowy creek, called for its principal inhabitants the Muskrat." He also noted, ". . .it is a favourite camping place for Indian. To-day a war party of Sioux rode in, *en route* to provide themselves with a few Shoshone scalps." (9:175) The station was "a terrible unclean hole: milk was not procurable. . .there was no sugar, and the cooking atrocious."(9:176-7) He did note that some volumes of natural history and agricultural reports were found there

as had been at other stations along the trail. Sleeping conditions were uncomfortable as the floor was knobby and it was full of bedbugs

Rocky Ridge area today. — *Hill photo*

and mosquitoes. This part of the country was known for its summer of hot dry days and cool nights, with the possibility of glacial storms which could bring snow and sharp colds at any time. Burton also noted that wolves and coyotes were plentiful and were bold enough to steal poorly secured food supplies.

For those who accept Buffalo Bill as a rider, this station was the end of his long ride that he made from Red Buttes to Rocky Ridge and then turned around and went back to Red Buttes. Charles Becker's route was from Plante Station just west from Devil's Gate to Rocky Ridge. He also was assigned to ride on the North Platte between Deer Creek and Red Buttes. (43:29)

Today there is a small stone marker to the north of the trail near the site off the ranch road. The geological formation known as Rocky Ridge is on the hills in the distance. The ridge was very difficult for Pony horses, stagecoaches and emigrant wagons. The Sweetwater entered a narrow canyon to the left and the early trail turned away, twisting and turning its way up and over the ridge. Another route was developed through the narrow canyon and then made a steep climb, but it missed the extremely rough rocky section of the trail.

SOUTH PASS/UPPER SWEETWATER STATION

The trail continued winding up and down rugged hills and broken hollows as it headed for the South Pass.

Historians agree that there were stage and express stations west of Rocky Ridge, but the specific ones and locations are harder to determine. A Rock Creek Station is listed on the 1861 Mail Contract.

159

On August 20, Burton describes two inhabited sites and implies or mentions two stops, but he uses almost contradictory statements. He also indicates in his itinerary the locations of some good camping areas with water and grass but doesn't mention any stations at them. Most historians generally agree that the last most western station in the Sweetwater Valley and also the last one before crossing the South Pass was the Upper Sweetwater or South Pass Station. Burton indicates, "At Ford No. 9 Canadian ranch and store." (9:571). Moellman made this sketch which he labeled South Pass Station, and Jackson's later painting of the station is very similar but with more landscape detail.

Burton noted, "At Ford No. 9, we bade adieu to the Sweetwater with a natural regret which one feels when losing sight of the only pretty face and pleasant person in the neighborhood….ten miles beyond Ford No. 9, hilly miles…led us to the South Pass, the great *Wasserscheide* between the Atlantic and the Pacific; and the frontier points between the territory of Nebraska and the state of Oregon." (9:178). Actually, the trail was then entering Utah Territory—the land of the Mormons. They played a major role in the development and running of the Pony Express.

SOUTH PASS/PACIFIC SPRINGS

On August 20 Burton writes, "A watershed is always exciting to the traveler. What shall I say of this, where on the topmost point of American travel, you drink within a few hundred yards of the waters of the Atlantic and the Pacific Oceans?" (9:179) The South Pass is not a narrow area between two towering mountains, but a broad saddle about twenty miles wide, rising so gently that it's almost imperceptible as to where the specific dividing line lies. James Wilkins made a painting he labeled South Pass. If the light colored slightly arched line is the trail, perhaps he was trying to represent the actual point of the watershed.

Continuing Burton writes, "But we have not yet reached our destination, which is two miles below the South Pass. Pacific Springs is our station; it lies a little down the hill, and we can sight it from the road. The springs are a pond of pure, hard, and very cold water surrounded by a strip of shaking bog, which must be boarded over before it will bear a man. The hut would be a right melancholy abode, were it not for the wooded ground on one hand and the glorious snow

South Pass - Upper Sweetwater Station. — *C. E. Moellman, American Heritage Center, University of Wyoming, ah 002264*

peaks on the other side of the "Pass." We. . .dined without delay; the material being bouilli and potatoes —unusual luxuries." (9:180) Later he writes, "The shanty was perhaps a triffle more uncomfortable than the average; our only seat was a kind of trestled plank, which suggested

Area today. — *Hill photo*

Approach to true South Pass today. — *Hill photo*

a certain obsolete military punishment, called riding on a rail." And
". . .the log hut being somewhat crannied and creviced, and the door
had a porcelain handle, and a shocking bad fit—a characteristic
combination. We had some trouble to keep ourselves warm. At sunrise
the thermometer showed 35° Fahrenheit." (9:183) Pacific Springs was
a station for both the Pony Express and the stage.

Rider Calvin Downs said that Joseph (Jack) Slade finally caught
up with Old Jules Reni, the leader of a gang of horse thieves, at Pacific
Springs. He was shot trying to escape. Slade brought him back, tied
him to a corral post and used Jules for target practice. Once he was
dead, he reportedly cut off his ears, nailed one to a post as a warning
to other thieves and carried the other in his pocket. (61:128) Twain's
account of the Slade-Jules incident places it near Rocky Ridge to the
east but still in the vicinity of the South Pass. (72:69). However, the
most recent research indicates Slade may not have done the actual
killing. Jules had been wounded when captured by two of Slade's men
east of Fort Laramie. He was brought to nearby Cold Spring Station.
When Slade arrived, Jules was already dead. But, he did cut off his
ears.(59:230) The old lore is certainly more exciting.

The old buildings of the Halter and Flick Ranch shown in a modern
view would be in the area where the original hut was located.

Harry Lamont was another rider assigned to ride the segment to
Fort Bridger.

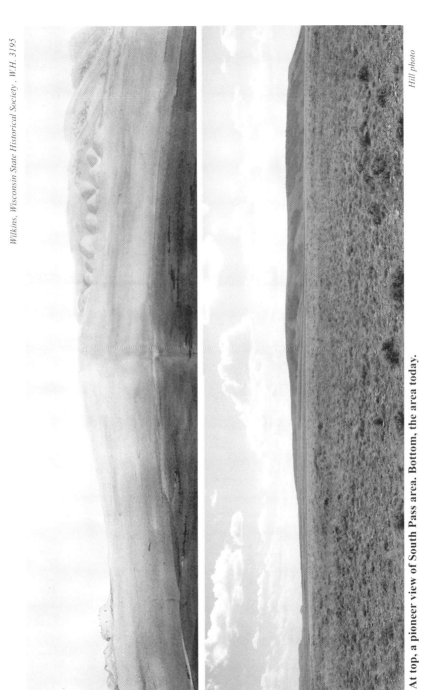

Wilkins, Wisconsin State Historical Society, W.H. 3195

Hill photo

At top, a pioneer view of South Pass area. Bottom, the area today.

Pacific Springs. — *Wilkins, Wisconsin Historical Society, W.H. 3196*

Pacific Springs today. — *Hill photo*

Pacific Springs today. — *Hill photo*

164

The next stations were the Dry Sandy, Little Sandy, Big Sandy, Big Timber, and then Green River.

BIG SANDY CROSSING

In Jackson's painting of Big Sandy Crossing, the view is looking towards the northeast from very near the site of the Big Sandy Station. The Wind River Mountains are in the background. The water was refreshing. Burton noted, "After a long stage of twenty-nine miles [from Pacific Springs], we made Big Sandy Creek, an important influent of the Green River; the stream, then shrunken, was in breadth not less than five rods, each = 16.5 feet, with a clear swift current through a pretty little prairillon. . . .The Indian, in their picturesque way, term this stream Wagahongopa, or Glistening Gravel Water.(9:84-5)

Today the area immediately along the creek is still green and flowered. The painting was made by the bridge where U.S. Highway 187 crosses the Big Sandy at the edge of Farson, Wyoming, where the trail crossed the highway. Travelers today can refresh themselves with some of the best and largest ice cream cones in the country at the corner store in Farson.

Burton described the Big Sandy Station noting, "We halted for an hour to rest and dine; the people of the station, man and wife, the latter very young, were both English, and of course Mormons; they had but lately become tenants of the ranch, but already were thinking. . .of making their surroundings 'nice and tidy'." (9:185) In a corral some

Big Sandy Crossing. — *Jackson. Harold B. Lee Library, Brigham Youn University. M55 1608 #651*

Big Sandy Crossing today. — *Hill photo*

mules were in the process of being broken and taught to take a harness by the station hands. Each mule had a bell so if they got away they could be found by the sound. The trail forded the Sandy and went up the steep bank and headed for the Green River about thirty-two miles away to the southwest. Burton noted, "Beyond the Glistening Gravel Water lies a *mauvaise terre*, sometimes called the First Desert, and upon the old road water is not found in the dry season within forty-nine miles—a terrible *jornada* for laden wagons with tired cattle. We prepared for the drought by replenishing all our canteens. . . . ."(9:185) Burton was referring to the Sublette Cutoff which had split off earlier near the Little Sandy Creek Station.

The Big Sandy Station site is just west of the main intersection in Farson, Wyoming. To follow the trail west from Farson, take either the old Lower Farson Cutoff or continue west on Hwy 28 to the Green River. The trail closely follows 28 or is under its right of way for much of the distance.

SIMPSON'S HOLLOW

Before reaching the Green, the trail crossed Simpson's Hollow. It was here in October 1857 that some Mormons under Lot Smith had surprised twenty-three of General Johnston's supply wagons. They ran off all the stock and burned the supplies and wagons. Burton noted, "Two semi-circles of black still charred ground. . . .the Mormons fell upon a corralled train of twenty-three wagons, laden with provisions

166

and other necessities for the Federal troops. . .The wagoners, suddenly attacked. . .could offer no resistance. . .the whole convey was set on fire. . .no blood was spilt." (9:186) As it happened, these were the wagons of Russell, Majors, and Waddell. The resulting financial loss here of $85,000.00 and additional losses at other places farther west during Johnston's advance, and the company's inability to get reimbursed from the government, helped to cause the later financial problems which finally led to their bankruptcy.

Nearby Twain noted the scattered skeletons of mules and oxen. Later at midnight it turned dark and a violent thunderstorm hit. He wrote, "The stage was wandering about the plain with gaping gullies

Simpson's Hollow. — *Jacking, Harold B. Lee Library, Brigham Young University, M55 1608 #651*

Simpson's Hollow today. — *Hill photo*

167

in it, for the driver could not see an inch before his face nor keep the road, and the storm pelted so pitilessly that there was no keeping the horses still."(72:89) It took almost two hours before the trail was found and they could continue on to the Green.

Heavy rains made the trail dangerous for the riders. The gullies could quickly fill with water, the trail become muddy and slick, and the ponies could lose their footing. During one storm on another section of the trail, Erasmus Egan's horse slipped and fell. Egan had to finish his ride by walking to the next station and getting a new mount.

For the express rider, Big Timbers was the next station near where the trail again approached the Big Sandy and an alternate trail crossed Big Sandy and headed for Green. Burton noted, ". . .we approached the banks of the Big Sandy River. The bottom through which it flowed was several yards in breadth, bright green with grass, and thickly feathered with willows and cottonwoods. It showed no signs of cultivation." He made no mention of a station there. Little is known about it or its specific site location. The trees were cut long ago.

Green River Ferry

James Wilkins made this painting of the crossing of the Green by ferry at the Lombard Ferry. The site today has changed very little. It is now part of the Seedskadee National Wildlife Refuge. It was a little north of the area of where the later Green River Station was built. The station was a home station for both the Pony Express and the stage. It was after Big Timber and before reaching the Green that Burton recorded that they met a Pony Express rider, and they stopped to exchange the news. The station was the home of the coach driver, Mr. Macarthy. It was like "an oasis in the sterile." (9:188) There was a wide variety of grass and plants, shrubs, willows and aspen. The station had sheep, horses, cattle, cows and mules. The food was very good and even included fresh fish. There was even a separate store. It was like a small settlement. While maps frequently indicate the station was on the west bank, Burton seems to indicate that it was on the east side by noting that when they departed on the morning of August 22, "we forded the pebbly and gravelly bed of the river. . ." (9:190) In the drier months the river could be forded, but in spring and early in the summer it was deeper and had to be ferried. Israel Benjamin, traveling east, had to cross by ferry. He wrote, "Green River Ferry Station is on

Ferry at Green River. — *Wilkins, Wisconsin Historical Society, W.H. - 3197*

the other side of the river. . ." (1:257) That seems to confirm Burton's comment about the station's location.

Mark Twain, who had visited the station earlier, also commented on the good food. He wrote, "At Green River station we had breakfast—hot biscuits, fresh antelope steaks, and coffee—the only decent meal we tasted between the United States and Great Salt Lake City, and the only one we were ever really thankful for."(72:90) Surely, the Pony riders enjoyed their stay at this station.

Green River Station area today. — *Hill photo*

Ham's Fork/Granger South Bend Station

The trail was now headed for Fort Bridger, passing a number of relay stations, including Martin's Station and Hams Fork Station. There and farther down the trail Burton noted more evidence of Russell, Majors & Waddell's additional loss of animals and wagons during the 1857 Mormon War. More ox bones were still scattered around parts of the trail.

The Pony Express and the stage lines had stations at Hams Fork. An old rock building and shed listed as the South Bend Stage Station is in the present small town of Granger on the Hams Fork. Although the Pony station was in the general area, its precise location has not been identified. The Granger Station does not appear to be the one used by Burton, nor by the Pony Express. It appears to postdate the Pony Express. It is more likely that it is associated with the Overland Trail that crossed southern Wyoming and intersected with the older Oregon-California-Mormon-Pony Express trails. A few miles west of the river crossings all the trails joined and followed the Blacks Fork to Fort Bridger. One variant crossed about one and one half miles up the Hams Fork, and the Pony Express crossed a half mile farther up the river. It would be logical that in this crossing area the Pony Express and the C.O.C. & P.P. stage used the same stations.

Burton arrived on August 22 and noted, "At mid-day we reached Hams Fork, the north-western influent of Green River, and there we found a station. The pleasant little stream is called by the Indians Turugempa, the "Blackfoot Water."

Hams Fork area today. — *Hill photo*

"The station was kept by an Irishman and a Scotchman—'Dawvid Lewis;' it was a disgrace; the squalor and filth were worse almost than the two—Cold Springs and Rock Creek—which we called our horrors, and which had always seemed to be the *ne plus ultra* of western discomfort. The shanty was made of dry-stone piled up against a drawf cliff to save backwall, and ignored doors and windows. The flies—unequivocal sign of unclean living!—darkened the table and covered everything put upon it: the furniture, which mainly consisted of the different parts of a wagon, was broken, and all in disorder; the walls were impure, the floor filthy. The reason was at once apparent. Two Irishwomen, sisters, were married to Mr. Dawvid, and the house was full of "childer," the noisiest and most rampageous of their kind.... it boasted only of one cubile, and had only one cubiculum."[bedroom and bed].

"To give the poor devils their due, Dawvid was civil and intelligent, though a known dawdler. . .Moreover his wives were not deficient in charity; several Indians came to the door and none went away without a "bit" and a "sup." (9:193-4)

Examining the site today, it is clear that the station was not built into a small cliff. The Pony Express station was located on the east side of the river, against the riverbank on a different trail variant to the north. It had been called a dugout which seems to be more similar to Burton's description of the station using the cliff as one wall.

CHURCH BUTTE

Church Butte was a major landmark on the Pony Express Trail on the way to Fort Bridger. Burton wrote, ". . .we passed Church Butte, one of the many curious formations lying to the left hand or south of the road. This isolated mass of stiff clay has been cut and ground by wind and rain into the folds and hollow channels which from a distance perfectly simulate the pillars, groins, and massive buttresses of a ruinous Gothic cathedral. The foundation is level, except where masses have been swept down by the rain, and not a blade of grass grows upon any part." (9:194) Burton does not mention a station nor a stop, but some historians indicate a station near or west of the butte.

The Savage photo shows the view that Burton and the riders saw as they rode by. It was taken from near the trail. The topography of the area has changed little since the days of the Pony Express. Remnants of the old Lincoln Highway passes close to the formation. It remains hot

Church Butte. — *Savage, Harold B. Lee Library, Brigham Young University, MSS 1608 #651*

Church Butte today. — *Hill photo*

and dry and lonesome. There is still disagreement over the existence and location of a Church Butte Station. It was not mentioned in the 1861 US mail contract.

Millersville Trail swales

There still is evidence of the Pony Express Trail looking west where it crossed a dry bed about a mile before it reached Millersville Station, about nine miles east of Ft. Bridger. The station was large, constructed with many wagon parts and had comfortable accommodations. It was named after A. B. Miller, a partner of Russell and Waddell when they opened a store there in 1857. Burton described the station as "a large ranch with a whole row of unused and condemned wagons drawn up on one side. . .the chairs had backs of yoke bows, and the fences which surrounded the corral were of the same material. The station was kept by one Holmes, an American Mormon. . . .His wife was a pretty young Englishwoman." The party was supplied with "a supper which was clean and neatly served. . . ." (9:195) The passengers spent the night there. Someone played the violin or fiddle and Burton read some of Holmes's books before going to bed. His stay there was comfortable. (9:196)

Some believe that Millersville also served as a Pony Express home station. There was also a trading post nearby. Nothing is left of the old station, but here is the trail coming off a bench by the site of the station.

Millersville trail swales today. — *Hill photo*

FORT BRIDGER

Aside from the fort's sutler, private businesses, such as the Pony Express were usually not allowed to operate on military forts/reservations as was the case at Fort Kearny and Fort Laramie, nor would their animals be allowed to forage. Even emigrant wagon trains usually had to camp off military grounds. However, it does seem that the Pony Express would have been allowed. Russell, Majors, and Waddell had contracts with the military at Fort Bridger, and stages stopped there. The distance to the nearest stations east and west of the fort would fit the pattern for the fort to have served as a relay site.

Ft. Bridger Pony Express stable today. — *Hill photo*

Sutler's store today. — *Hill photo*

Twain noted, "At 5 P.M. we reached Fort Bridger, one hundred and seventeen miles from the South Pass. . ." (72:90) Burton mentions a forty-five-minute layover there, with time to visit the store and talk with Judge Carter, the fort's sutler, and the fort's officers. (9:198)

Within the fort is the Sutler's complex. Located in the northwest corner next to the carriage house is a portion identified as the Pony Express Barn. This white building housed the post office and store complex run by Judge W. A. Carter, the sutler. Carter had been appointed as the Pony Express agent by William Russell. (43:101) The restored store has displays about the Pony Express.

Muddy Creek Stage and Pony Express Station

This was the first station west of Fort Bridger. The photo on page 176, shows Muddy Creek Station during the early to mid 1860s. Burton stopped there for a short time, perhaps only fifteen minutes. The station keeper was named Jean-Baptiste. He had an English wife. Burton was impressed by the quality of the milk and cream. (9:199) Burton wrote, "We bade adieu to Little Muddy at noon, and entered a new country, a broken land of spurs and hollows, in parts absolutely bare, in others clothed with thick vegetation. Curiously shaped hills, and bluffs of red earth capped with clay that resembled snow…growths of tall firs and pines…and tall note-paper-coloured trunks of ravine-loving quaking asp." (9:199) There may have been a relay station at Quaking Aspen. Continuing west, the Pony passed some famous landmarks—Bear River Crossing, the Needles, and Cache Cave and more relay stations at the Bear River and the Needles on the way to Echo Canyon in present-day Utah.

The Muddy has cut the bank back, washing away part of the trail in front of the cabins. Markers in the sage mark what is probably the remnant of the old chimney. The site is on private property.

The last station in modern Wyoming was at the ford of the Bear River south of Evanston off Hwy 150. It was a stage and Pony Express station. Burton described part of the route, "the land is broken and confused, up heaved into huge masses of rock and mountains broken by deep canyons, ravines, and water-gaps, and drained by innumerable streamlets. The exceedingly irregular lay of the land makes the road devious, and the want of level ground. . ." (9:201) Riding in this terrain was difficult for both the pony and rider. Later Burton notes,

Muddy Creek Station. — *American Heritage Center, University of Wyoming, ah 100972*

Muddy Creek area today. — *Hill photo*

"Beyond a steep terrace, or step which compelled us all to dismount, the clear stream, about 400 feet in width, flowed through narrow lines of willows, cottonwood, and large trees, which waved in a cool refreshing wind; grass carpeted the middle levels, and above all rose red cliffs and buttresses of frowning rock. We reached the station [Bear River]. . . ." (9:201) Mr. Myers was the station keeper. There was a fireplace in the structure, and there seemed to be more furniture than at most of the other stations Burton described. As was typical in many places, he slept on the floor.

THE NEEDLES

After fording the Bear River, the trail passed The Needles on the north side of the road. Burton wrote, "we passed over rough ground and, descending into a bush, were shown on a ridge to the right a huge Stonehenge, a crown of broken and somewhat lanceolate perpendicular conglomerates or cemented pudding stones called not inappropriately Needle Rocks." (9:203)

The Needles today. — *Hill photo*

CACHE CAVE

The trail crosses over the watershed between the Bear and Weber rivers. On August 24 Burton noted, "...we ascended Yellow Creek Hill, a steep chain which divides the versant of the Bear River eastwards from that of the Weber River to the west. ...In front the eye runs down the long bright red line of Echo Canyon, and rests with astonishment upon its novel and curious features. ...On the right, about half a mile north of the road, and near the head of the kanyon is a place that adds human interest to the scene. Cache Cave is a dark, deep natural tunnel in the rock, which has sheltered many a hunter and trader from the wild weather and wilder men." (9:203)

For a Pony Express rider, the storm would have had to have been pretty severe for him to have taken shelter there. For him, the mail had to go through. Cache Cave is on private property.

Cache Cave. — *Carter, LDS Church Archives*

Cache Cave today. — *Hill photo*

HEAD OF ECHO CANYON PONY EXPRESS STATION

As the coach entered Echo Canyon, Burton noted, "Echo Kanyon has a total length of twenty-five to thirty miles, and runs in a south-easterly direction to the Weber River. Near the head it is from half to three quarters of a mile wide, but its irregularity is such that no average breadth can be assigned to it."(9:203-4) After the trail entered the head of the canyon, it passed a sandstone formation called the Castle. This was the site of a relay station called Head of the Canyon, Castle, or Frenchie's. The station was a log structure. Burton noted an "unfinished station at entrance."(9:573) This photo might show the finished building. Some of the structures are believed to be from the post-express period. The original express station may have been down the canyon at the former site of Castle. The station was purchased by "Frenchie" in 1867 and moved to the site in the old photo. (37:22)

178

William Page was one of the regular riders along the section between Fort Bridger and Salt Lake City. He knew the territory very well. He had first traveled through the area as a member of the Willie's Handcart Company in 1856. Then during the Mormon War 1857-58 he was stationed with the Mormon militia in Echo Canyon. (43:101) There are local stories that during the early months of the Pony Express, the station keepers had trouble with horse thieves who would later try to sell the stolen horses back. Once the express horses were branded with PX, the rustling stopped. (23:13). This sounds reasonable, but it still remains a "story."

ECHO CANYON

Burton wrote, "The height of the buttresses on the right or northern side varies from 300-500 feet; they are denuded and water washed by the storms that break upon them under the influence of southerly gales; their strata here are almost horizontal; they are inclined at an angle of 45°, . . .The opposite or southern flank, being protected from the dashing and weathering of rain and wind, is a mass of rounded soil-clad hills or slopping slabs of rock, earth veiled, and growing tussocks of grass. Between them runs the clear swift bubbling stream in a pebbly bed now hugging one then the other side of the chasm: it has cut its way deeply below the surface; the banks or benches of stiff alluvium are not unfrequently twenty feet high. . .and everywhere

Head of Echo Canyon today. — *Hill photo*

Echo Canyon. — *Jackson, National Archives, #57-H5-33*

Echo Canyon today. — *Hill photo*

the watery margin is of the brightest green and overgrown. . . . Echo Kanyon has but one fault: its sublimity will make all similar features look tame." (9:204)

Twain wrote, "Echo Canyon is twenty miles long. It was like a long, smooth, narrow street, with a graceful descending grade, and shut in by enormous perpendicular walls of coarse conglomerate, four hundred feet high in many places, and turreted like medieval castles. This was the most faultless piece of road in the mountains, and the driver said he would "let his team out." He did. . . ."(72:91) Pony riders also could fly down this section.

Jackson's photo taken a decade after the Pony Express, shows the old trail the Pony took hugging the base of the tall cliffs on the right which Burton called "the gigantic red wall." (Burton-p.204) The railroad was then being constructed on the bench above where the stream had cut its bed. The modern photo shows a more recent road. However, the interstate used today is parallel, but off to the left on the other side of the canyon.

WEBER STATION

There is some indication that another station, Halfway, Daniels, or Emory was located near the present-day Emory exit. Weber Station was located at the junction of Echo and Weber Canyon near the old landmarks of Pulpit Rock and Hanging Rock. Burton described, "As we advanced the bed of the ravine began to open out, the angle of the descent became more obtuse; a stretch of level ground appeared in front where for some hours the windings of the kanyon had walled us in. . .we debouched upon the Weber River Station. It lies at the very mouth of the ravine almost under the shadow of the loftly red bluffs. . ." He noted that the station keepers were Mormons and "The station was tolerably comfortable, and the welcome addition of potatoes and

Weber Station. — *Edward Martin, Harold B. Lee Library, Brigham Young University*

Weber Station area today. — *Hill photo*

onions to our usual fare was not to be despised." (9:208) It is believed that the building that served as the station had been constructed in 1853. From here the trail turned to the northwest along the Weber for three or five miles toward Henefer before turning to cross the Wasatch Mountains. Highway 65 closely follows the trail passing the Brimville site by Henefer, East Canyon, Wheaton Springs, and then Mountain Dell.

The area at the junction of Echo Creek with the Weber River has been subject to extensive grading, leveling and filling to make possible the junction of the Interstates.

Entrance To Salt Lake Valley

There was no station at Big Mountain Pass, but it was here that the Pony and travelers saw their first view of the Great Salt Lake Basin and Salt Lake City. Twain noted, "At four in the afternoon we arrived on the summit of Big Mountain, fifteen miles from Salt Lake City, when all the world was glorified with the setting sun, and the most stupendous panorama of mountain peaks yet encountered burst on our sight. We looked out upon this sublime spectacle from under the arch of a brilliant rainbow! Even the Overland stage-driver stopped his horses and gazed!" (72:91) The route of the Pony had diverged from the California-Mormon trail route near East Canyon as it climbed to

Big Mountain Pass. — *Hall, LDS Church Archives*

Big Mountain Pass today. — *Hill photo*

the pass. The modern highway does the same and closely follows the Pony's route as it passes Wheaton Springs Station site. However, at this pass and down the west side, all the old trails were once again the same. They went over the pass and straight down the mountainside heading towards Mountain Dell Station. Burton called the descent "an impracticable slope." The passengers had to walk down while the coach wheels were rough-locked.

The view today looks almost the same. A modern highway winds its way down to the valley floor. The trail went straight down near the tree to the left. Burton's coach stopped at the pass where they had a "few minutes delay to stand and gaze," but more likely to rest the mules after their long climb up the mountain. He noted, "The summit of the Pass was well nigh cleared of timber. . . .[and] are exposed to the heat of summer." (9:211) Today the same is still true. Travelers can also stop and gaze. For the descending rider, he didn't have time to enjoy the view. The mail had to go through and time was of the essence, but he would have to hold his pony back a little.

184

Mountain Dell Station. — *Utah State Historical Society, #9657*

Ephram Hanks' Home at Mountain Dell

This painting depicts Ephram Hanks' home which was used by the Pony as a relay station. He had built the place as a stagecoach station in 1858. It was also the last station before the trail went over Little Mountain Pass and down Little Emigration Canyon into Salt Lake City. The view is looking back northeast. The station was listed as Mountain Dale in the Overland Mail contract but was also known as

Mountain Dell area today. — *Hill photo*

185

Hank's Station, or Big Canyon Creek Station. However, Hanks had named the valley were he lived Mountain Dell.

In 1934, a marker was placed by the Pioneer Trails and Landmarks Association near what was believed to be the site. The site is under water and today there is a park along the lake. From the marker, the modern highway soon turns to wind its way up and over Little Mountain, but not the old trail. It continued down the valley through the present reservoir for about two miles before it took a turn to the right and went almost straight up Little Mountain. Burton writes, "After two miles of comparatively level ground we come to the foot of "Little Mountain," and descended from the wagon to relieve the poor devils of mules. The near slope was much shorter, but also it was much steeper than "Big Mountain." The counter slope was easier, though by no means pleasant to contemplate…" (9:212) The Pony rider could not take pity on his mount and walk up. His pony had to be strong enough to carry his rider up the mile to the summit and then down the other side.

The Pony was headed straight down into Emigration Canyon. Burton wrote, "Beyond the eastern foot. . .we were miserably bumped and jolted over the broken ground. . . .The road was a narrow shelf along the broader of two spaces between the stream and the rock, and frequent fordings were rendered necessary by the capricious

Descending Little Mountain. — *Jackson, Scotts Bluff National Monument*

wanderings of the torrent. . . .we saw in more than one place, unmistakable signs of upsets in the shape of broken spokes and yoke bows. (9:213) The modern road winds its way up and down the other side, crossing the trail as it nears the summit and again on the other side. Jackson's painting depicts this area.

Emigration Canyon. — *J. Willard Marriott Library, University of Utah*

EMIGRATION CANYON

A rider heading east out of Salt Lake City up Emigration Canyon in the 1860s would have seen a view similar to a drawing made in that period. The canyon bottom was very narrow. It was there, in 1846, that the Donner Party finally gave up cutting their trail along the winding stream through the narrow bottom which was thick with vines, brush, trees, and rocks. They decided to climb up and over a hill, which was off to the right of the picture. That hill, known today as Donner Hill,

Emigration Canyon today. — *Hill photo*

seemed to have blocked their route. When the Mormons came the following year, they arrived at Donner Hill, but instead of climbing the hill they decided to cut their way through the brush. In about four hours they had cleared a route through the trees, brush, and rocks into the valley.

The area remains narrow and the stream is still there. However, it has been graded some, the road widened and the rock formation removed. There is less water in the stream, its bed altered, and the waterfall is no more. However, around the bend on the other side, just south across the stream, one can see that steep hill the Donners double teamed and pulled their wagons up and over, "Donner Hill." Coming out through this gap, Burton noted, "In due time, emerging from the gates and portals and deep serrations. . . .The valley presently lay before our sight." (9:213)

PARLEY'S CANYON

The typical route of the Pony Express crossed Big Mountain to Mountain Dell, then over Little Mountain and down Emigration Canyon into Salt Lake City. However, a major snow storm blocked Big Mountain in April 1860 and forced the first riders to take an alternate, somewhat longer, route until mid-May. They took Parley's Golden Pass route. At Weber Station at the mouth of Echo Canyon they turned south. Taking the new road, they changed mounts at Synder's Mill near Kimball Junction and then went down Parley's Canyon and northwest into Salt Lake City.

Today I-80 closely follows the route taken by the Pony Express during those early months. The floor of the canyon has been leveled, widened, and filled and raised in places, but the many twists and turns are still there. Traffic is heavy and moves quickly. Be careful looking for this site.

Salt Lake House. — *From Burton's The City of the Saints, Hill Collection*

SALT LAKE HOUSE

The Salt Lake House served as a home station. It was also the last station in Division Three. It was located at about 143 S. Main Street near Temple Square. It was reputed to be the finest hotel in Salt Lake City and one of the finest in the West. Richard Burton arrived there on August 25, 1860. He described the hotel/station, "Nearly opposite the Post-office, in a block on the eastern side, with a long verandah, supported by trimmed and painted posts, was a two storied, pent-roofed building, whose sign-board, swing to a tall, gibbet-like staff, dressed for the occasion, announced it to be the Salt Lake House, the principal, if not the only establishment of the kind in New Zion. In the Far West, one learns not to expect much of hostelry; I had not seen aught so grand for many a day. Its depth is greater than its frontage, and behind it, secured by a *porte cochère*, is a large yard, for corralling cattle. . . .We looked vainly for a bar on the ground. . .a bureau for registering names was there. . . .upstairs we found a Gentile ball-room, a tolerably finished sitting-room, and bed chambers, apparently made out of a single apartment by partitions too thin to be strictly

189

Salt Lake House site today. — *Hill photo*

agreeable." (9:222) It had taken Burton nineteen days to make the journey. The Pony Express was expected to do it in just over five.

Salt Lake City was the major population center between the two ends of the express. Like most cities it seems to have been the center of romance. That was true for the Pony riders.

Thomas O. King had signed on to the Pony Express in March, 1860. His first assignment was to help deliver the stock to the relay stations east of Salt Lake City into present-day western Wyoming. Like most riders he was young, hardy and had an interest in girls. He later recalled that his "longest ride was from Salt Lake to Hams Fork, 145 miles, and returned next day making the trip in thirteen hours, and I remember that I went out walking with my best girl in the evening." (43:87)

Another story is about the friendship bond between two riders, Richard Erasmus "Ras" Egan and Billy Fisher. It could be called "A Ride Exchanged for Romance" and involved "Ras" Egan's longest ride of 330 miles. Billy "was riding west from me and had a sweetheart in Salt Lake City whom he desired to see, but could get no leave of absence to go see her and I naturally had sympathy for him, so we got our heads together and agreed to accidently (on purpose) pass each other in the night, and he would have to ride his route and continue on

190

mine. But he had all night in Salt Lake to rest or spark as he choose and return the double route next trip.

But with me it was different for after I had rode the double route, 165 miles I met the "Pony" from west and had to turn around without any rest and ride over the double route again, making a continuous ride of 330 miles and again I was tired." (20:281) It's interesting to note that in 1861, Ras married Billy's sister Minnie.

The Pony Express route west from Camp Floyd to the Nevada line can still be traveled today by using the Pony Express Byway. The route is not easy as most of it is a rough dirt road. A flat tire would not be an uncommon incident, as it happened to the author. There is not much traffic there, but you can view the beauty and feel the loneliness the riders experienced.

The hotel stands no more. Only a plaque marks the site by the Salt Lake Tribune Building.

From the Salt Lake House, the trail headed south to Camp Floyd. There were three relay stations. First was Trader's or Traveler's Rest run by Absalom Smith. Next was Rockwell's Station run by Orin Porter Rockwell, one of Brigham Young's bodyguards. Joe's Dugout served briefly as the third. None of the structures from the Pony Express period exist today.

Ras Egan recounted a dunking incident on his Dad's ride, ". . .he started his first ride. It was a stormy afternoon, but all went well with him till on the 'home stretch.'

The pony on this run was a very swift, fiery and fractious animal. The night was so dark that it was impossible to see the road, and there was a strong wind blowing from the north, carrying sleet that cut the face while trying to look ahead. But as long as he could hear the pony's feet pounding on the road, he sent him ahead at full speed.

All went well, but when he got to Mill Creek, that was covered with a plank bridge, he heard the pony's feet strike the bridge and the next instant pony and rider landed in the creek, which wet Father above his knees, but the next instant, with one spring, the little brute was out and pounding the road again." (20:199-200)

Mill Creek is between the Salt Lake House and Trader's/Travelers Rest. It crosses the trail about four miles south of the site of the Salt Lake House. This is the present crossing of Mill Creek on State Street where Egan took his spill. It is no longer a plank bridge, but a wide

Mill Creek Bridge Crossing today. — *Hill photo*

paved road with an almost undetectable crossing. The creek still flows, but it is greatly reduced. It flows under the road through a culvert. The dark suburban heading north is crossing the creek. Look closely on the right side at some dark bushes. The narrow creek is behind the fence there as it goes under the road. Egan would certainly not recognize the site today.

JOE'S DUGOUT

Joe's dugout was located about nine miles from Camp Floyd. Joe Dorton was the station keeper. The station included a two-room adobe house, a log barn, a well and a dugout for Joe's young Indian helper. (21:43) The old photo shows the old well site that was dug to get water. The attempt failed.

Billy Fisher's section was west of Salt Lake City. On one of his rides to the city, a fierce blizzard hit him east of Rush Valley. He barely made it to Camp Floyd, but was able to make his change of mounts and continued on. East of there he nearly rode right into a mule team because he could barely see in front of himself. Then somewhere past Dug Out he lost the trail and got off his horse. He recalled "As I sat there holding the reins, I began to get drowsy. That snow bank looked like a feather bed, I guess; and I was just about to…take a good nap when suddenly something jumped on to my legs and scared me. I looked up just in time to see a jacket-rabbit jumping through the snow….A man who goes to sleep in the snow might keep on sleepin'." (19:148-9). He started up again, found his way for awhile and then

192

Joe's Dugout Station — *Utah State Historical Society, Charles Kelly Collection, #5801*

Joe's Dugout site today. — *Hill photo*

lost the trail again. In the morning he finally found his way to Salt Lake City and home. The story is generally substantiated by rider Ras Egan. (20:248)

Another rider in this section was Michael Whalen. He rode for two months during the spring of 1861 between Salt Lake and Camp Floyd.

Camp Floyd, 1859. — *Mills, Library of Congress, LCMS - 65612-4*

CAMP FLOYD

Camp Floyd was established at the end of the so-called Utah War after Johnston's Army had entered Salt Lake City. By agreement, the army was not to stay in the city after marching in, but could establish a post nearby. A site to the south was selected near Fairfield in Cedar Valley.

The view shown here is looking northeast across the old fort's parade grounds.

Camp Floyd today. — *Hill photo*

Camp Floyd Museum. — *Hill photo*

One building on the site was part of the original camp. It served as the commissary. At one time as many as 3,000 troops were stationed at the Camp Floyd. Its name was changed to Fort Crittenden after Secretary of War John Floyd joined the South. Shortly after the Civil War started, most of the troops were withdrawn to fight in the east, and the fort was soon abandoned. The structure was moved to its present site and used as a house.

Today the building serves as the park's headquarters and houses a small museum about the camp's history. It is across the street from the Carson Inn.

John Carson had built an adobe home and inn in 1858 in Cedar Valley. It was used as a stage stop and later part of the express station and a place for riders to sleep. The area was also selected by the U.S. Army for its new fort. Today it is part of the Camp Floyd and Stagecoach Inn State Park.

Nearing the end of his journey from Carson City, one traveler noted, "There is a post-office here and a store where all necessary articles may be bought and where one may rest somewhat from the hardships of the journey." [1:221]

Riders faced dangers of all kinds. George Thatcher rode between Salt Lake City and Camp Floyd. One winter day, George faced an unexpected enemy. The deep snow had forced George to walk his horse. A wolverine attacked, knocking him down. Rolling into a ball

Stagecoach Inn today. — *Hill photo*

for protection and kicking with his feet, he succeeded in driving the wolverine away. He got up, ran to his horse and got away. (43:125).

Night travel and weather was a major problem facing express riders and stages in the West. After leaving Camp Floyd, Burton wrote, "About 4 P.M., as we mounted, a furious dust-storm broke over the plain. . . .The road to the first mail station, "Meadow Creek," lay over a sage barren; we lost no time missing it. . . ." (9:505) The coach missed the road and wandered around for six hours. They finally determined they had wandered about twenty-five miles and were now about sixteen miles from their next station. They arrived there the next day and spent another day recruiting. (9:506)

Ras Egan recalled leaving Fort Crittenden (Floyd) "at sun down for Rush Valley in a very heavy snow storm, and the snow knee deep to my horse. I could see no road, so that, as soon as darkness came on, I had to depend entirely on the wind. It was striking on my right cheek, so I keep it there, but, unfortunately for me, the wind changed and led me off course, and instead of going westward I went southward and rode all night on a high trot, and arrived at the place I had left at sundown the evening before with both myself and horse very tired." (20:281)

East Rush Valley Station monument. — *Hill photo*

EAST RUSH VALLEY STATION

The first station west of Camp Floyd was called Pass or East Rush Valley. It was built as a dugout. Today a monument marks the site. Water still collects in the low spot and more vegetation grows in it.

Russell, Majors, and Waddell grazed their stock in Rush Valley. Chorpenning had erected a stone stage stop there in 1858. It was located nineteen miles west of Camp Floyd. Henry Jacob "Doc" Faust served as the station-keeper for Chorpenning's line and then for the Pony Express. The station has been called Rush Valley, Bush Valley, Pass, Faust Station and Meadow Creek. It is believed that the station served as a home station. Faust also acted as an alternate rider when

Stone building ruins. — *Hill photo*

197

needed. One traveler noted, "At this station I paid 75¢ for a cup of black coffee with sugar. . .a price that I report herewith to console all those in Europe who are complaining about the high price of coffee." (1:221)

The past fifty years has been hard on the old stone building that is believed to have been part of Faust Station. Then it was two levels, with a cellar and a raised floor and roof, but without care it has collapsed to its present state.

PASS SPRING STATION

Now the westbound pony was heading to Point Lookout or Lookout Pass Station. The trail crossed the rest of the valley and then headed up Johnson's Pass. In April, Howard Egan built a log station there near a small spring. Mr. Jackson was the keeper. During the June and the July Paiute War, the station was abandoned. In September, Burton reported the station was in ruins, but it was later rebuilt. Today the trail is still evident, the small spring still has some water, and only a later pet cemetery is nearby.

Pass Spring today. — *Hill photo*

SIMPSON'S SPRINGS

The territory the Pony was entering was becoming harsher. Finding good and sufficient water was becoming more difficult. Seventeen more miles brought the Pony to Simpson's Springs.

There may have been a later relay station at Government Creek. The mileage between Lookout Pass and Simpson's Springs stations would fit the later pattern for stations. Burton doesn't mention a stop there, but that was still early in the Pony's history. A telegraph station was there in late 1861 which also coincided about the time when additional stations were added along the express route. David E. "Pegleg" Davis was the operator. (21:58)

Simpson's Springs reconstruction. — *Hill photo*

The springs in this area had long been known and used by the Indians. Howard Egan had located them, and Chorpenning and Simpson used them. Chorpenning first occupied the site in 1851. A stone station and stables with a wooden corral were soon built there by Chorpenning for his stage line, and like his other stations, were used by the Pony Express when the C.O.C. & P.P. took over his route in June 1860. The express station is said to have had two or three rooms. The station keeper was George DeWees (Dewees). The springs are now called Simpson Springs in honor of the explorer, but the site was also known as Pleasant Valley, Egan's Springs and Lost Springs. It served as a relay station where the rider could get a refreshing drink of water, which in this area was a real luxury. The next good water was about 42 miles west at Fish Springs after the rider changed mounts at Riverbed, Dugway, and Black Rock stations.

The present structure is a reconstruction built in 1975 based on local information and excavation. However, it may have been constructed on the site of a later stage stop. The actual site of the station is believed to be about 300 feet to the west near the original spring. (21:61) According to some locals, the smaller and drier stone masonry construction used on the old 1890s Anderson house behind a chain link fence nearby, and perhaps even some of its stones, had been used in the original express and stage station.

In early May of 1860, riders George Washington Perkins and Billy Fisher had left the Ruby Valley Station bearing the news of the Indian raids. When they reached Simpson's Springs Howard Egan had Billy continue to Salt Lake with the news. He took Perkins back with him to check on the condition of the stations. Perkin's normal run was between Egan's Station and Ruby Valley. (43:103)

Looking out from there in late September, Burton wrote, "Standing upon the edge of the bench, I could see the Tophet (hell) in prospect for us till Carson Valley; a road narrowing in perspective to a point. . . All was desert: the bottom could no longer be called a basin or valley; it was a thin fine silt, thirsty dust in the dry season, and a putty-like mud in the spring and autumn rains. The hair of this unlovely skin was sage and greasewood: it was warted with sand-heaps; in places mottled with bald and horrid patches of salt soil, whilst in others minute crystals of salty, glistening like diamond-dust in the sunlight, covered tracts of moist and oozy mud." (9:509)

RIVERBED STATION

The next station west was Riverbed or River Bed Station. It was not until 1861 near the end of the express that this station was constructed with upright logs, similar to the construction used at Ruby Valley. Some question its use by the Express. It was about eight miles west

Riverbed Station. — *LDS Church Archives*

Riverbed site today. — *Hill photo*

of Simpson's Springs. A well was dug there which was also used to provide water for Dugway. Prior to its establishment, William Egan recounted, "When we arrived at Simpsons Springs the pony rider told us we could not cross the river bed until the road was repaired, as there had been a big flood that had torn the whole bottom out: road and all. The rider on the previous trip, going west, as he started down the bank, heard a sound like a very heavy wind among the trees. He stopped to listen; the sound was coming from the east and increasing rapidly. He put spurs to the pony and, just as he made the opposite side of the bed, he could see a wall of water, brush and other debris, twelve or fifteen feet high, spread from bank to bank, rolling down the bed at race horse speed. If he had been one-fourth of the distance back across the bed, when he first saw the flood, he could not have escaped with his life." (20:218) Another reported problem facing the station keepers was hauntings by "desert fairies." (21:68) William Hosiepool, Oscar Quinn, and George Wright were all station keepers who reported being afraid of the hauntings. Perhaps it was really the sound of the dry desert winds.

Today nothing is left of the structures, except the pile of rocks from the chimney. A marker identifies the site north of the present road, but south of the old trail.

Desert View. *Utah State Historical Society, #10416*

This painting depicts the barren flats west of Simpson's Springs that Simpson's expedition of thirteen wagons and men, and later the Pony Express riders, crossed and was described earlier so vividly by Burton.

Desert View area today. — *Hill photo*

Here is the same area today. It is flat, hot, and dry. The terrain and present road can be pretty tough. Within a mile of the area we encountered a car and an RV with flat tires.

DUGWAY STATION

On September 29 Burton recorded, "After twenty miles over the barren plain we reached, about sunset, the station at the foot of the Dugway. It was a mere "dug out"—a hole four feet deep, roofed over with split cedar trunks, and provide with a rude adobe chimney. The tenants were two rough young fellows—station master and express rider—their friend, an English bulldog. . . .Water is brought to the station in caskets." Burton noted that three wells had been attempted, one 120 feet, but still no water found. (9:513) William Egan recounted that on one visit the well was at 130 feet and still no water. Later, the well was bored forty feet farther before giving up. He did note that "it made a nice place to dump the stable cleaning." (20:219)

Here is the station site monument. The author is standing in the hole or "dug out." It is still extremely hot and dry here. Water may have been found by July of 1861 as one visitor reported, "we came to Dug Spring Station, where a well has been dug; but this water, too, is not fit for drinking." (1:220)

Dugway Station site today. — *Hill photo*

BLACK ROCK

The Pony now headed up Dugway Pass and then on towards Black Rock and the distant Fish Springs Station. Little is known about Black Rock Station. There is some evidence to indicate that the station may have been south of the rock formation in a cleared area near large scattered rocks where the trail cut over the small rise. The station was not listed on the 1861 mail contract, and Burton did not mention it by name. The site seems to have derived its name from a volcanic outcrop of black basalt on the tip of a bench. Burton wrote, ". . .after eight miles rounded Mountain Point, the end of a dark brown butte falling into the plain." (9:514) This "dark brown butte" would be the Black Rock. He continued, "Opposite us under the western hills, which were distant about two miles, lay the station, but we were compelled to double, for twelve miles, the intervening slough, which no horse can cross without being mired. The road hugged the foot of the hills at the edge of the saleratus basin. . ." (9:514)

It is thought that the stone station had been built shortly after July 1861 when the Overland Mail Company took over the Pony Express. (21:73) The Pony Express Trail had been skirting the twists and turns of the southern portion of the Great Salt Lake Desert and its marshy areas.

An earlier site for the station may have been a mile or two to the east. [37:90]

Black Rock (Butte or Desert) Station area today. — *Hill photo*

Indian ambush of a Pony rider. — *Jackson, Harold Warp's Pioneer Village, Minden, Nebraska*

Horses played a significant role in the success of the Pony. Riders were not expected to fight the Indians, but to outrun them. During the period of Indian raids, Nick Wilson had been assigned the section between Fish Springs and Simpson's Springs with Billy Fisher. He recalled, "If the mail was to be carried at all, one horse had to make that distance, all the stations had been burned between, or the keepers killed. Only the best animals could be used there. . . .One day I had to

Similar area today. — *Hill photo*

take the mail from Fish Springs east. There was a certain point on the trail that was pretty dangerous—just a little way from Fish Springs. The water from the springs there spreads out and makes a swamp which reaches up pretty close to a rocky point of the mountain which is covered with cedars. This point made a good hidin' place for the Indians, and they used it to get up close to the trail and shoot at the riders. . .just as I reached the danger point, I touched N. . . lightly with my spurs. He leaped into a dead run. . . .A few bullets and some arrows came whizzing past me. By good luck none of them hit either my horse or me. . . .I looked back over my shoulder and saw them comin'. . .as hard as they could. . . .N. . .'s grain-fed muscles soon got me out of the danger. . . .Their grass-fed ponies couldn't keep long within gunshot." (19:67) After another incident of outrunning the Indians they made it safely to Simpson's Springs. Three days later he made the return run and had similar encounters. However, he had informed the Army, and they were waiting nearby. "We did not have any more trouble with them after that. The way stations were rebuilt, and N. . .was given a good rest." (19:69)

FISH SPRINGS

When Burton passed through this area later, he confirmed what Wilson had said about earlier conditions. Burton wrote, "About 3 A.M., cramped with cold, we sighted the station, and gave a "Yep! Yep!" A roaring fire soon revived us; the strong ate supper and the weak went to bed. . . ."

"On this line there are two kinds of stations, the mail station where there is an agent in charge of five or six "boys," and the express

Fish Springs Station. — *Utah State Historical Society, Charles Kelly Collection #5798*

Fish Springs Station. — *Hill photo*

station—every second—where there is only a master and an express rider. The boss receives $50-$75 per mensem, the boy $35. It is a hard life, setting aside the chance of death—no less than three murders have been committed by the Indians during this year—work is severe; the diet is sometimes reduced to wolf-mutton, or a little boiled wheat and rye, and the drink to brackish water; a pound of tea comes occasionally, but the doughty souls are always "out" of whiskey and tobacco. At "Fish Springs," where there is little danger of savages, two men had charge of ten horses and mules. . . .The fish from which the formation derives its name, is a perch-like species, easily caught on cloudy days." (9:515) Based on the 1860 census, Ferd Bath was listed as a station keeper and William Eckels as a rider or stockman. (37:96)

There is some debate about the station's construction. In 1859 Simpson commented about Chorpenning's station. He wrote, "There is a mail station at these springs, where we camped. At present the only shelter is a thatched shed." (66:50) Simpson's use of "at present" and Burton's later comment about the station and its "roaring fire" seems to imply something more substantial had been built by the time of the Pony Express—such as the old stone structure.

Today the deteriorated stone ruins of the Thomas Ranch are no more. The former site is now part of the Fish Springs National Wildlife Refuge. The marshy area is still nearby and a picnic grounds is located at the old site.

There is still some debate as to whether the express riders sometimes went west from Fish Springs over a pass in the mountain or followed the flat route along the base of the mountain which was used by the stages. That route is parallel to the modern Pony Byway which makes a big loop to the north and then back south along the old stage road which meets the cut-off trail coming in from the east. Either way, the riders were heading towards Boyd's Station.

BOYD'S STATION

A few miles west of the Fish Springs, Burton met Lieutenant Weed and his command of ninety dragoons and ten wagons. He noted, ". . .they had been in the field since May, and had done good service against the Gosh-Yutas." Farther down the trail Burton noted, "We halted to bait at the half-way house. . . ." (9:516) This was Boyd's Station. It had been built by "Bib" George Washington Boyd around 1855. It was a small stone structure with gunports, not a log one as sometimes described. Boyd also served as station keeper and continued to live there for more than forty years. The next station would be Willow Springs, eight miles to the west.

The Pony Express Trail went west from Boyd's while the old stage route continued to the south before looping back to the north. The remnants of the express trail can be seen.

The ruins of the rock station were subject to limited excavation and stabilization by the BLM in 1974/5. There is also an interpretive sign.

Boyd's Station ruins today. — *Hill photo*

Willow Springs today. — *Hill photo*

Willow Springs

Arriving on September 30, Burton noted, "The station lay on a bench beyond the slope. The express rider was a handsome young Mormon, who wore in his felt hat the effigy of a sword; his wife was an Englishwoman, who, as usual under the circumstances, had completely thrown off the Englishwoman. The station keeper was an Irishman. . . .Nothing could be fouler than the log hut, the flies soon drove us out of doors; hospitality, was not wanting, and we sat down to salt beef and bacon, for which we were not allowed to pay. . .As the hut contained but one room we slept outside." (9:517.) The Pony rider was Josiah A. Faylor.(43:59) Earlier in June the station had been attacked.

An 1868 photo doesn't match Burton's description. The house appears to be adobe and the barns wood. The Bagley Ranch and town of Callao has grown up around the springs and station site. However, there appears to be the ruins of a building that might have been the old station. The adobe building served as an Overland stage station.

Here is what is believed to be that old adobe station. It has been covered with wood which was often done to protect it from the elements, but the thick adobe walls are evident when inside. Part of one of the old cottonwoods recently blew down in a storm. Luckily it just missed the old structure. It is on private property.

From Willow Springs, the trail headed northwest to enter Overland Canyon about twelve miles away. Later, an additional station may have existed at Six-Mile or Willow Creek. A very short-lived station was located in the canyon. Canyon Station was located at the head of the Overland Canyon near the flats. The stations were built by Howard Egan for the Pony Express and used for the stages. [37:117] The canyon route was dangerous. A portion of Burton's description of the route also included comments about an express rider. He noted, "After six miles we reached Mountain Springs. . . .After twelve miles over the bench we passed a dark rock. . .and we halted to form up at the mouth of Deep Creek Canyon (Overland Canyon). This is a dangerous gorge, some nine miles long. Here I rode forwards with 'Jim,' a young express rider from the last station, who volunteered much information upon the subject of Indians. He carried two Colt's revolvers, of the dragoon or large size, considering all others too small. I asked him what he would do if a Gosh-Yuta appeared. He replied, that if the fellow were civil he might shake hands. . .if surly he would shoot him, and in all events, when riding away, that he would keep a "stirrup eye" upon him: that he was in the habit of looking round corners to see if anyone was taking aim, in which case he would throw himself from the saddle, or rush on, so as to spoil the shooting—the Indians, when charged, becoming excited, fire without effect. . . .He pointed out a place where Miller, one of the express riders, had lately been badly wounded, and lost his horse. Nothing, certainly, could be better fitted for an ambuscade than this gorge, with its caves and holes in snow cuts, earth drops, and lines of strata, like walls of rudely piled stone; in one place we saw the ashes of an Indian encampment; in another a whirlwind, curling as smoke would rise, from behind a projecting spur, made us advance with the greatest caution."

As we progressed the valley opened out." (9:517-8)

BURNT STATION

The station received its name "Burnt Station" in 1863 after the Pony had ended. Indians attacked, killed all the inhabitants and burned the station as an act of revenge. Earlier a party of California Volunteers attacked a nearby Indian camp. Everyone, including the women and children, had been killed. See Egan for a more complete account of

Canyon "Burnt" station site and Monument. — *Hill photo*

the circumstances. (20:263) The station was never rebuilt there, but one was built near the mouth of the canyon.

There is still some evidence of the old station. Markers in the sagebrush identify the site. The modern photo shows the site of the station with an old monument in the distance.

DEEP CREEK STATION

The trail now made another loop north through Deep Creek Canyon before entering Deep Creek Valley. Burton wrote, "At 4 P.M. we reached the settlement, consisting of two huts and a station house, a large and respectable-looking building of unburnt brick, surrounded by fenced fields, watercourses, and stacks of good adobe. We were introduced to the station-master, Mr. Sevier, and others. They are

Deep Creek area today. — *Hill photo*

211

mostly farm labourers, who spend the summer here and supply the road with provision: in the winter they return to Grantsville, where their families are settled." "The Mormons were not wanting in kindness; they supplied us with excellent potatoes, and told us to make their house our home. We preferred, however, living and cooking afield. The station was dirty to the last degree: the flies. . .could be brushed from the walls in thousands." (9:519) In the foreground are some of those wheat fields.

Matthew Orr also served as the station keeper. Deep Creek was also the home of Major Howard Egan, the Division Three Superintendent. The ranch also provided much of the hay, grain, beef and mutton to the other nearby express stations.

While many of the buildings are old, they are all from the post Pony Express period. The name Deep Creek is not derived from its depth, but from the fact that it has cut itself deep into the land.

ANTELOPE SPRINGS

Now the Pony was beginning its ride through what is today modern Nevada. Remember how Burton described the land that lay ahead while at Simpson's Spring. There are some paved roads that can be used to find some of these sites, but a good four-wheel drive vehicle with high clearance and good maps would be best if you want to find all of them once off the main roads.

The next station, Antelope Station was about thirty miles west. However, another station, Eight-Mile Station may have been added in between after July 1861 near Eight Mile Creek southwest of Deep Creek. It was not there when Burton passed by. However, later when Nick Wilson was assigned to the run between Shell Creek and Deep Creek, the station existed. Wilson noted, "The station was a stone building about twelve by twenty feet in size, with a shed roof covered with dirt, so that no timbers were sticking out for Indians to set fire. There were portholes in each end of the building, and one on each side of the door in the front." (76:149) It had a cellar and had been built on the low ground so water seeped in. The station was run by an old man who had accepted care for two boys after their emigrant parents had died. After the old man left, the two boys, about eleven and fourteen years of age, ran the station. The station was attacked by Indians when Wilson was there. They brought the horses in and held the Indians off

Antelope Springs ruins today. — *Hill photo*

for three days. Finally, some of Johnston's soldiers came and broke the siege. (76:150-1)

Antelope Springs Station was constructed in 1859 as a stage stop on Chorpenning's line. It later became a Pony Express Station. On October 4, Burton and party reached Antelope Springs. He wrote, "it had been burned by the Gosh-Yutas in the last June, and had never been rebuilt. "George," our cook, who had been one of the inmates at the time, told us how he and his *confrères* had escaped. Fortunately, the corral still stood; we found wood in plenty, water was lying in an adjoining bottom, and we used the two to brew our tea." Burton noted, "Beyond Antelope Springs was Shell Creek, distant thirty miles by long road and eighteen by the short cut." Two express riders who were at the station agreed to take them over a short cut to Shell Creek station. (9:523) Sometime later, the station was reconstructed at Antelope Springs.

Today all that remains of the later Antelope Station is a pile of rocks and a few logs, the springs and a dilapidated corral from more recent times.

Site of Rock Springs. — *Hill photo*

ROCK SPRINGS

Another station, Rock Springs was added on the shortcut or summer express route. It cut over the southern tip of the Antelope Mountains with the intent of reducing distance and time. Nothing remains of either Rock Springs or Spring Valley Stations.

After July 1861, Spring Valley Station was added on the longer or winter route that made a dip around the tip of the mountains. It was at that station that rider Nick Wilson received a head wound which left a scar on his head that he later tried to hide by wearing a hat. He wrote, "That spring I was changed back into Major Egan's division and rode from Shell Creek to Ruby Valley.

"Things grew worse that summer. More stations were burned, some hostlers and riders were killed, and I got very badly wounded. It happened this way. I had been taking some horses to Antelope Station, and on my way back, I made a stop at Spring Valley Station. When I got there, the two boys that looked after the station were out on the wood pile playing cards. They asked me to stay and have dinner. I got my horse and started him towards the station, but instead of going into the stable he went behind it where some other horses were grazing. Pretty soon we saw the horses across the meadows towards the cedars with two Indians behind them. We started after them full tilt and gained on them a little. As we ran I fired three shots at them with my revolvers, but they were too far off for me to hit them. They reached the cedars a little before we did. I was ahead of the other two boys, and as I ran around a large cedar one of the Indians shot me in the head with a flint-tipped arrow. It struck me about two inches above the left eye. The two boys were on the other side of the tree. Seeing the Indians run, they came around to find me lying on the ground with the arrow sticking in my head. They tried to pull the arrow out, but the shaft came away and left the flint in my head. Thinking that I would surely die, they rolled me under a tree and started for the next station as fast as they could go. There they got a few men and came back the next morning to bury me; but when they got to me and found that I was still alive, they thought they would not bury me just then. They carried me to a station at Cedar Wells, and sent to Ruby Valley for a doctor. When he came, he took the spike out of my head and told the boys to keep a wet rag on the wound, as that was all they could do for me.

I lay there for six days, when Major Egan happened to come along. Seeing that I was still alive, he sent for the doctor again. When the doctor came and saw I was no worse, he began to do something for me. But I knew nothing of this. For eighteen days I lay unconscious. Then I began to get better fast, and it was not long before I was riding again.

If Mr. Egan had not happened along when he did, I think I should not be here now telling about it. But oh, I have suffered with my head at times since then!" (76:147-8)

SHELL CREEK STATION

This was another of Chorpennings stage stations, which became a Pony Express Station. On June 8, 1860, during the Paiute War, the station came under attack. Depending on the accounts, the station may have been destroyed (but not according to Burton), the stock scattered or stolen and the inhabitants escaped, or three killed. On August 28, Egan's Station was attacked and on August 29, Shell Creek. Burton passed through on October 5 noting, "At the foot of the descent we saw a woodman, and presently the station. Nothing could more want tidying than this log-hut, which showed the bullet marks of a recent Indian attack." The station was manned by the keeper and three express riders. He noted, "There is a cold creek 200 yards below the station and closed by the hut a warm rivulet. . ." (9:522)

Shell Creek ruins area. — *Hill photo*

Nothing is left from the express period. The Overland Mail Company established one of its regional headquarters there in 1862. Workers and craftsman were brought in and new structures built in to keep the stages in good repair and running. The old buildings and ruins are from that period. It became known as Schellbourne or Fort Schellbourne.

EGAN'S STATION

Leaving "the filthy hole-still full of flies," the trail headed towards Egan's Station and canyon.

Burton wrote, "it was cold comfort to find when we had cleared the kanyon that Egan's Station at the further mouth had been reduced to a chimney stack and a few charred posts. The Gosh-Yutas had set fire to it two or three days before our arrival in revenge for the deaths of seventeen of their men by Lt. Weed's party. We could distinguish the pits from which the wolves had torn up the corpses, and one fellow's arm projected from the snow." (9:523) With no protection from the weather-snow and sleet, and a real fear for their lives from attack, they prepared for the worst. Fortunately, an hour later additional men, animals and wagons arrived and they were off to Robber's Roost Station. The incident that had caused the army's action occurred in mid-July. About eighty Indians took over the station and held Mike Holten, the keeper, and Henry Woodville "Slim" Wilson, a rider, captive as they ransacked the station for supplies. As rider William Dennis approached, he saw the Indians. He returned to find Lt. Weed and his patrol of sixty soldiers that he had met earlier. They returned to Egan's

216

Station and freed the two men and killed a number of the Indians. Such were the dangers and conditions at these isolated stations. The station was rebuilt and continued to serve as a Pony Express station until it ended, and then as a stage station until 1869. (71:52)

BUTTE STATION

From Egan's Station, the party headed to Butte Station or Robber's Roost. (9:524) The station may have been built where the later trail crossed present day Hamilton Butte near Pony Springs. Egan writes that he built a new Butte station and had needed a thirty foot ridge pole for his rock station. (20:227) Burton noted on October 6, "arriving at the end of the stage, Butte Station. The road was six inches deep with snow, and the final ascent was accomplished with difficulty. The good station-master, Mr. Thomas, a Cambrian Mormon . . .bade us welcome, built a roaring fire, added meat to our supper of coffee and doughboy, and cleared by summary process amongst the snorer places for us on the floor of "Robbers Roost," or Thieves' Delight," as the place is facetiously known throughout the country-side." Burton stayed for more than a day and gave one of his best descriptions of a station "we will glance around the "Robber's Roost," which will answer for the study of the Western man's home."

"It is about as civilized as the Galway shanty. . . ..A cabin fronting east and west, long walls thirty feet, with portholes for windows, short ditto fifteen; material, sandstone and bog ironstone slabs compacted with mud, the whole roofed with split cedar trunks, reposing on horizontals which rest on perpendiculars. Behind the house a corral of rails planted in the ground; the enclosed space a mass of earth, and a mere shed in one corner the only shelter. Outside the door—the hingeless and lockless backboard of a wagon, bearing the wounds of bullets—and resting on lintels and staples. . ., a slab acting stepping-stone over a mass of soppy black soil strewed with the ashes, gobs of meat offals, and other delicacies. On the right hand a load of wood; on the left a tank formed by damming a dirty pool which flowed through a corral behind the "Roost." The inside reflected the outside. The length was divided by two perpendiculars, the southern of which, assisted by a half-way canvas partition, cut the hut into unequal parts. Behind it were two bunks for four men; standing bedsteads of poles planted into the ground. . .covered with piles of ragged blankets. Beneath the framework were heaps of rubbish, saddles, cloths, harness, and straps, sacks of wheat, oats, meal, and potatoes, defended from the ground by underlying logs, and dogs nestled where they found room. The floor, which also frequently represented bedsteads, was rough, uneven earth, neither tamped or swept, and the fine end of a spring oozing through the western wall kept part of it in a state of eternal mud. A redeeming point was the fireplace, which occupied half of the northern short wall: it might have belonged to Guy of Warwick's great hall; its ingle nooks boasted dimensions which one connects with an idea of hospitality and jollity; whilst a long hook hanging down it spoke of a bouillon-pot, and the iron oven of hot rolls. Nothing could be more simple than the furniture. The chairs were either posts mounted on four legs spread out for a base, or three-legged stools with reinforced seats. The tables were rough dressed planks, two feet by two, on rickety trestles. One stood in the centre for feeding purposes; the other was placed as buffet in the corner near the fire, with eating apparatus——coffee-pot and gamelles, rough knives, "pitchforks," and pewter spoons. The walls were pegged to support spurs and pistols, whips, gloves, and leggings. Over the door in a niche stood a broken coffee-mill, for which a flat stone did duty. Near the entrance, on a board shelf raised about a foot from the round lay a tin skillet and its "dipper." Soap was provided by a handful of gravel, and evaporation was expected to act towel. Under the board was a pail of water with a floating can, which enables the inmates to supply drainage of everlasting chaws. There was no sign of Bible, Shakespeare, or Milton: a Holywell Street romance or two was the only attempt at literature. *En revanche*, weapons of the flesh, rifles, guns, and pistols, lay and hung all about the house, carelessly stowed as usual, and tools were not wanting—hammers, large borers, axe, saw, and chisel." (9:525-26.) Leaving the station on October 7, Burton describes the descent down the mountain into Long Valley.

Some archaeologists agree with Burton and believe that his description is probably pretty typical of most express station as it fits some of the studies of other sites. (29:123)

RUBY VALLEY STATION

The Pony now aimed for Ruby Valley Station about twenty-two miles away. Sometime later, probably in July of 1861, Mountain Springs Station was built about ten miles to its east. Ruby Valley Station was situated in the fertile valley. It originally served as a stop on the Chorpenning stage route and became part of the C.O.C. & P.P. Burton arrived on October 7. He noted, "Ensued another twelve miles' descent, which placed us in sight of Ruby Valley, and a mile beyond carried us to the station. . . .Ruby Valley is a half-way house, about 300 miles from G. S. L. City and at the same distance from Carson City. It derives its name from the small precious stones which are found like nuggets of gold in the crevasses of primitive rock . . . .We were received at the Ruby Valley station by Colonel Rogers, better known as "Uncle Billy." . . .He is now assistant Indian agent, the superintendent of a Government model farm. . ." (9:517)

Old Ruby Valley Station. — *Northeastern Nevada Museum*

Uncle Billy's house was built of stone with primitive furniture. Chief Chokup, as called by the Whites, was there and much of his band who lived in the Ruby Valley. Two miles to the north was a large lake full of water fowl of all kinds. The site provided food and hay for other stations in the area. Frederick William Hurst served as station keeper. It was also one of the few stations that escaped attack during the Paiute War. Rogers had befriended the Indians during the brutal winter a few months earlier, and Company B from Camp Floyd was stationed near there from May to October 1860. Mose Wright was an express rider from a neighboring station.

Ruby Valley Station today. — *Hill photo*

The next day Burton left, "After ten miles we reached the place where the road forks; that to the right passing through Pine Valley fall into gravelly ford of the Humboldt River, distant from this point eighty to eighty-five miles." (9:538) That road was the last segment of the Hastings' Cutoff of the old California Trail.

The monument at the original Ruby Valley site was recently vandalized and destroyed. In the 1960s the upright log station was dismantled and brought to the Northeastern Nevada Museum in Elko. It was reconstructed to resemble its original appearance. You can follow the Hastings route mentioned by Burton to Elko and the Northeastern Nevada Museum. There one can also visit the new California National Historic Trail Interpretive Center on the main California Trail. Both museums are well worth the side trip to Elko.

George Scovell was with the Pony Express when it began. His first assignment was to deliver horses to the relay stations along the route to his home station. He was assigned to ride between Ruby Valley and west to Roberts Creek. He carried the first eastbound mail over that section to Ruby Valley. He remembered the terrible loneliness of that first ride and how he thought Indians were hiding behind the trees and rocks just waiting to get him. (43:117) Billy Fischer was also a rider assigned to the Ruby Valley Station. However, his segment was to the east to Egan's Station. He was with the Pony Express when it began and took the first east bound mail from George Scovell on to Egan's Station. (43:63)

Winters in this area could be quite brutal. Burton had encountered six inches of snow in October.

DIAMOND SPRINGS STATION

This station was built of limestone slabs. It was one large room with a fireplace at one end. The photo shows a plank addition which would have been added later. William Cox was the station keeper.

Diamond Springs Station. — *Nevada Historical Society*

Diamond Springs ruins. — *Hill photo*

During the Paiute War it served as a gathering place. Richard Burton stopped here on October 9, 1860. He mentioned that the keepers were Mormons and stated that it was named "Diamond Springs, from an eye of warm, but sweet and beautifully clear water bubbling up from the earth. A little below it drains off in a deep rushy ditch, with a gravel bottom, containing equal parts of comminuted shells: we found it agreeable and opportune bath." (9:539)

Today, only part of the wall with the fireplace remains of the old Diamond Springs Station.

ROBERTS STATION

From Diamond Springs, the Pony rider aimed for Roberts Creek Station, and then Dry Creek Station. Burton wrote on October 6 about Roberts Creek, "Like all the stations to the westward, that is to say, those now before us, it was burned down in the late Indian troubles, and has only been partially rebuilt."

"About the station loitered several Indians of the White-Knife tribe, which boast. . .never to have stained its weapons with the blood of a white man. . . .These men attend upon the station, and herd the stock. . ."(9:540) Roberts Station was the western end of Bolivar Roberts' Division Four. Thirty-five more miles brought the riders to Dry Creek Station in Division Five.

GRUBBS STATION

About fifteen miles west of Robert's Creek Burton noted, "we reached some wells whose alkaline waters chap the skin." (9:542) This was the future site of the Grubbs Well Overland Stage Station which was believed to have been used by the Pony briefly at the end of its run. It is thought that the original station was a tepee like structure made of upright poles covered with brush. Israel Benjamin was traveling east, noted "Beyond Dry Creek, too, the road was good and after fifteen miles we came to Grub Station and, twelve miles farther on reached Roberts Creek." (1:216)

The current structure was probably built after the Pony. The old photo shows a building with a smooth surface, however, the present photo shows a construction very similar to the old Ruby Valley Station. Most of the old surface covering has weathered off, leaving only the old logs. An early Pony Express monument is located nearby along the trail.

Grubbs Station. — *Northeastern Nevada Museum*

Grubbs site today. — *Hill photo*

DRY CREEK STATION

Continuing on, Burton wrote, "Twenty miles further led to the west end of the Sheawit Valley, where we found the station on a grassy bench at the foot of low rolling hills. It was a mere shell, with a substantial stone corral behind, and the inmates were speculating upon the possibility of roofing themselves in before the winter. Water is found in tolerable quantities below the station, but the place deserved its name, Dry Creek." The new station-keeper was Col. Totten. (9:543) Benjamin traveling in July, 1861 found no water available for the animals. (1:26)

Gravestone today. — *Hill photo*

Dry Creek was the eastern end of Division Five which ran to San Francisco. It may have served as a home station. This was the scene of an attack on May 21, 1860 by Paiutes that resulted in the deaths of station-keeper Ralph Roiser and John Applegate who, severely wounded, committed suicide. Burton made an interesting observation about life and the state of division end stations. "Dry Creek is on the eastern frontier of the western agency; as at Roberts' Creek, supplies and literature from Gt. S. L. City east and Carson City west are usually exhausted before they reach these final point. After a frugal feed, we inspected a grave for two, which bore the names of Loscier and Applegate, and the date 21st May." (9:542-3) Burton and others slept in a hay stack.

Another incident involved Thomas Flynn (Flyman) who normally rode the section between Genoa and Carson's Sink. However, on one run in 1861 to Carson, Flynn arrived with the east bound mail, but there was no rider to take the mail east to Dry Creek, the next home station. Mindful that the mail had to go through, Flynn continued east all the way to Dry Creek. When he arrived, he found six emigrants barricaded in the station and the keeper had been killed. (61:90)

The building ruins are overgrown by sagebrush. The grave of Applegate and Roiser is on the crest of the hill nearby. Beginning in late 1861, the Overland Stage Company used a different station.

SIMPSON'S PARK AND REESE RIVER

Continuing west, Burton and the Pony Express stopped at Simpson's Park and then Reese River. Both stations suffered attacks and destruction in the summer of 1860. James Alcott, the station-keeper, had been killed and Simpsons Park was being rebuilt.

Burton noted, "The Station in the Reese River Valley had lately been evacuated by its proprietors and burnt down by Indians: a new building of adobe was already assuming a comfortable shape. The food around it being poor and thin, our cattle were driven to the mountains." Commenting about the daily temperature shifts that faced those living in the desert, "At night, probably by contrast with the torrid sun, the frost appeared colder than ever: we provided against it, however, by burrowing into the haystack, and despite the jackal-like cry of the coyote and the near trampling of the old white mare, we slept like tops."(9:545)

SMITH CREEK STATION

"Before 8 A.M. we were under way bound for Smith's Creek. Our path stretched over the remainder of Reese's Valley, an expanse of white sage and white rabbit brush. . . .After a long and peculiarly rough divide, we sighted the place of our destination. It lay beyond a broad plain or valley, like a huge white splotch" in the centre, set in dirty brown vegetation backed by bare and rugged hills which snow topped only on the north; presently we reached the "splotch" which changed its aspect from that of a muddy pool to a yellow floor of earth so hard that the wheels scarcely made a dint. Except where a later inundation had caused the mud to cake, flake, and curl. . . .Beyond that point, guided by streams meandering through willow thickets, we entered a kanyon—all are now wearying of the name—and presently sighted the station deep in the hollow. It had a good stone corral and the usual haystack, which fires on the hill tops seemed to menace. Amongst the station folk we found two New Yorkers, a Belfast man, and a tawny Mexican named Anton. . . .The house was unusually neat, and displayed even signs of decoration in adornment of the bunk with osier work taken from the neighbouring creek. We are now in the lands of the Pa Yuta, and rarely fail to meet a party on the road. . . .I observed, however, that none of the natives were allowed to enter the station-house. . . ." (9:546)

Smith Creek Station. — *Central Overland Route and Transcontinental Telegraph through Nevada*

Smith's Creek Station reportedly served as a home station for the Pony Express.

One story about Smith's Creek was reported in the August 1860 *Virginia City Territorial Enterprise.* "One day last week H. Trumbo, station keeper at Smith's Creek, got into a difficulty with Montgomery Maze, one of the Pony Express Riders, during which Trumbo snapped a pistol at Maze several times. The next day the fracas was renewed when Maeze shot Trumbo with a rifle, the ball entering a little above the hip and inflicting a dangerous wound. Maze has since arrived at this place (Carson City) bringing with him a certificate signed by

Smith Creek Station today. — *Hill photo*

various parties, exonerating him from blame in the affair and setting forth that Trumbo had provoked the attack." (45:22)

In another incident, two riders, William Carr and Bernard Chessy, got into an argument. Carr later shot and killed Chessy. Carr was arrested, found guilty, and had the dubious distinction of being the first man legally hanged in the Nevada Territory in Carson City. (45:22)

Rider William "Bill" James used Smith's Creek Station on his run between Cold Springs and Simpson Park. He recalled it as a desolate region inhabited by Indians, and that he was lonesome and he rarely made the journey without wondering if he would make it there and back. He rode California Mustangs which were considered the fastest ponies in the area. His run was sixty miles, but he remembered making a round trip in twelve hours, changing ponies five times each way. (56:130)

The old photo shows the adobe and rock portion. It is believed by some that the original station was the adobe, and the rock portion added. (45:22) The station, on private property, is being privately renovated. From here the Pony looped north to Cold Springs Station.

EDWARDS CREEK STATION

After leaving Smith Creek Station, the trail followed the creek up the Desatoya Mountains to where it crossed the summit and down to where it met and followed Edwards Creek out of the mountains. Burton described the route, "Our route lay through the kanyon, whose floor was flush with the plain; the bed of the mountain stream was the initiative of vile travelling, which, without our suspecting it was to last till the end of the journey. The strain upon the vehicle came near to smashing it. . . .The divortia aquarum was a fine watershed to the westward, and the road was in V shape. . . ." (9:546) This section is still much like Burton described. It is also largely on private property.

Edwards Creek Station was established near the mouth of the canyon as a stage station and listed on the 1861 mail contract. It was used briefly by the Pony Express. It was not there when Burton passed through. Israel Benjamin arrived on July 11, 1861. He wrote,"…we reached Edwards Creek. This station has its name for the little stream that flows nearby. Here there was fresh bread, Zwieback, and brandy, but so dear that a bottle of brandy cost from three to four dollars. The mules were changed here." (1:214) It was also the site of some

Edwards Creek Station ruins today. — *Hill photo*

Indian conflicts. Here are the station's ruins with the creek in the background.

COLD SPRINGS AND SAND SPRINGS

The next two stations have the unique status of being the subject of an extensive archaeological study and survey in the summer of 1976. The report provides an interesting perspective into the development of Pony Express station life based primarily on the use of artifacts and how they shed light on the life at express stations. One of the findings mentioned is that Cold Springs and Sand Springs stations were more or less rectangular, similar in construction and were the largest stations in Nevada. (29:32) The *Sacramento Union*, July 2, 1860 reported that many of the stations that had come under attack were being rebuilt and "fortified." That report seems to have been verified by the survey of both buildings, noting the existence of gunports and room and wall modifications and additions. Cold Spring's overall measurements are 121' x 53,' while Sand Springs averaged about 100'x 53'. Each had a living space, smithing area, corral and stable area. There was a fireplace in the living area of both stations. The survey seemed to support the written reports of attacks by a number of indications and findings. (This author has served briefly as a volunteer at an excavation of a stage station in Wyoming, a fur trade fort in North Dakota and some colonial sites on Long Island. The work is hard, but the findings

228

can be very rewarding. Anyone with the slightest interest should read the whole report.)

Smith's Creek, Cold Springs & Sand Springs are all parts of "Pony" Bob Haslam's story of his longest ride in Pony history during the height of the Piaute War. His regular section was from Friday's to Buckland. But when he reached Reeds, no horses were available. They had been seized by volunteers who needed them to find and attack the Indians. He continued on to Buckland where he found that the next rider, Johnson Richardson, refused to take the mail. Accepting an offer of an extra $50.00 from the superintendent C. W. Marley, who happened to be at the station, Halsam rode on. He arrived safely at Carson Sink and pushed on to Sand Springs, changed his horse again and rode to Cold Springs. He made it to Smith's Creek, 190 miles, where J. Kelly continued the run east. Nine hours later he started his return run. At Cold Springs he reportedly found the station burned, the keeper killed and no horses. He arrived safely at Sand Springs, changed horses and persuaded the station keeper to return with him. At Carson Sink the men were badly frightened after seeing fifty warriors nearby. Haslam rested briefly and went on to Buckland's and again met the superintendent who raised his offer to $100.00. He rested briefly and then continued his run back to Friday's. The total distance was 380 miles and he had kept the schedule. (73:40-1)

Cold Springs Station was built in March 1860 under the direction of Bolivar Roberts and Jay G. Kelly and others. They had been moving east, building stations as fast as they could in order to be ready for the Pony's opening run in April. Jim McNaughton was its first station keeper. Kelly was appointed assistant station-keeper. It was one of the strongest and largest stations built. However, like other stations, it had been under attack starting as early as May 11. John William, the stationkeeper, was killed and the stock run off, and in late May, C. H. Ruffin, an employee, reported that eight animals had been stolen or run off and the men forced to evacuate the station. (45:20) Shortly after that a Placerville newspaper reported that Bartholomew Riley, an express rider, died from an accidental discharge from his friend's weapon while at the station. (45:21) Near the end of May the home station was attacked again and parts burned. It was enlarged and rebuilt with small openings as gun ports in thick stone walls. (29:55)

On October 15 Burton wrote, "As we progressed, however, the valley became more and more desert, the sage more stunted, and the hills more brown and barren. After a mid-day halt. . .we resumed our way along the valley southwards, over a mixture of pitch-hole and boulder, which forbids me to forget that day's journey. At last. . .we made Cold Springs Station. . . .The station was a wretched place half built and wholly unroofed; the four boys, an exceedingly rough set, ate standing, and neither paper or pencil was known amongst them. Our animals found good water in a rivulet from the neighboring hills and the promise of a plentiful feed on the morrow, whilst the humans, observing that a "beef" had been freshly killed, supped upon an excellent steak. . . .We slept. . .under the haystack, and heard the loud howling of the wolves, which are said to be larger on these hills than elsewhere."(9:546-7)

The station was built of rock with walls about two and a half feet thick. While Burton mentioned no roof at the time, the archeaological evidence suggests that a roof did exist in one of the rooms. The wall was peaked and a post hole was in the center. (29:53) The site is about a mile off the U.S. Highway 50. Along the highway are the ruins of the old telegraph station and the 1861 stage station.

Sand Springs served as both an Overland Stage stop and a Pony Express station. Burton's description on October 17, 1860 noted that "Sand Springs Station deserved its name. . . .the land is cumbered here and there with drifted ridges of the finest sand, sometimes 200 feet

Cold Springs Station today. — *Hill photo*

high and shifting before every gale. Behind the house stood a mound shaped like the contents of an hour glass, drifted up by the stormy S.E. gale in esplanade shape falling steep to the northward or against the wind. The water near this vile hole was thick and stale with sulphury salts: it blistered even the hands. The station house was no unfit object in such a scene, roofless and chairless, filthy and squalid, with a smoky fire in one corner, and a table in the centre of an impure floor, the walls open to every wind, and the interior full of dust. . .Of the *employés*, all loitered and sauntered about. . .except one, who lay on the ground crippled and apparently dying by the fall of a horse upon his breast bone." (9:548) Life for the station keeper and stockmen was hard.

The photo shows the view to the west with the corral clearly visible and the living quarters section on the right. On the other side of the distant hazy hills lies Carson Lake. The station is listed on the National Register of Historic Places, and the ruins have been structurally stabilized. The wind still blows, the fireplace is there and the sand piles up in those 200 foot hills.

Sand Springs Station today. — *Hill photo*

Richard Burton describes the area west of Sand Springs that he traveled over on October 17, 1860, ". . .we set off t0 cross the valley the ten miles of valley that stretched between us and the summit of the western divide still separating us from Carson Lake. The land was a smooth saleratus plain, with curious masses of porous red and black basalt protruding from a ghastly white. . . .It was smooth except where broken up by tracks, but off the road was dangerous ground: in one place the horses sank to their hocks and were not extricated without difficulty. . . .Arrived at the summit, we sighted for the first time the Carson Lake, or rather the sink of the Carson River." (9:548-50) Burton's lithograph depicts the view from Simpson Pass, the summit mentioned by him and the same view the Pony Express riders would have seen. Today the lake has greatly receded. Where once there was a large lake, there are only many smaller lakes, ponds, marshes and dried water holes. The majority of the lake bed is dry and covered with sage brush, a very different view. The first view looks back east towards Sand Springs and the other west to Carson Lake. After Sand Springs, the Pony passed through Carson Sink Station, Smith's, thought by some to be perhaps William's Station, and then to Buckland - Fort Churchill. During the last few months of the Pony Express, another station, Desert/Hooten Wells Station, may have been added between Carson Sink and Fort Churchill. Burton continues, "From the summit of the divide five miles led us over a plain too barren for sage, and a stretch of stone and saleratus to the watery margin [of Carson Lake] which was troublesome with sloughs and mud....we proceeded to finish the ten miles which still separated us from the station, by a rough and stony road, perilous to wheeled conveyances, which rounded the southern extremity of the lake. After passing a promontory whose bold projection had been conspicuous from afar, and threading a steep kanyon leading towards the lake, we fell into its selvage. . . .A long dull hour still lay before us, and we were approaching civilized lands. "Sink Station" looked well from without; there was a frame house inside an adobe enclosure, and a pile of wood and a stout haystack promised fuel and fodder. The inmates were, however, were asleep. . . .At last appeared a surly gripple, who presently disappeared to arm himself with his revolver." He was not hospitable, granting no water, fuel or food."(9:550-1)

First view of Carson Lake. — *From Burton's The City of the Saints, Hill Collection*

Burton's drawing shows what riders saw looking west from the summit of Simpson's Pass.

The location of the station would have been about fifteen miles west of the summit, about four miles past the far side of the "promontory whose bold projection" shown jutting into the lake from the left or south in the sketch. The station site was first used in 1859 by Chorpenning as a stop for his stage line. In March of 1860 Bolivar Roberts and Jay Kelly and crew built an adobe station there. Kelly recalled that when building the station, they had to make the adobe by tramping the mud in their bare feet. The alkali in the mud caused their feet to swell to appear as "hams." (6:58) A marker now identifies the approximate location.

Leaving the station the next day Burton described the route ahead, "Crossing a long plain bordering on the Sink, we "snaked up" painfully a high divide which a little engineering skill would have avoided. From the summit. . .we could descry. . .the Sierra Nevada. When the deep sand had fatigued our cattle, we halted an hour to bait in a patch of land rich with bunch grass. Descending from the eminence, we saw a gladdening sight: the Carson River, winding through its avenue of dark cotton woods, and afar off, the quarter and barracks of Fort Churchill." (9:551) That place where Burton halted could have been the future site of the Hooten Wells Station.

Rider Nicholas Wilson was transferred to the Fort Churchill for a short time by Howard Egan after Nick had a narrow escape with some

233

View from Simpson's Pass, today. — *Hill photo*

Indians on his Deep Creek run. Nick also remembered the sand, "I was sent further west…to ride from the Carson Sink to Fort Churchill. The distance was about seventy-five miles and was a very hard ride, for the horses, as well as for me, because much of the trail led through deep sand." (76:147) He continued, "Some things were not so bad, however, for I had no mountains to cross, the weather in winter was mild, and the Indians were a little more friendly here."(43:141)

Today the general view is the same, only the lake has disappeared. The trail taken by the Pony and Burton as they descended and entered the old lake bed is still visible, just as it was drawn by Burton.

Before arriving at Buckland's, Burton spent the night at Smith's. At least one historian, Roy Bloss believes that Smith's station might be the same as William's Station. Burton wrote, "Mr. Smith, who hospitably insisted upon our becoming his guests. He led us to a farmhouse already half roofed in against the cold, fetched the whiskey for which our souls craved, gave to each a peach. . .and finally set before us a prime steak. Before sleeping we heard a number of "shooting stories." (9:552) It is interesting to note that Burton does not indicate that any of the stories told to him related to the killing were the very ones at William's Station that precipitated the Paiute War. If Smith's was William's Station, then it would seem logical that those killings would surely have been the subject of at least one of those stories told to the guests. Perhaps after the killings at William's Station, the

Pony Express ceased using it. The next morning Burton and party left Smith's. He noted they crossed the Carson and soon found the next station-house, Buckland's. The site of Williams Station is not known. Some think it might be under the waters of Lake Lahontan of the Carson River.

BUCKLAND RANCH

Samuel Sanford Buckland came to settle the area on the Carson River in 1859. There he built his log house, barns & corral, and a trading post. In March of 1860 Bolivar Roberts contracted with him to use his ranch as a stage station and then as a Pony Express home station. W. C. Marley served as the station-keeper. Once the Paiute War broke out, there was a lot of concern about the safety of the stations along the Carson and the country to the east. During the late summer or early fall, the Pony Express ended the use of Buckland's and transferred its operation to the new fort. This appears to have been the only military fort which actually was used by the Pony Express as a station.

This is the two-story Buckland ranch house that had been constructed with salvage parts from Fort Churchill, which closed in 1869. The house is believed to have been built on the site of the original cabin and station. Today the site is part of the Fort Churchill

Buckland Ranch today. — *Hill photo*

state park complex.

FORT CHURCHILL

Fort Churchill was one of the most expensive forts constructed at the time. Construction began near the end of July under the direction of Captain Joseph Stewart. It was built in response to the fear created during the Paiute War of 1860 and located within eyesight of the Buckland Ranch. It then replaced the ranch as a home station.

On August 19 Burton wrote, "From the station-house we walked, accompanied by a Mr. O.,—who, after being an editor in Texas, had become a mail rider in U.T.,—to the fort. . . .A well-disposed cantonment, containing quarters for the officers and barracks for the men. Fort Churchill had been built during the last few months: it lodged about two companies of infantry, and required at least 2000 men. Capt. F. F. Flint (6th Regt.) was then commanding....We went straight to the quartermaster's office and there found Lieut. Moore, who introduced us to all present, and supplied us with the last newspapers and news. The camp was Teetotalist, and avoided cards like good Moslems: we were not, however, expected to drink water except in the form of strong waters, and the desert had disinclined us to abstain from Whiskey. Finally, Mr. Byrne, the sutler, put into our ambulance a substantial lunch, with a bottle of cocktail, and another cognac, especially intended to keep the cold out." (9:553) The next station was Miller's.

The January 7, 1861 *San Francisco Daily Bulletin* described Fort Churchill. "This post is situated at the Big Bend of the Carson, 25 miles below Chinatown, was designed on an extensive scale, being intended to accommodate a thousand troops or more. The original plans, however, has been somewhat curtailed, those in high quarters becoming a little uneasy about the expense required for its completion. As it is, the work will cost the government a good round sum. For what purpose so large an amount has been expended at this point it would be hard to say. . . .The scheme had its origin in the war department, and they are here simply to carry out orders.

Had Captains Flint and Moore, or Lieutenant Gibson been consulted, they would have advised the plan of stationing small garrisons at various points in the Indian country, with squads of dragoons to traverse the mail and immigrant routes, making Carson City a depot for supplying them. This would have been a much more effectual as

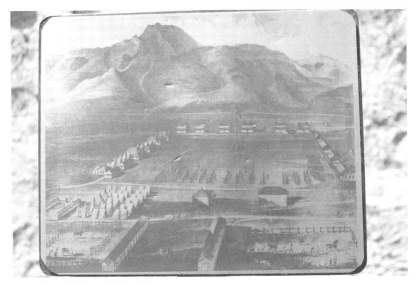

Fort Churchill -- old drawing. — *Hill photo*

well as economical system than the present, and one which all military men would have counseled."

"The fort stands on a handsome eminence which slopes gently down to the river. It is on the west bank of the stream, and about a quarter of a mile from it. The river bottoms in this vicinity are extensive, and being covered with a heavy growth of grass. The post has the essentials, wood, water, and feed for animals, convenient. The buildings are erected on three sides of a square of some eight or ten acres in extent, and are mostly composed of adobe with stone foundations. They are neat and substantial, giving evidence throughout of care and good workmanship. The soldiers barracks occupy the south side of the square, the officers the west, and the barns, stables and arsenal the north—the east being open to the river. There are about 300 hundred soldiers in the garrison at present."

This view of the fort is part of a display. The drawing was made from the hill south of the river and fort. The fort was deactivated in 1869. As with most adobe structures that were abandoned, the wooden parts were salvaged or sold.

Today it is a state park. The ruins of the fort have been stabilized. One can walk the grounds and visit the ruins of the old headquarters and officers' quarters which served as the Pony Express station. This

Ft. Churchill Headquarters ruins today. — *Hill photo*

is the old headquarters. It is the single story building located at the far right corner in the old illustration of the fort.

MILLER'S STATION

Millers Station served as a stage and express station on the Carson River. It had developed earlier as a resting spot on the old California Trail. In 1859, Simpson's westward expedition coming up from the south met the Carson River about a mile or two west of the future site of Fort Churchill. They continued to follow the river on the south side. The later Pony Express met and crossed the Carson River a few miles east of Fort Churchill and Buckland's and then continued on the north side of the river. Simpson continued on the south side hoping to raft across the river. The river in the area of the valley was "from ten to fifteen feet." A few days earlier he had sent a man ahead to find an area to cross or to make a raft. He made arrangement for Miller to make a raft from logs hauled about three miles. They were in the vicinity of the area known as Pleasant Grove. Simpson recorded "we arrive. Find the raft ready, made of cottonwood-trees of an old log-house belonging to Mr. Miller, the agent of the California Mail Company at this station, and which was pulled down for the purpose. This point a good one for ferry or ford : banks on either side low and firm. . . .We have now at Pleasant Grove, for the first time, got into the

Carson Crossing - Miller's Station—*Utah State Historical Society*

Carson Crossing - Miller Station area today—*Hill photo*

old Humboldt River and Carson Valley emigrant-road. The California Mail Company have a station here, under the charge of Mr. Miller, who occupies quite a good, weathered-boarded house. The grove of cottonwoods near it gave the place its name." (6:88-9) The sketch shows the ferry and Miller's Station in the background. It is the only known representation.

The Pony Express did not cross the Carson River here, but had already crossed it east of Buckland's. It now followed the north side or west bank of the Carson River.

Continuing on October 19, Burton wrote, "Our next station was Miller's, distant 15-16 miles. The road ran along the valley of Carson River, whose trees were a repose to our eyes, and we congratulated ourselves when we looked down the stiff clay banks, 30 feet high, and wholly unfenced, that our journey was by day. The desert was now "done." At every few miles was a drinking 'calaboose:" where sheds were not a kettle hung under a tree, and women peeped out of the log huts."

"At Miller's Station, which we reached at 2:30 p.m., there really was one pretty girl. . . .Whilst the rain was heavy we sat round the hot stove, eating bread and cheese, sausages and anchovies. . . ." (9:553-4) Shortly after they finished lunch they were off again towards Carson City.

Other relay stations were added during the next year along the Carson. On July 1, 1861, G. W. Reed became the owner of the station. After that, it was sometimes called Reed's Station.

Today the site is on private land and the buildings gone. There is much less water in the river today, but the cone hill remains and trees line the river.

CARSON CITY

The Pony Express was heading for Carson City. Twain noted, "Visibly our new home was a deset, walled in by barren, snow-clad mountains. There was not a tree in sight. There was no vegetation but endless sage-brush and greasewood. (72:144) By and by Carson City was pointed out to us. It nestled in the edge of a great plain and was sufficient number of miles away to look like an assemblage of mere white spots in the shadow of a grim range of mountains overlooking it, whose summits lifted clear out of companionship

Carson City—*Harper's Monthly, January 1861, Hill Collection*

Carson City today—*Hill photo*

241

and consciousness of earthly things. . . .It is a "wooden" town. . .The main street consisted of four or five blocks of little white frame stores . . .They were packed close together, side by side, as if room were scarce in that mighty plain. The sidewalk was of boards. . .In the middle of the town, opposite the stores was the "plaza." (72:145). The station had been located on Carson Street between Fourth and Fifth. Little is known about the station. From there the Pony continued to Genoa.

It was here in Carson City, late in the evening of April 5, that Warren "Boston" Upson carrying the first mail east arrived after his eighty-five mile ride. He had left Sportsman Hall April 4.

According to some, he handed off the mochila to Pony Bob Haslam who continued the relay east.

On April 13 at 1:30 p.m. Upson started his first run back west to Sportsman Hall. His ride over the Sierras took him twenty-two hours. The telegraph sent word ahead to Placerville and Sacramento where celebrations of the Pony's arrival were quickly planned.

GENOA

Genoa served as a Pony Express station. Genoa was also the goal of Simpson's 1859 expedition. He arrived there on June 12, 1859. A drawing shows members of the Simpson Expedition entering Genoa.

Arrival at Genoa—*A. John Young, sketched by H. V. A. Von Beckh, Utah State Historical Society*

Genoa area today—*Hill photo*

He reported, "Genoa, at the present time, has 28 dwellings-houses, 2 stores, 2 hotels, 1 printing establishment, and 1 electric-telegraph office." (66:93) The second building to the left in the drawing appears to be the old Mormon station. Simpson recorded, "Just as we entered town, were saluted by the citizens with thirteen guns and the running up of the national flag, in honor of the party's having successfully accomplished the object of exploration—the opening of a new and short road across the Great Basin from Camp Floyd, and thus facilitating the mails and emigration." (66:92-3) The corral could be part of the Tingham Livery Stable that was later used by the Pony Express. Today the area is part of the park and picnic area.

Perhaps Warren Upson, the first Pony rider, upon entering the town, had a similar experience. His arrival represented the fulfillment of what the Californians had dreamed of and what Simpson made possible.

The view today is from a slightly different spot. Trees and other houses crowd the area.

Mormon Station, 1860—*Nevada Parks, Mormon Station*

MORMON STATION

The 1860 photo is part of a display at Genoa. It shows the old Mormon Station. It was the oldest building in town. Note the burned log below the photo. Unfortunately the old station burned down in the early 1900s. The log is the only known original part of the station that exists.

Today there is a reproduction of the station. Inside is a nice little museum. Included is a piano from the old Kauber Store where Pony Express employees often relaxed and were entertained. As with

Mormon Station today—*Hill photo*

244

Rider at Lake Tahoe in the winter. —*Jackson, Denver Public Library, WHJ 10659*

other sites there are more trees in the area than when the Pony came through.

A painting shows a rider as he approached Lake Bigler/Tahoe on his way down after crossing Daggett Pass.

Winters were tough on the Pony Express. This was true in the mountains of the Sierras and Wasatch or in the Great Basin or on the Great Plains. Even the scheduled delivery times were increased. Trips could take two weeks or more.

FRIDAY'S/LAKESIDE STATION

As the trail entered California, not only did the topography of the land change, but also the nature of the typical stations. They were

Vischer's Friday's/Lakeside Station—*From The Saga of Lake Tahoe, by Edward Scott*

more permanent and civilized when compared to the crude, rugged stations of the Great Basin.

The distance from Genoa to Friday's was 21.5 miles. However, this was an extremely difficult ride for the Pony. If winter snows made it impassable, the rider took an alternate route along the established Carson River Wagon Route. The regular route had the Pony climb about 2,500 feet in less than ten miles over the 7,334-foot Daggerts Pass. Martin K. "Friday" Burke and James Washington

Area today—*Hill photo*

246

Small managed the Lakeside or Friday's home station. It included a one room log cabin, a two and a half story hostelry including a dining room, kitchen, storeroom, a woodshed and a large building that served as a stable and hay barn. It was the last station in Nevada. This drawing was made by Edward Vischer. It shows the hostelry, what appears to be the cabin and part of the barn. During the Pony's first month of operations, the Daggett trail was not used. However, by the beginning of May, Rollon Daggett granted the Pony the free use of his toll road over the pass. (26:211)

Lake Bigler/Tahoe

The difficult climb over the Sierra Nevada started. Simpson recorded, "In 1.5 miles from Genoa, pass Warm Springs (Wallys Hot Springs), at foot of the Sierra Nevada; 1.5 miles farther brought us to the Daggett trail, which we take. . . .Find the trail up to Daggett Pass quite steep. It runs along the side-hill, and at times is dangerous. It is possible, however, that a better grade might be got along the ravine of the road. In about 3.5 miles from foot of the sierra reach summit of pass 7,180 feet above the sea, and lying about 4 miles to the northwest of us could see Lake Bigler, beautifully embosomed in the Sierra. Descending by tolerable grade, 2.5 miles farther brought us to Lake Valley. . .which we thread. . .about 12.5 miles southwardly to the Mail Station." (66:95-6)

Today the old route up to Daggett Pass is closed. Highway 50 is nearby and longer, but still climbs up to the pass and over to Lake Tahoe. The area around Lake Tahoe (Bigler) and the shoreline have been built up, but the view and the lake are still beautiful.

View of Lake Bigler—*Utah State Historical Society, #10418*

Lake Tahoe today—*Hill photo*

Today a similar view can be seen from Pioneer Trail Road. The boulders are still there, but the growth of the trees blocks part of the view.

YANK'S OR MEYER'S STATION

Yank's Station was established in 1851 by George Douglas and Martin Smith, who operated a stage station and hostelry in the 1850s. Then in 1859 the station was bought by Ephraim "Yank" Clement and his wife, Lydia. They enlarged the station as it appears in the Edward

Yank's Station—*Edward Vischers, Special Collections, Libraries of the Claremont Colleges*

Yank's or Meyer's site today—*Hill photo*

Vischer drawing, which was made during the summer of 1861. The station was a three story, fourteen room hostelry, with a large stable and barn, outbuildings and corral. It served as an express relay station during the Pony Express era and also continued as a stage station. Nearby were a saloon, store, blacksmith shop, a cooperage and meat-processing facility and a water flume and mill. Warren Upton was one of the first riders on this section. In 1873 it was purchased by George D.H. Meyers and was then known as Meyers station. It was destroyed by a fire in 1938.

The station site today is in the town of Meyers. It is still a major area of congestion. The marker is in front of the store. As with other sites there are more trees in the area that block the mountains in the background.

STRAWBERRY STATION

In 1856 a Mr. Swift and a Mr. Watson opened up a hostelry that catered to travelers. In 1859, Mr. Berry managed the station for the Overland Mail and the Pony Express. It was the first station west of Echo Summit of the Sierras. According to some, Mr. Berry would feed the horses straw when he had been paid for hay, hence, the name Strawberry Station. (64:463) Vischer also sketched this view of Strawberry's in 1861. On the far side hidden by the three story hostelry were two more barns and corral. The large bald rock cliff formation behind the station is known as "Lover's Leap."

249

Strawberry Station—*Edward Vischers, Special Collections, Libraries of the Claremont Colleges*

A few years after the express ended, a traveler along the route east wrote, "As we left Strawberry, we began to travel through some of the finest scenary in the State. On our right stood a rock on the side of the mountain, thousands and thousands of feet high. All of granite." (15:236)

Strawberry Lodge today—*Hill photo*

The Pony riders didn't have time to sightsee. They had the mail to deliver.

Today the "rock" and the beautiful views prevail. The present lodge is about 1,000 feet west of the original site. It was moved after the highway was realigned. Strawberry Lodge remains a major stopping place along U.S. Highway 50 for travelers, but the lodge today is a far cry from the original. The rooms are nice, the food is good, hiking facilities are available and it is a major attraction for rock climbers who want to conquer Lover's Leap.

Sugar Loaf House/Station

Sugar Loaf was one of the original stations that served as a relay station. Then in 1861 it was also listed as a mail contract station and served as a stage station. It also became very popular with the teamsters, as did the others on the Placerville to Carson route. An old drawing shows Sugar Loaf House in the mid 1860's. The name is derived from a nearby mountain of that name.

Sugar Loaf Station—*Edward Vischers, Special Collections, Libraries of the Claremont Colleges*

251

Sugar Loaf Station site today—*Hill photo*

Today the site is on private property. Trees have since overgrown the area. A monument is located by the fire station on US 50 less than one mile west of Kyburz. The next station was Moore's. Today only a monument marks the site on Highway 50.

BROCKLISS BRIDGE CROSSING

Anthony Richard Brockliss built the first wooden bridge across the American River about 1855/6. A drawing shows the bridge underneath the larger and more substantial bridge which the express riders used. After the crossing, the road began a steep climb up Peavine Ridge. Westbound riders descended the steep and winding road before crossing the bridge. The road was narrow and steep on both sides. Those who drove wagons and coaches on it had to have lots of skill and nerves of steel.

In today's view, one of the supports of the bridge can still be seen on the far side. The building on the right no longer stands, but in the same place in the bushes are some old large wooden timbers. There is even some talk about rebuilding the bridge for hikers.

Brockliss Bridge—*Edward Vischers, Special Collections, Libraries of the Claremont Colleges*

Brockliss Bridge crossing site today—*Hill photo*

Sportsman's Hall Station

This station served as a home station for riders. The "hall" or hostelry was built in 1852 by John and James Blair. It had a large barn and corral reportedly capable of stabling about one thousand horses and mules. It was famous for its service and accommodations for travelers. It was located about thirteen miles east of Placerville and fifty miles from Sacramento.

Sportsman's Hall Station—*California History Room, California State Library.*

It was here that William "Sam" Hamilton and Warren Upson exchanged mochilas during the first ride. Sam had made the sixty mile run east through the heavy rain and muddy trail in four hours and three minutes. (50:41) Upson rode the section east out of Sportsman

Sportsman's Hall site today—*Hill photo*

Hall over the high Sierras. He had to fight a terrible winter storm. Bolivar Roberts had taken extra precautions to combat the storm. Mules were constantly taken over the trail and special relays were set up to shorten the lengths of the rides. Even with these, the ride was extremely difficult and slow.

The hall burned down in April of 1898 and was rebuilt. It is located off Highway 50 on the Pony Express Trail about three miles west of Pollock Pines. The hall has just been remodeled again. Inside are Pony Express materials.

Pleasant Grove today—*Hill photo*

PLEASANT GROVE

This house was originally constructed in 1850-1 by Rufus Hitchcock. It was a large two-story frame house on the north side of the road. It was a popular inn and served as a relay station for the Pony Express. This is not related to the Pleasant Grove described earlier by Miller's Station. Ira Rounds Sanders may have acted as station keeper for Henry Wickwire, the owner. (26:219) The inn became a relay station when the route was changed July 1, 1860 and used until June 30, 1861 when the route changed again. From there the Pony headed to Folsom.

The house has had some alterations since the Pony Express period. The old barn with its shed remains standing.

FOLSOM, CALIFORNIA

Although Sacramento is usually thought of as the terminus for the Pony Riders, Folsom served as the end for a longer time. The Sacramento Valley Railroad was extended to Folsom and the mail was then carried by train. Starting on July 1, 1860, and until June 30, 1861, Folsom served as the terminus.

The Wells Fargo building today looks much the same as it did in 1860. A museum is next door.

Wells Fargo office today—*Hill photo*

Folsom's Wells Fargo office—*Display photo*

256

PLACERVILLE

Placerville was known as Hangtown during the gold rush. From April 1860 until June 1861 a relay station was located there. Then from July 1, 1861 until October 26, 1861, Placerville served as the western terminus of the Pony Express. A monument is located near the site of the station.

Old Placerville—_California Historical Society Collection at the University of Southern California_

Placerville today—_Hill photo_

257

Arrival in Sacramento. -- *Center for Sacramento History*

SACRAMENTO

The Alta Telegraph Company and California State Telegraph with their offices in the Hastings Building served the receiving agents from April 1860 until March 1861. William "Sam" Hamilton has been identified as the rider who, on April 4, brought the first mochila east out of Sacramento. It was 2 a.m. during a terrible rainstorm that he started on his historic ride east. The weather was terrible, rain in the lower elevations and a harsh winter storm in the Sierras made the route heavy in the lowlands and almost impassable in the mountains.

On April 14, the first mail west arrived in Sacramento. Hamilton arrived around 5:30 p.m. to a gala celebration. It very different from his sendoff. Beginning in March, 1861 the station relocated to the Adams Express Building at 1014 Second Street when Wells Fargo acted as agent for the Pony Express. In the sketch it is two buildings down and has the large flag on top.

Today there is a nice museum in the old Alta Telegraph Company which has been restored to look as it did during its Pony period. It is located at J and Second in Old Sacramento. Across the street in the Old Sacramento State Historic Park is the statue of the Pony Express rider coming in with the mail. The old Adams building still stands.

Here is the express rider, William "Sam" Hamilton, arriving with the first mail to Sacramento as depicted in the *New York Illustrated News*. The scene was fairly accurate, except there should be a mochila, not a bag of mail. Hamilton was met by crowds of people, including the mayor. Men on horseback met him at Sutter's Fort and followed

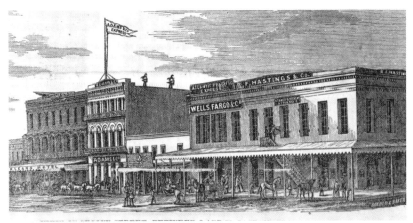

Hastings Building. -- *Center for Sacramento History*

him through town down J Street. Canons were fired and church bells rang out. Here is the account as reported by *The Sacramento Bee* on April 14, 1860.

> "THE PONY EXPRESS --- It having been announced that the Pony Express left Placerville at five minutes before two o'clock yesterday afternoon, it was figured up that the pony would arrive here about half-past five o'clock, and true to his time, at twenty-five minutes past five the first gun announced the approach of the pony. This gun was answered by the ringing

Hastings Building today—*Hill photo*

of the church and engine house bells and was re-echoed by salutes in different portions of the city. Crowds rushed to and lined J Street on either side, and the excitement became intense. Amid the clouds of dust, a troop of horsemen could be partially seen approaching at break-neck speed and in most delightful confusion. On they came amid the shouts and cheers of the assembled multitude. Which is the pony? Where is the pony? resounded on all sides, and at last the roan pony appeared, and was greeted with a hearty cheer. Down J Street he came at a rattling pace, a detachment of the Sacramento Hussars acting as escort. On arriving in front of the agent's office on Second Street between J and K, the arrival of the Pony Express received another hearty cheer, and the Union Brass Band struck up an inspiring air. The rider, W. Hamilton, dismounted and the pony's wants were carefully attended to a neighbor ingestible. Between Placerville and this point Hamilton had four relays of horses. In a few minutes the Pony Express letters were transferred to the steamer Antelope, which at once moved off, a gun fired at the foot of P Street giving here a parting salutation. The Antelope arrived at San Francisco soon after eleven o'clock and a grand demonstration took place there."

The April 14, 1860 San Francisco *Daily Evening Bulletin* reported "The boat waited for the Pony Express at Sacramento until 5 o"clock

The *Antelope*. -- *Center for Sacrament History*

yesterday afternoon. The instant it arrived it came on board, and the *Antelope* put on all steam to accomplish an early trip."

Once at Sacramento, the rider and mail boarded a steamer to San Francisco. William Hamilton took the side-wheeled steamer *Antelope*. However, if the rider missed the steamer there were three additional relay stations: Benicia, Martinez, and Oakland, and two more ferries to take. Between Benicia and Martinez, the ferryboat *Carquinez* took the Pony across the river, and at Oakland, the "Oakland" ferry brought the rider to San Francisco. (6:10) That is exactly what happened on April 22, 1860.

Ferryboat *Carquinez—Courtesy Tom Crews*

The April 23, 1860 *Daily Evening Bulletin* reported, "The Pony Express last arrived, left St. Joseph in Missouri at 5 p.m. of the 13th, and reached San Francisco in 9 days 17 hours. The swiftest riding we have heard of on the route, was Mr. Bedford's from Martinez to Oakland, which 24 miles he accomplished in one hour and 45 minutes; yet the Pony did not shed his shoes, his rider did not break his neck, nor was there any appreciable smell of fire upon his garments when he came in. The distance from Sacramento to Benicia Mr. Hamilton rode this morning between 1 and 7 o'clock. Very few letters brought the Pony.

Dreadful slow people live on the other side of the mountains."

SAN FRANCISCO

The Alta Telegraph office was at 153 Montgomery Street. It served as the western headquarters of the Pony Express. The first east bound messenger was so excited by the cheering crowds and his horse all decked out with flags, he reportedly mounted his horse from the wrong side. Leaving at 4:00 p.m., he only rode the few blocks to the dock and the awaiting steamer the *Antelope*. In the mochila were eighty-five letters. The real ride started out of Sacramento.

On the first west trip, the Pony arrived in San Francisco shortly after midnight on April 14, but the late hour did not deter another celebration. As the *Antelope* approached the harbor, other steamers blew their whistles. As the ship docked, cannons boomed, rockets were fired and bonfires lit. As the rider disembarked from the *Antelope,* the band played "See, the Conquering Hero Comes." Night was turned into day as bonfires were lit and a torch light parade ensued. He only had a few blocks to go. The first ride was over. It proved that the central route was not only feasible, but practical!

On July 13, 1852, Wells Fargo's first office opened on this site, today's corporate headquarters and

Wells Fargo office—*Wells Fargo Museum*

Wells Fargo today—*Hill photo*

On April 14, 1860, the San Francisco *Daily Evening Bulletin's Local Matters* reported on the celebration earlier that morning under the title "Glorification of the Pony."

"It took seventy-five ponies to make the trip from Missouri to California in 10 1/2 days, but the last one—the little fellow who came down in the Sacramento boat this morning had the vicarious glory of them all. Upon him an enthusiastic crowd were disposed to shower all their compliments. He was the veritable Hippogriff who shoved a continent behind his hoofs so easily; who snuffed up sandy plains, sent lakes and mountains, prairies and forests, whizzing behind him, like one great river rushing eastward; who left a wake like a clipper's, "carried a bone in his mouth,' and sent his fame rippling off north and south, as nothing has done before for years; who frightened whole tribes of Indians, that thought it was an arrow whittled into a pony's shape that whizzsed by; who made eagles and all swift-winged birds heartsick, and sent them into convention to devise measures to keep their reputation up; who crossed the railroad track, fifteen miles out of Sacramento, just as the cars had passed and got to the City of the plains just as the same cars arrived. . . .all we could do was to go down and glorify him on his arrival this morning."

The article continued to describe the celebration—the waiting, the arrival, the band and music, the bonfires, the bell ring, the police, the fire departments, the parade, the speech makers, the distribution of the letters, the cheering, and, of course the decorated Pony. The people celebrated into the morning, but the article ended with, "Long live the Pony." And it has!

The historic run was over. The last of the mails were delivered on November 18, 1861 to Sacramento. It arrived in San Francisco shortly thereafter. Note the iron shutters on all the windows and the door for protection. They were painted a bright green and at the time were similar to a trademark for the company.

Today the office of Wells Fargo has expanded. Inside is a terrific museum that focuses on the whole history of Wells Fargo, including its brief association with the historic Pony Express.

Arrival in San Francisco—*New York Illustrated News, May 19, 1860 - Courtesy of the California History Room, California State Library.*

Chapter Six

The Riders — Folklore and Fact

These three men, Buffalo Bill, Pony Bob Haslam, and Bronco Charlie are found on most lists of Pony Express riders. All three of them have been considered to have been some of the most famous riders and each has had his supporters. This was especially true when they were living. Their stories relate to being the youngest, having made the longest ride, or having made one of the most dangerous rides. Each of them became famous as a Pony Express rider after the Pony Express had ceased its operations. There are no authentic documents of their accounts. All three were known for telling good tales and most of those have been printed. They seem to owe their fame to what they claimed to have done, which is also very difficult to prove. This was partially due to the fact that those who were actual participants in the stories and could have substantiated them had passed away. More often than not, there were some possible truths mixed in, perhaps just enough facts to make the accounts plausible. This will be only a brief highlighting of some of the problems with their stories. There are individuals who point to other material which support them.

* * *

Bronco Charlie's claim was that he was the youngest Pony Express rider, age 11, and was the last surviving rider. He died in 1955, that is, twenty-one years after William Campbell. It is known that he did work with Buffalo Bill's Wild West Show. He could handle horses, ride and shoot, was an expert with a whip, and enjoyed telling tales. He claimed to have been born January 1, 1850 in California and that his association with the Pony Express started in 1860. According to Charlie, he and his father saw a riderless express horse ride by them while in Sacramento. They followed it to the station. For some unknown reason the regular rider was unavailable, and there was nobody else around to ride. His father said that his son knew the route and could do it. With the station keeper's consent, he put his son on the horse and off went Charlie to Placerville. That started Charlie's career as a Pony Express rider.

Those who question Charlie's claim point to a number of points, of which only some will be mentioned. Charlie's early life as claimed is hard to document. The list of people he claimed to have known and been friends with included almost all the famous people in the West, including Zebulon Pike, Davy Crockett, Joseph Robidoux, Jim Bridger, Mark Twain, Richard Burton, Chief Joseph, Sitting Bull, Joseph Slade, Wyatt Earp, Bill Hickok, and Buffalo Bill. He even claimed to have met Abe Lincoln. The problem is some of the people whom he claimed to have known were dead, and to have met some he would have had to have been in two different places at the same time. Pike died in 1813 and Crockett in 1836. Living in California and meeting Lincoln in St. Joseph, Missouri would have been hard to do for a ten-year-old. Travel was slow and if by coach too expensive for most people. If his father truly put him on the express horse, then how could he have been an orphan? If he rode east to Placerville, then the mail being delivered would have to have come from San Francisco by boat. The ride from the boat to the station was only a few blocks. For the rider to have gotten lost would be highly unlikely. Some of Charlie's relatives said he was born in New York.

* * *

I had traveled 380 miles within a few hours of schedule time, and was surrounded by perils on every hand.—"Pony" Bob Haslam.

Haslam's heroic ride and longest ride in Pony Express history was mentioned earlier in the photographic journey. Part of the problem is that his name and story didn't appear at the time of the express.

The first documented appearance of Haslam's name is about seven years after the Pony ended. His own description of the claimed event was reported in Major's book. He said that his ride was about eight months after the Pony began, during the Paiute War. However, the Paiute War began the month after the Pony began and by eight months, the war had subsided. Eight months later he would have been riding in

December in the winter. In his story he mentioned the rider would not continue because of the Indians. Haslam could have made an honest error in the number of months. However, the rider he mentioned was a Johnnie Richardson. The only Richardson presently identified is a Johnson William Richardson. That person is the one often cited as the first rider out of St. Joseph. While today it's believed Johnny Fry was the first rider, Richardson could have been at the send off and the reporter mixed up the names. (See earlier comments about Richardson & Fry.) Richardson would have to have ridden out to the Carson Valley in only four weeks. That would be a record by itself. Perhaps Haslam had the name wrong.

Haslam said that he rode to Fort Churchill. However, the fort wasn't started until after the war had subsided and it was finished in the fall. Buckland was the station during the war. Now if Haslam did ride to Fort Churchill, then he did "make" his ride in December. Or perhaps he just made another error. There are no newspaper reports of a famous ride made by a person named Haslam. However, reportedly there was an account in the 1860 *Territorial Enterprise* about a person named Bartholemew Riley who made a similar ride. He was not an express rider. He was a survivor of the Battle of Pyramid Lake. When he arrived back at Buckland's, an (unnamed) rider was fearful of riding. Riley volunteered to take the ride and made it. On his return run back to Buckland's he was the victim "by an accidental discharge of a weapon in the hands of a friend." He died two weeks later. (4:11) If this report is accurate, it seems to parallel Haslam's later story of his famous ride.

The first newspaper article that mentioned Haslam by name appeared in 1868 in the *Territorial Enterprise*. It was about a twenty-two mile relay race from Reno to Virginia City. The riders were "Pony" Bob Haslam for Wells, Fargo & Company and Frank Henderson for the Pacific Union Express Company. Haslam won. He had been favored in the race. Haslam was known as an express rider for Wells, Fargo & Company. There seems to be little debate about his riding earlier for Wells, Fargo. However, seven years had passed since the Pony ended. Haslam's reputation could have been made while riding on a local express route which he even admits he rode two routes. One route was from Virginia City to Friday's Station, and the other was from Virginia City to Reno. These existed after the famous

C.O.C. & P.P. Pony Express. Wells, Fargo did get control of the Overland Mail Company. The article did refer to Haslam as "an old rider for the company (Wells Fargo) on the old Overland Pony Express route." (14:190)

* * *

There is no question that William "Buffalo Bill" Cody worked for Russell, Majors, and Waddell as a messenger in 1857 and that Cody and Alexander Majors were friends. After that the connection with the Pony Express becomes questionable, except that Cody became the major promoter of the Pony Express as the most Famous Pony Express rider made famous by his Wild West Shows.

Most of what we "know" about Cody and the Pony Express is based on information from Cody's own book first printed in 1879, from his Wild West Shows that started in the 1880s and from his sister, Helen Cody Whitmore's book. Cody's own account includes riding for the Pony Express for two years. He explained that he had gone to Colorado during the Pike's Peak gold rush, but had no luck. On his way back home to Kansas, he decided to get a job as a Pony Express rider. He was only 13, but was hired to ride out of Julesburg. He rode for two months and then had to resign so he could help his sick mother back in Kansas.

The following year, 1860, Cody returned and was hired by Joseph Slade. His assignment was farther west and this is where his various adventures occurred. One story was of his longest ride in one of the most dangerous sections of the trail. It took him from Red Buttes to Three Crossing and then to Rocky Ridge and back. The rider at Three Crossings had been killed and no one else could take the mail, so off went Cody. Majors attested to the story writing. "This round trip of 384 miles was made without a stop, except for meals and to change horses, and every station was entered on time. This is the longest and best ridden pony express journeys ever made." Note that Cody's ride was four miles longer than Haslam's ride. However, one problem is that the distance from Red Buttes to Three Crossings is only about seventy-six miles and to Rocky Ridge is another thirty-five miles. Even if a few miles are added, the one way trip was about 115 miles. Double that and one is still far short of 384 miles. Cody stated that he rode the summer before 1860 which would be 1859. That would be impossible since the Pony Express started in 1860. There are no known deaths of a Pony Express rider at Three Crossings. Cody's own sister's book about him mentions little about any Pony Express exploits, not even his claimed ride. It is also interesting to note that the latest in-depth work on Joseph "Jack" Slade's life and death doesn't mention Buffalo Bill.

While it is possible one or all could have ridden, there certainly seems to be good reasons to question them all. Writers and historians have disagreed in the past and there is much more to those differences than that which is mentioned here. Determining what the lore is, can be very interesting. By understanding the folklore of the trail, one also learns much about its history.

LIST OF RIDERS

The following is a list of riders. It is not necessarily complete. There is no authentic or official company list of riders that is known to exist. This list is based on earlier research and more recent work by that of the St. Joseph & Pony Express National museums, the National Pony Express Association and individuals. Rider's names are added as they are confirmed. Sometimes confusion is caused by the use ofnicknames, initials, partial names, missspellings or recordings and differences in handwriting.

Jack Alcott	Thomas Bedford
Andrew Ole Anderson	James Bentley
Anton	Asher Bigelow
John Anson	Charles Billman
Henry Avis	G.R. Bills
Rodney Babbit	"Black Sam"
L.W. "Little Baldy" Ball	"Black Tom"
Lafeyette Ball	Thomas Black
James Banks	Lafayette Bolwinkle
James Barnell	Bond
Jim "Boston" Baughn	William Boulton
Melville Baughn	James W. "Dock" Brink
Marve Beardsley	Hugh Brown
James Beatley (Foote)	James Brown
Charles Becker	James Bucklin

David (John) Burnett
Ed Bush
Henry Butterfield
William Campbell
James H. Carlen
Gustuavus Carlton
Alexander Carlyle
William Carr
William Carrigan
James Carter
Michael Casey
William F. Cates
Francis M. Cayton
James Clark
John Clark
Richard W. Clark
Richard Cleve
Charles Cliff
Gustavas Cliff
William F. Cody
Buck Cole
Bill Corbett
Edward Covington
Janes Cowan
Jack Crawford
James Cumbo
James Danley
Louis Dean
J.William Dennis
Frank Derrick
Alex Diffenbacher
"Captain" Thomas Dobson
J. Dodge
Joseph Donovan
Tom Donovan
W. E. Dorrington
Calvin Downs
David Drumheller

James Dunlap
William Eckels
Major Howard Egan
Howard Ransom Egan
Richard Erastus "Ras" Egan
Thomas J. Elliot
J. K. Ellis
Charles Enos
George Fair
Henry J. "Doc" Faust
Josiah A. Faylor
Johnny Fischer
John Fisher
William Fredrick Fisher
Thomas Flynn
Jimmie Foreman
Johnny Fry
William H. Fulkerson
Abram Fuller
George "Irish" Gardner
James Gentry
James Gilson
Samuel H. Gilson
James Gleason
Frank H. Gould
Thomas "Irish Tom" Grady
Martin Hall
Parley Hall
Sam Hall
Samuel Hamilton
William "Billy" Hamilton
James Bean Hamilton
George Harder
Handy
Robert "Pony Bob" Haslam
Theodore Hawkins
Sam Haws
Frank Helvey

Levi Hensel
William Hickman
Lucius Ludosky Hickok
Charles Higginbotham
Martin Hogan
Clark Huntington
Lester Huntington
Lot Huntington
"Irish Jim"
William James
David R. Jay
William Jenkins
Bob Jennings
Samuel S. Jobe
William Jones
William Kates
Jack H. Keetley
Hiram L. Kelley
Jay G. Kelley
Mike Kelly
Thomas Owen King
John Phillip Koerner
Harry La Mont
Thomas Landon
William Lawson
James Madison Lenhart
George Leonard
George Little
N. N. Lytle
Sye Macaulas
Joseph Malcom
Robert Martin
Elijah Maxfield
Montgomery Maze
Emmet McCain
Jay G. McCall
Charlie McCarty
James McDonald

Pat McEneany
David McLaughlin
James McNaughton
William McNaughton
Lorenzo Meacona
J. P. Mellen
Howard Mifflen
"Broncho" Charlie B. Miller
James Moore
John Mufsey
Jeramiah H. Murphy
Newton Myrick
Matthew Orr
Robert Orr
G. Packard
William Page
Chas Park
John Paul
"Mochila Joe" Paxton
George Washington Perkins
Joseph "Josh" Perkins
Edward Pollinger
Charles Pridham
Thomas Ranahan
Theodore "Little Yank" Rand
James Randall
Charles Reynolds
Thomas J. Renyolds
William Minor Richards
H. Richardson
Johnson W. Richardson
Sewel Ridley
Bartholomew Riley
Jonathan Rinehart
Don C. Rising
Harry Loren Roff
C.H. Ruffin
Edward Rush

271

John Rutsel
Thomas Ryan
Robert Sanders
G. G. R. Sangiovani
George Scovell
John Seebeck
Jack Selman
Joseph Serish
James Shank
John Sinclair
George William Smethurst
George Spurr
Edward Sterling
William Henry Streeper
Robert Sticklen
William Strohm
John Suggett
George Talcott
Billy Tate
George Washington Thatcher
J. J. Thomas
Bill Thompson
Charles P. "Cyclone"
    Thompson
James M. Thompson
Alexander Toponce
Elias Littleton Tough
William Sloan Tough
George Towne
Bill Trotter
Henry Tuckett
"Boston" Warren Upson
William E. "Pony Ned" Van
    Blaricom
Bill Vickery
John B. Wade
Henry Wallace
A. B. Wall Jun

Cap Weaver
Daniel Wescott
Michael Whalen
George O. Wheat
"Whipsaw"
J. Williams
H. C. Wills
Thomas Thornhill Willson
Elijah Nicholas White
Slim Wilson
Ira Wines
Joseph Barney Wintle
Henry Worley
James Worthington
George Wright
Mose Wright
Jose Zowgaltz

Chapter Seven

Stations

Some of these stations served as home stations, while most as relay stations. The functions of some may have changed over time as others were added or routes changed. Many of these were added after the initial few months. A few served for a few weeks. Some existed on alternate routes of which some were used only a few months. Some are listed with alternate names. Some were spelled slightly differently. Historians still debate a few of them. The same name may have been used for more than one station.

MISSOURI
St. Joseph

KANSAS
(Elwood-stables)
(Wathena-stables)
Atchison
Lancaster
Cottonwood Springs
Cold Springs / Lewis
Troy
Kennekuk
Kikapoo
Log Chain
Seneca
Ash Point
Guittard

Marysville
Cottonwood / Hollenberg

NEBRASKA
Rock House Oketo
Rock Creek / Turkey Creek /
Pawnee
Virginia City – (Lone Tree)
Big Sandy
Millersville / Thompson's
Kiowa
Oak Grove
Liberty Farm
Spring Ranch / Lone Tree
32 Mile Creek
Sand Hill / Summit
Kearny/ Valley / Hook's

(Ft. Kearny)
Dobytown
Platte / Seventeen Mile
Garden
Plum Creek
Willow Island /Willow Bend
Midway / Cold Water
Gilmans
Machette's
Cottonwood Springs
Cold Springs
Fremont Springs
Dansey's / O'Fallons / Elkhorn
Alkali
Gill's Sand Hill
Diamond Springs
Beauvais Ranch

COLORADO
Frontz
Overland City / Julesburg

NEBRASKA
Nine mile Lodge Pole
Pole Creek #2
Pole Creek #3
Midway Station
Mud Springs
Courthouse Rock
Chimney Rock
Ficklin's Springs
Scott's Bluff
Horse Creek

WYOMING
Spring Ranch / Cold Springs /
Junction House
Bordeaux / Verdling's Ranch
Fort Laramie

Sand Point / Ward's / Nine Mile/
Central Star
Cottonwood Creek
Horsehoe Creek
Elk Horn
LaBonte
Bed Tick
La Prele / Lapierelle
Box Elder
Deer Creek
Little Muddy / Muddy Creek
Bridger
Platte Bridge / North Platte
Red Buttes
Willow Springs
Greasewood / Horse Creek
Sweetwater
Devil's Gate
Plantes
Split Rock
Three Crossings
Ice Slough / Ice Springs
Warm Springs
Rocky Ridge / St. Mary's
Rock Creek / Strawberry
Upper Sweetwater / South Pass
Pacific Springs
Dry Sandy
Little Sandy
Big Sandy
Big Timber
Green River
Michael Martin's
Ham's Fork
Church Butte
Millersville
Fort Bridger
Muddy Creek

Quaking Aspen / Aspen / Springs
Bear River / Biggs

Utah
Needles / Needle Rocks
Head of [Echo] Canyon /
Frenchies / Castle Rock
Halfway / Daniel's
Weber
Henefer / Brimville
Carson House
East Canyon / Dixie Hollow
Wheaton Springs
Mountain Dell / Dale
Salt Lake House
Traveler's Rest / Trader's Rest
Rockwell's
Dugout / Joe's Dugout / Seven
Mile
Camp Floyd / Fort Crittenden/
Cedar City/ Carson's Inn
East Rush Valley / Pass
Faust's / Rush Valley / Bush
Valley
Point Lookout / Lookout Pass
Government Creek
Simpson's Springs / Egan's
Spring / Lost Springs / Pleasant
Springs
Riverbed
Dugway
Black Rock
Fish Springs
Boyd's / Desert
Willow Springs
Willow Creek / Six Mile
Canyon / Overland Canyon /
Burnt

Deep Creek

Nevada
Eight Mile / Prairie Gate
Antelope Springs
Rock Spring
Spring Valley
Schell Creek
Egan Canyon / Egan's
Butte / Robber's Roost
Mountain Spring
Ruby Valley
Jacob's Well
Diamond Springs
Sulphur Springs
Roberts Creek
Grub's Well / Camp
Dry Creek
Cape Horn
Simpson Park
Reese River / Jacob's Spring
Dry Wells
Smith's Creek
Castle Rock
Edwards Creek
Cold Springs
Middle Gate
West Gate
Fairview
Mountain Well
Stillwater / Salt Well
Old River
Bisby
Nevada
Ragtown
Desert Wells
Sand Springs
Sand Hill

Carson Sink
Williams
Desert / Hooten Wells
Buckland's
Fort Churchill
Millers / Reed's
Dayton / Spafford's Hall
Carson City
Genoa
Friday's / Lakeside

CALIFORNIA
Woodford's
Fountain Place
Hope Valley
Yank's
Strawberry
Sugar Loaf House / Webster's

Moore's / Moss / Riverton
Sportsman's Hall
Placerville
Mud Springs/ El Dorado/
Nevada House
Mormon Tavern / Sunrise House
Pleasant Grove
Duroc
Folsom
Fifteen Mile House
Five Mile
Sacramento
Benicia
Martinez
Oakland
San Francisco

Chapter Eight

Museums and Displays

For those interested in following the Pony across the country, there are numerous museums, visitor centers and historic sites that will assist the traveler in understanding and appreciating the conditions faced and overcome by the young riders of the Pony Express as they made history and helped to provide a service so sorely needed, if only for a brief time. Most of these places are near main Interstate or state highways, others are usually off easily accessible local roads. Only a few are in "out of the way" places. All levels of government, federal, state, and local are responsible for these sites and their interpretation, and most are well done. Some of the museums will take a few hours to thoroughly examine and appreciate, while some sites may only take a few minutes. There are many more historic sites and local museums than are listed here. Some are just small interpretive signs along the state highways placed by state or local historical societies. For most travelers concerned with time, they will be passed by. However, for the ardent Pony Express enthusiast, they should be seen.

Many of the sites have markers or monuments placed by different individuals and historic groups. Some were placed almost a century ago. Others have been placed recently with the support of or by trail organizations such as the National Pony Express Association, Pony Express Trail Association, and the Oregon-California Trail Association. Even the trail itself has been marked with the cooperation of the federal government, trail organizations and land owners. Because most of the route used by the Pony Express overlapped the emigrant and military trails, many of the museums and centers are primarily focused on those aspects. However, one cannot easily separate them since their respective histories are intertwined. All help to tell significant aspects and to make it easier to more clearly understand the history of the Pony Express.

MUSEUM & DISPLAYS

JEFFERSON NATIONAL EXPANSION MEMORIAL, ST. LOUIS, MISSOURI

The Gateway Arch represents the portal through which the west was opened. It is located at the site of the original city of St. Louis. Inside the Arch's base is the Jefferson National Expansion Memorial. Radiating out from the statue of Jefferson, beginning with the Louisiana Purchase, the expansion and settlement of the West unfolds. The related movements and major milestones are depicted in displays that are both interesting and informative.

The Arch is located off I-55 and I-70 on the west bank of the Mississippi River and is open year round. There are numerous other historic sites, unrelated to the Pony Express in the area that are well worth a visit, and numerous others within an hour or two. Nearby are the old Church, the Courthouse, Missouri Historical Society Museum, Jefferson Barracks, and Old St. Charles, and across the river in Illinois are Cahokia Mounds, Cahokia Village, and Camp River DuBois. These are but a few in the greater metropolitan area. One can easily spend a few hours in the Arch and a few days visiting the other sites.

LEXINGTON HISTORICAL MUSEUM, LEXINGTON, MISSOURI

Although Lexington is probably better known for its Civil War history and the Battle of Lexington, it was also the home town for William Russell and William Waddell, both of whom established stores there and became partners in 1852. Today the small museum has interesting artifacts and memorabilia about the Pony Express worth seeing. Other items there deal with the general history of Lexington and the Battle of Lexington. Waddell's home, which was purchased after the Express, still stands, but is not open to the public. William Waddell is buried in the Machpelah Cemetery south of town. Also nearby is the Battle of Lexington site and center for those who have additional time.

The Lexington Historical Museum is located at 104 South 13 Highway, just south of Main Street. It is open on a limited basis during most of the year and most afternoons during the summer.

St. Joseph, Missouri Area

St. Joseph, Missouri, is one of those historic western towns that has something for everyone. For the Pony Express, this is where it started. The **National Pony Express Museum** is housed in the old Pikes Peak Stables that originally could hold 200 horses. These were the stables for both the Pony Express and the Patee House. Today there are lifelike displays and other exhibits relating to the start of the Pony Express, the original well, express saddle and mochila reproductions, archaeological displays, a children's area, dioramas, a video, a gift shop and more. This museum is the perfect place to start, and it is located at 914 Penn Street. It is open daily.

Up the hill is the **Patee House Museum National Landmark**. This was the office for the Central Overland California and Pikes Peak Express Company, also known as the Pony Express, owned by Russell, Majors, and Waddell. Inside the hotel is a reproduction of the office with displays about the Pony. Within the hotel are other displays and museum sections relating to the "Streets of Old St. Joe," a transportation section with antique automobiles and fire trucks, an engine from the old Hannibal-St. Joseph Railroad, a large model railroad and the working old "Wild Thing Carousel." It is located at 12th and Penn Street and is open daily April through October and weekends the rest of the year.

The **Riverfront Park** is where the old steamboats docked and the Pony Express embarked for its trip across the river. Nearby are the **Pony Express Monument,** a bronze larger than life statue, and **site marker** for the Hannibal and St. Joseph railroad station.

For those interested in other historic periods, there is the **Robidoux Row Museum,** housed in a building constructed in the 1840s by Joseph Robidoux, about the founding of St. Joseph; the **St. Joseph Museums** with its fascinating centers about St. Joseph's early history and culture, black history, psychiatric care, and Victorian St. Joseph; the **Jesse James Home Museum** where Jesse was shot; and the **Mount Mora Cemetery** where two Pony Express riders are buried.

Pony Express Preservation Society Museum, Seneca, Kansas

During the first few months of the Pony Express, Seneca was the site of the first home station west of St. Joseph. Joseph Smith had built the hotel in 1858, a part of which later served as the station. Today only a monument identifies its former location.

The museum is located diagonally across from the site on the corner of Main and Eighth. Inside are some displays about the Pony Express, including some furniture and artifacts from the Smith Hotel. Other displays relate to different aspects of frontier life. This is one of those small sites that have the potential for the development of a quality museum. It is open on a limited basis.

PONY EXPRESS BARN MUSEUM, MARYSVILLE, KANSAS

Marysville served as a home station for most of the express period. Today the inside of the old barn has been restored to its appearance during the Pony Express. Inside are the blacksmith shop and the stables. Attached to it is a fine museum constructed in 1991 devoted to the Pony Express and early history of Marysville. It is also a site in the annual Pony Express re-ride. Marysville was also on the St. Joe emigrant wagon road and an alternate of the Oregon Trail from Alcove Spring, a lower fording area of the Big Blue. The Pony crossed the Big Blue on a ferry located in Marysville on the St. Joe Road or forded it during low water. Today the former site of the ferry is a park. The river has moved west a little.

The Pony Express Barn is open daily April through October and is located at 106 South 8th Street. The large Pony Express statue is located two blocks away on US 36.

For those interested, a trip about six miles south to **Alcove Spring** on East River Road is well worth the small detour. Excellent examples of trail swales, the Oregon Trail ford of the Big Blue, and the famous spring, associated with the Donner Party, can all be visited.

COTTONWOOD/HOLLENBERG PONY EXPRESS STATION AND VISITOR CENTER, HANOVER, KANSAS

Cottonwood Station was constructed by Gerat Hollenberg in 1857. The station house is open and has displays relating to both its emigrant and Pony Express periods. It also served as stage stop. The structure is actually a composite of three main building periods. The major additions were made by the time it was used by the express riders. The station's first floor is open and has exhibits about its trail history and also its construction. It is one of the few structures still standing on its original site. It is a Kansas State Historic Site and operated by the

280

Kansas State Historical Society. Trail swales are in the area and a nice visitor center provides a cool place to relax and see the video, examine additional displays and purchase some books. This is also one of the relay stations used in the annual re-ride in June.

The site is located about one mile east of Hanover off Kansas Highway 243. It is open daily, April through October, and is well worth the trip. The site supervisor Duane Durst has been there for over two decades and has lovingly watched over its development. He has a wealth of knowledge about the site.

WASHINGTON COUNTY HISTORICAL SOCIETY, WASHINGTON, KANSAS

This is one of those small town museums that isn't known to outsiders, but has a lot to offer. One room in particular is devoted to the artifacts related to the Pony Express and the Hollenbergs. As with other small museums, it has other unique collections and displays related to the local history.

The museum is located on the town square of Washington, Kansas. It is well worth the small side trip.

ROCK CREEK STATION, VISITOR CENTER, FAIRBURY, NEBRASKA

This is what I consider to be one of the jewels of the Nebraska Game and Parks Commission. The creek fording area was first settled in 1857 by S.C. Glenn who built a small cabin and store which served the emigrant traffic. David McCanles purchased the site and built his ranch and toll bridge there in 1859. It was later rented out and served as stage station and then as a Pony Express station. I have watched its development since the early 1980's under the direction of Wayne Brandt as it progressed from an old farm, through its archaeological investigation, to its reconstruction to look as it did in about 1860. Structures on both the east and west side of Turkey or Rock Creek have been rebuilt along with the toll bridge. Part of the original well that the express riders would have used still exists. The visitor center is on the west side. Huge swales, weathered by time, are evident where hundreds of wagons, stagecoaches, and express riders climbed up and down the hills. There is also a picnic area and a fine campground which our family loves to camp at when passing through.

This is also the site where James Butler "Wild Bill" Hickok served as stockman for the Pony Express and the site of the infamous Hickok-

McCanles shootout. This is also one of the relay sites used during the annual Pony Express re-rides.

The park is located about seven miles east of Fairbury off Nebraska Highway 8. It is open from April to October.

HAROLD WARP PIONEER VILLAGE, MINDEN NEBRASKA

This "village," reconstructed from historical buildings and loaded with over 50,000 artifacts, has something for everyone no matter where one's interests lie. A reportedly original Pumpkinseed Creek Stage and Pony Express Station, the subject of one of William Henry Jackson's paintings, is located there. A special exhibit area inside the main building relates to many of Jackson's paintings and the Pony Express.

The village is located in Minden, Nebraska, at the intersection of SR 10 and U.S. 6/34. It is open daily.

FORT KEARNY STATE HISTORIC PARK, NORTH PLATTE, NEBRASKA

Fort Kearny (Childs) was built to protect the emigrant traffic along the Platte River. Construction was started by Lt. Woodbury in 1848. The Pony Express did not have a station or stables on the military reservation. They had a station seven miles to the east near Lowell and another perhaps a few miles west. Nothing remains of those sites. However, because it was a military fort and the telegraph was soon completed to it, the express riders did stop there briefly. Today, only the eastern portion of the original fort site is within the park grounds. The rest is under cultivation. Only a few of the trees originally planted in 1848 are still alive on the parade grounds. On the grounds are a fine visitor center, a reconstructed blacksmith shop, arsenal and replica of the 1864 stockade. The displays and video in the visitor center contains information about the fort's role and its history. The center has specific exhibits and artifacts relating to the Pony Express, including rider Robert Cleve's pistol and holster. The outline of many of the fort's buildings can be seen as one tours the grounds. Today the area is treed and irrigated, much different than it would have looked to the Express riders, but for the modern traveler it is just fine.

From Kearney, the fort is located about two miles south of the I-80 exit 272 and about four miles east of Highway 44 on V Road at 1020 V Road. It is open daily during the summer. Although camping is not allowed on the fort grounds, camping is possible just to the east at the Kearny State Recreation Area.

For those interested in another aspect of the significance of the Platte River, this area is located on the main north-south flyway. One of the main attractions in the early spring and fall is the arrival of hundreds of thousands of Sandhill Cranes and other migratory birds.

THE GREAT PLATTE RIVER ROAD ARCHWAY, KEARNEY, NEBRASKA

This is a private concern, but the trip through the Arch is well worth it. Using life-like displays and a multimedia approach, the history of the Platte River Valley from the Indian period through today is told. The focus is on the economics and transportation systems that have followed the Platte River. It puts the Pony Express into its historical perspective.

The Arch is located right over I-80, but the entrance to it is located off the Kearny Exit 272 on the north side service road. It is open year round.

WILLOW BEND/ISLAND STATION, COZAD, NEBRASKA

Here is the Willow Island Pony Express and Stage Station. It was moved from its original site by the local American Legion in 1938 from the south side of the Platte southeast of Darr to the park in Cozad. The structure is very similar to both the Midway Station and Machette's at Gothenburg and North Platte.

Today the station resides in the Cozad's Veterans Park at 9th and E Street. It is open on a limited basis.

MIDWAY STATION, (PRIVATE), GOTHENBURG, NEBRASKA

Today Midway Station is on private property on a working ranch, but it may still be visited. It has never been moved from its original site. There is a monument and plaque. If the owners or caretakers are present, they often open it to the public to see the Pony Express related materials.

It is located about three miles south of Gothenburg, a mile east of Highway 47 on the Lower 96 Ranch.

GOTHENBURG PONY EXPRESS STATION (MACHETTE'S), GOTHENBURG, NEBRASKA

The station was moved from its original location to its present site in Ehman Park. Inside this easily accessible station are some nice displays and souvenirs related to the Pony Express. It is run by the local Gothenburg Chamber of Commerce and called the Pony Express capital.

It is located in Gothenburg's Ehmen Park at 15th and E Street.

SCOUT'S REST RANCH, BUFFALO BILL STATE HISTORIC PARK, NORTH PLATTE, NEBRASKA

This was the home of Buffalo Bill Cody. Cody built this eighteen room mansion in 1878. At that time the area was generally treeless and the third floor room had a commanding view of the area.

Today the state historic park is open daily to the public from April to October. The house can be toured and also the large show barn. The displays cover all aspects of Cody's life and legend from his days as a freighter, a Pony Express rider, Indian fighter, scout, hunter, and of course the leader of his Wild West Shows.

The park is located at 2921 Scouts Rest Ranch Road, in the northwest end of town north off U.S. Highway 30 on Buffalo Bill Avenue and west on Scouts Rest Ranch Road. It is open weekdays from April through October.

Around the corner is the **Lincoln County Historical Museum** with a recreated frontier railroad town. One of the structures is an old log building associated with the Pony Express. It is believed to have served as a blacksmith shop, bunkhouse and storeroom at the old Machette's Station. Inside are blacksmith exhibits. Two other structures are from Fort McPherson.

Also in the area are the **Rough Riders Rodeo** and the **Golden Spike Tower** and visitor center at the largest railroad switching yard in the United States. On the south end of town just off the interstate is **Fort Cody Trading Post**. This is not associated with Buffalo Bill's ranch, but it does have displays and artifacts about the west, one of the widest selections of souvenirs and books available for the travelers, and the world famous model of the Wild West Show including 20,000 hand carved items by Ernie and Virginia Palmquist encompassing all aspects of Buffalo Bill's Wild West Show.

O'FALLON'S BLUFF, REST AREA, SUTHERLAND, NEBRASKA

This rest stop on I-80 is just south of Sutherland, Nebraska. While there is a rest stop on both the east and west sides, the trail display and swales are located only on the eastbound side. There is a kiosk and walkway that leads to the swales as the trail climbs the bluffs to bypass the area where the Platte River had cut close to the bluff and made the passage difficult. The construction of the interstate cut into the bluff, and it does not seem as menacing as it did a century and a half ago

It is two miles east of exit 158. Take a short rest in the shade and then walk on the trail where the Pony rode.

JULESBURG, COLORADO

There are a number of points of interest in this area. The Colorado Welcome Center is off I-76 & US 385. Outside it is the statue of the Pony Express Rider. Inside are displays about Julesburg and information about a short driving tour for local points of interest related to the Pony Express and the history of Julesburg. This is not the site of the original Julesburg station. That was located near County Road 88 on the south side of the river and west about six and a half miles. Markers about the site are along side the road. About a mile farther west is the site of the real Fort Sedgwick of *Dances With Wolves* fame. These are part of the auto tour.

In present Julesburg are the Depot Museum with small displays about the early settlements and railroad period and the Fort Sedgwick Museum with displays about the fort and the history of all the Julesburgs. These two museums are located in present day Julesburg on US 138. They are open seasonally.

The site of **Mud Springs Station** can be visited by following U.S. Highway 385 north towards Bridgeport, Nebraska. Signs direct one to a small park and the monument where the old station stood. The site is about seven miles north of Dalton and about two miles west off 385, or about eighteen miles south of Bridgeport, Nebraska. It is surrounded by private property.

COURTHOUSE AND JAIL ROCK SITE, BRIDGEPORT, NEBRASKA

Courthouse and Jail Rock is a Nebraska State Historic Site. It was one of the major landmarks along the Platte River. The site is located about five miles south of Bridgeport, Nebraska. It was near here that the Pony Express Trail came up from Mud Springs Pony Express Station. The Pony Express riders passed nearby.

Today there is a viewing area to the east of the formation off Highway 88. The location of the Pony Express Station was south off the main highway by Pumpkinseed Creek now on private land.

CHIMNEY ROCK, VISITOR CENTER, BAYARD, NEBRASKA

Chimney Rock is a national historic landmark and another Nebraska State Historic Site. It was the most frequently recorded landmark along the Platte and on the trails west. There is an excellent visitor center just east of the rock. The displays deal with the geology of the area and the history of the landmark on the trails that passed nearby.

The visitor center is located just west of Bayard about a mile south of Highway 92. It is open daily.

There is a marker for the site of Chimney Rock Pony Express Station on Highway 92 just west of the turnoff to the visitor center. The station site was north of the marker in the field.

SCOTTS BLUFF NATIONAL MONUMENT, OREGON TRAIL MUSEUM, GERING, NEBRASKA

This is where the Pony Express riders were forced to go through a narrow gap in the Scotts Bluff/Mitchell Pass formation. Today visitors can walk through the gap that the Pony rode and thousands of the emigrants took their wagons as they traveled to Oregon, Utah and California. The museum focuses on the artistic works of William Henry Jackson and many of the artifacts found nearby. Living history programs are held on weekends and a walk or ride to the top gives one a broad overview of the surrounding area.

The original Oregon Trail bypassed Scotts Bluff and went through Robidoux Pass. However, in 1851 a trail was broken through Mitchell Pass, and that is the route the Pony Express followed. There was no station in Mitchell Pass itself. Two stations were located in the vicinity. The marker for Ficklin's Station is located east of Gering on Highway 92, one mile west of Melbeta. The Scotts Bluff station is thought to be located at or near the site of the later Fort Mitichell, constructed just after the Pony Express period. It was located about two and a half to three miles west of Mitchell Pass. The site is presently unmarked but a monument is nearby.

The museum and Mitchell Pass are located on Old Oregon Trail Road/Highway 92 just west of Gering. It is open year round. The North Platte Valley Museum has fine displays on all the trails.

Nearby a historic old barn has been converted into the Barn Anew bed and breakfast. It is much more comfortable than sleeping on the prairie. It is decorated with old and modern art and artifacts all related to the old west.

Ft. Laramie N.H.S. Visitor Center, Fort Laramie, Wyoming

This was one of the major military forts in the West. Today it is a National Historic Site. It is considered to be one of the jewels of the National Park Service. It is well worth all the time it takes to tour the grounds and buildings and to talk with the park docents. The officers' quarters, called Old Bedlam, and the sutler's store both date back to 1849. Other buildings have been restored and have displays in them. The sutler's store also acted as the post office during the 1840s, 50s and 70s, but its role during the Pony Express era is unknown. The history of the fort encompasses more than its role during the Pony Express era. In the immediate area a number of fur trapping forts were also established, including Fort William, the first "Fort Laramie" painted by Alfred J. Miller in 1837.

The military fort is located three miles west of the town of Fort Laramie off U.S. 26 on Highway 160 or Gray Rocks Road and is open daily.

Between Fort Laramie and Fort Caspar there are no major visitor centers. However four sites deserve mentioning. **Nine-Mile Station or Sands Point's** location was between the two Oregon Trail sites of **Register Cliff** and **Guernsey Trail Ruts** just south of Guernsey, Wyoming. From Fort Laramie the general route of the Pony Express can be followed on dirt roads which will take the traveler to Register Cliff and Guernsey Ruts. Both can be visited. The express station was located west of Register Cliff. Only a marker identifies the express station, but be sure to visit Register Cliff and walk the area of the Guernsey Ruts. One will have a better appreciation for the conditions the riders faced.

Horseshoe Station was a home station and the last station in Division Two. It was also the home of Joseph Slade, the infamous Division Two superintendent. Nothing is left of the once large station complex. Only a marker identifies the general site by the present farm house and its buildings. It is just east of where I-25 crosses Horseshoe Creek east of Sibley Peak about two miles south of Glendo on highway 319.

The **Wyoming Pioneer Memorial Museum** is located in Douglas on the Douglas County Fair Grounds. The museum has fine exhibits on a wide variety of themes including Indian life and culture, emigrants and pioneer life, ranching and many others representing the history of the area. Also nearby is the site of old **Fort Fetterman** with its focus on the military period.

Deer Creek Station site is located in Glenrock. The site, which is marked, and the general area is shown in the pictorial journey. There is a local museum in Glenrock near the rock, but it is open on a limited basis.

FORT CASPAR MUSEUM AND THE BLM HISTORIC TRAILS INTERPRETIVE CENTER, CASPER, WYOMING

Casper is the location of a number of important sites relating to the whole period of western migration. Most are associated with different crossings of the North Platte, the Mormon Ferry, the early Reshaw Bridge, and the Guinard trading post and bridge.

Today there is a fine reproduction of **Fort Caspar** which was built in 1936 on the location of the old Platte River Bridge Station at Louis Guinard's old site. Evidence of the old log and stone cribs that held the bridge the Pony Express used is still visible along with a partial reconstruction of the bridge and a replica of the Mormon Ferry. The reconstructed buildings are open to visitors. There is a fine expanded visitor center and museum with displays that cover the whole history of the site, the Indians, pioneer migrations, the fort's history, local agriculture, oil development, and Casper's history.

The fort is located on its original site located at 4001 Fort Caspar Road. It is open daily in the summer months and Tuesday through Saturday in the winter.

288

Another very worthwhile center is the **National Historic Trails Interpretive Center**. In it are a variety of life-like displays about the Indians, mountain men, the Oregon, California, Mormon, and Pony Express trails. There are many knowledgeable people for additional help and an excellent multimedia program.

It is located at 1501 North Poplar Street off I-25, exit 189, on a hill overlooking Casper. It is open daily in the summer and Tuesday through Saturday in the winter months.

BESSEMER BEND SITE, WYOMING

Today there is a small park with kiosks located on the north bank near where those emigrants using the last fording area of the North Platte crossed. The Red Buttes Station, a stage and Pony Express station, was located near the site, but the specific location is not known and nothing exists today. It is believed to have been at the site of the old Goose Egg Ranch house which is marked on private land. The Pony Express rejoined the main Oregon Trail and headed for the Sweetwater River.

The site is located southwest of Casper off Highway 220 on Bessemer Bend Road by the bridge after crossing the North Platte.

From Fort Caspar to Fort Bridger there are no museums but there are numerous historic places associated with the trails. There are also a few segments which, although on dirt roads, are also worth the slower drive that allows the traveler to see the area in a relatively unchanged environment. From either Fort Caspar or Bessemer Bend one can take a **driving route over the Oregon Trail Road** to the Sweetwater Valley and also see some of the sites in the pictorial chapter. To pick up the section from Fort Casper, cross the river to the north side in Mills continuing north and west about a mile where Poison Spider Road intersects from the west. Take it west and follow it until it meets the Rd 319, the Oregon Trail Road. From Bessemer Bend continue north from the park where the road turns west and continue to follow it about five miles where Bessemer Bend Road meets Rd 319, the Oregon Trail Road.

Along the Oregon Trail Road are **Rock Avenue**, **Willow Springs**, **Prospect Hill**, and the site of **Horse Creek**/Greesewood Station. The most impressive are Rock Avenue and Prospect Hill. These sites are also described in the pictorial journey. The BLM has a pull-off and kiosks at the top of Prospect Hill. Continuing west, the road intersects with highway 220.

INDEPENDENCE ROCK STATE HISTORIC SITE, WYOMING

The Oregon Trail Road joins Highway 220 about 10 miles east of the rock. Independence Rock is a State Historic Site. There is a rest area and a kiosk describing some of the history associated with the site. A path with a small walking bridge leads over the trail to Independence Rock. People today climb the rock as earlier travelers did. The Pony Express riders did not have time to stop. However, Sweetwater Station was located about a mile east along the riverbank.

Independence Rock is located on Wyoming Highway 220 about fifty miles west of Casper.

DEVIL'S GATE AREA, WYOMING

The Pony Express followed the main Oregon-California Trail through this area. It passed through Rattlesnake Pass by Devil's Gate and the former site of the famous Sun Ranch. Today the Mormon Martin's Cove Center is located there. While the site was significant to all travelers, the visitor center's emphasis is on the Mormon experience in that area. The main entrance is west of Independence Rock and west of Devil's Gate off Highway 220. The BLM has interpretive pull-off at Devil's Gate and Split Rock.

SOUTH PASS/PACIFIC SPRINGS SITE, WYOMING

The interpretive site is located off Highway 28, about four miles west of the actual pass. From the pull off area, Pacific Springs and the South Pass can be seen by looking east. This was the area through which almost all trail traffic was funneled. Only those who followed the Lander Road west did not use the South Pass.

For those who don't mind some bumps, dust and dirt, there is a road to the actual pass. High clearance is required. Return east on 28 about four and one half miles. Take the dirt road at the sign to the right/east about three miles. Turn right on the trail and proceed about one mile. You are now at the Great South Pass. Pacific Springs, the site of the Pony Express Station lies a few miles west. That road is a little rougher and depending on recent conditions may require one to back track to get out. The buildings there are on private property and are not from the Pony Express period.

Big Sandy Crossing site, Farson, Wyoming

There is no museum in Farson, but this was the site of the Big Sandy Station. Today a marker identifies the private property site. It is at the intersections of Highway 28 & U.S. 191. It is also the site of the author's favorite ice cream stop.

For those wishing to see the landscape of the trail, the **driving route between Farson & the Green River**, west of Farson along Highway 28, will give the traveler a good view of what the trail was like. The area has not changed much. A few years ago the road was a narrow dirt road that followed the trail very closely with its many small twists and turns. Today it has been widened and paved with gentle curves, but the general experience is still there. It will take the traveler to the Green River where it meets Highway 372 and includes some of the sites in the pictorial chapter. There are two interpretive sites on the route. The **BLM Pilot Butte** site is a few miles past **Simpson's Hollow** and the **Lombard Ferry** site in the Seedkadee National Wildlife Refuge after crossing the Green. This route was used by those following the Oregon, California, Mormon, and Pony Express trails to Fort Bridger.

Ft Bridger State Historic Site, Visitor Center, Fort Bridger, Wyoming

This is a Wyoming State Historic Site. This fort has had a varied history. It was started as a fur trading post, which has been reconstructed near the original site. It was expanded as a fort under the Mormons (part of the Mormon Wall stands), and then served as a U.S. military post from which most of the present buildings date. Many of the buildings have been restored and are open. All of them have appropriate displays for their time and function. There is a fine museum and restoration is a continuing process. The Pony Express exhibits are primarily located in the sutler's complex, but the whole fort with its visitor center is interesting and informative to tour. The archaeological exhibit of Bridger's original site is by the Visitor Center.

It is located off I-80 exit 34 on business I-80 in the western end of the town and is open daily May through September and weekends in October.

SALT LAKE CITY SITES & MUSEUMS, UTAH

Although there is no specific museum about the Pony Express in Salt Lake City there are a number relating to the whole emigration period and the Mormons. Near the "This is the Place" monument is the statue depicting the Pony Express relay, the Pioneer Trail State Park and Old Deseret Village. The Museum of Church History and Art, Temple Square, the Beehive House, the Family History Library, the Daughters of Utah Pioneers Museum, and the Utah Historical Society Museum have related historical material. All are worth the time and should not be missed.

CAMP FLOYD STAGECOACH INN STATE PARK, FAIRFIELD, UTAH

Camp Floyd was set up as a result of the Mormon War. The camp was active from 1858-1861.

It was also the site of a Pony Express Station. Today the Stagecoach Inn, which housed the company's employees, has been restored with period furniture. Across the street is one of the old buildings from the fort. Inside are displays relating to the fort's short history.

The park is on SR 73. The Inn is open daily, but during the winter is closed on Sundays. It is located at 18035 West 1540 North in Fairfield, Utah. Today trees provide nice shade for the visitors and travelers.

For those desiring to get a better feel of the Pony Express experience in Utah, the **driving tour along the Pony Express Trail Road** west from Fairfield/Camp Floyd to the Nevada border will do just that. It generally parallels the original route which can frequently be seen along side. It is a dirt road which can be tough on tires. On one trip over the route with about six or seven other cars we totaled two flat tires and one minor engine problem. On another, we encountered two vehicles with flats and one that ran out of gas. It is hot and dry and no services exist, but the adventure is still there. Be sure the car –a four wheel drive is better, is in good condition with plenty of water, gas and a good spare. Also, two adventurers are better than one.

Monuments along the route locate the Pony Express sites. Most are right along the road or nearby. The route includes many of the sites in the pictorial chapter.

SIMPSON'S SPRINGS SITE, UTAH

Today there is a modern reconstruction of the old Simpson Springs Station building. There are no displays in it, but it is the area of the site that is relevant. It is the beauty, the desolation, and the hardships associated with the trail that is experienced here. There are dry camping facilities available at the site. It is located on the Pony Express Trail Road about forty-three miles west of Camp Floyd.

Some of the other sites include the **Boyd Station ruins** and the site of the former **Fish Springs Station** with a nice picnic area. Monuments identify other sites shown in the photographic journey.

Northeastern Nevada Museum; Ruby Valley Station, & the new BLM Museum, Elko, Nevada

Elko was a major camping area for the California bound emigrants. The Pony Express Trail did not follow the Humboldt River, but was farther south. However, the Northeastern Nevada Museum has the Ruby Valley Pony Express Station. It was altered slightly after its move to the museum in 1960. It stands outside the entrance. Unfortunately, the marker at the original site has been vandalized and no longer exists. Inside the museum are exhibits on a variety of subjects including Indians, the emigrant trails, pioneer life, mining, animals and art.

The station and museum are located at 1515 Idaho Street, Business I-80 by the park. It is open Tuesday through Sunday.

The Hasting Cutoff rejoined the main California Trail a few miles south and west of Elko. Near the junction is the new **California National Historic Trail Interpretive Center**.

The Hastings Cutoff had made a loop south around the Ruby Mountains. At that southern point, the Pony Express Trail and the Hastings Cutoff followed the same route for a few miles. The Hastings Cutoff then turned back north to meet the Humboldt, while the Pony Express turned southwest heading for Carson City. The focus of the new museum is the California Trail and the emigrant experience. Both museums will provide visitors with a wealth of information.

Cold Springs Station Ruins site, Nevada

This was one of the largest stations constructed on the Pony Express Trail. The ruins were the subject of an extensive archaeological study of two stations in 1976. The site gives one a sense of the isolation and vulnerability of the stations.

There is an interpretive site on Highway U.S. 50 a few miles west of Cold Springs. The ruins are located one and a half miles off U.S.

Highway 50, 65 miles west of Austin or about fifty-two miles east of Fallon. Nearby, across from the interpretive site, are the ruins of another stage station and telegraph station from about the same period.

SAND SPRINGS STATION RUINS SITE, NEVADA

This site is located in one of the harsher environments on the trail. It was hot, sandy, with no shade and water that was barely fit to drink. The site was the other focus of the 1976 archaeological study. Until it was unearthed, the site had been covered with sand. The ruins were stabilized in 1977. Today signs help to interpret the different areas of the ruins of the basalt structure. It is a National Historic Site under the jurisdiction of the BLM. The site is also part of the Sand Springs Desert Study Area. Along the one-half mile trail are signs with information about the history, plants, wildlife, and geology of the area.

It is located twenty-five miles east of Fallon just north off U.S. 50 and is easily accessible.

CHURCHILL COUNTY MUSEUM, FALLON, NEVADA

This is another of the fine local museums found along the trail. The museum deals with the history of Churchill County and the city of Fallon. Thus, its focus is wider than the Pony Express era, including the local Indians, the Paiute life and culture, the California Trail and hardships experienced, pioneer life, and mining and geology. It has research facilities with collections of old newspapers and photos and a bookstore and gift shop. There are displays on a wide variety of interests. It seems that its holdings and displays are constantly expanding.

It is located at 1050 South Maine Street and is open daily.

FORT CHURCHILL & BUCKLAND RANCH STATE HISTORIC PARK, SILVER SPRINGS, NEVADA

Buckland Ranch served as a home station during the first few months of the Pony Express. At that time the house was a log structure. The present house stands on the site of the original structure. Once the fort was constructed, it replaced Buckland Station as an express and stage stop. When the fort was deactivated in 1869, materials from the fort were used to build the present Buckland ranch house in 1870 that replaced the original log station. Today the ranch house is being restored and can be toured on a limited basis.

Fort Churchill was built in 1860 by Captain Joseph Stewart and his command. It was built as a direct response to the Paiute or Pyramid Lake War. It was one of the most expensive forts built at the time. The present visitor center was constructed in the style of the headquarters building. Today the fort's ruins have been stabilized. The old headquarters and officers' quarters that served as the Pony Express Station still stand. Camping and picnic areas are available.

The state historic park is located eight miles south of Silver Springs off US 95 Alternate on CR 2B, U.S. Alternate Route 50. It is open daily.

DAYTON HISTORICAL SOCIETY MUSEUM, DAYTON, NEVADA

This small local museum located near the site of the Pony Express Station in the old section of Dayton, or Chinatown as it was also called. Its focus is on mining and local history with limited Pony Express material. It is open on a limited basis.

For those interested in a side trip, Virginia City is nearby. This was the site of the famous Comstock Lode and silver rush.

NEVADA STATE MUSEUM, CARSON CITY, NEVADA

Carson City became the capital. It was the site of a Pony Express relay station located off Carson Street. The site is unmarked. In Carson City are the Nevada State Railroad Museum and the Nevada State Museum. Both have interesting exhibits on their related themes.

MORMON STATION HISTORIC STATE PARK & GENOA COURTHOUSE MUSEUM, GENOA, NEVADA

Mormon Station, Reese's Trading Post, was first constructed on June 1, 1851 to serve the emigrant traffic on the Carson route of the California Trail. It burned down in 1910. The area was given the name Genoa by Orson Hyde, because it reminded him of the mountains behind Genoa, Italy. Genoa was the goal for Captain Simpson during his exploration expedition of the Great Basin for a central route to California. On the original site is a reproduction of the old Mormon trading post and corral and stockade. It is believed that Tingham Livery Stable, the Pony Express livery stable was next to Mormon station in today's the picnic area. Inside the station is a piano from the

Klauber store frequented by Express employees. A monument across the street identifies the site of the Pony Express Station.

Mormon Station is located on Jacks Valley Road, SR 57 off I-395 in Genoa. It is open daily from late spring to early fall.

The Courthouse and Jail Museum across the street includes displays about the Pony Express, emigrant trail, local Indians and other topics relating to its early role in Genoa's history. The Carson Valley Museum is located in nearby Gardnerville and has additional displays about the history of the Carson Valley.

EL DORADO COUNTY MUSEUM, PLACERVILLE, CALIFORNIA

Placerville, also known as Old Dry Diggin's and Hangtown, played an important role in California's history. It was on one of the main California Trail variants. It became a center for the gold rush. It was a Pony Express stop and for awhile its terminus. The museum reflects all its history.

It is located at 104 Placerville Drive and is open Wednesday through Sunday.

FOLSOM HISTORY MUSEUM - WELLS FARGO BUILDING, FOLSOM, CALIFORNIA

The museum is on the original site used by the Pony Express. It is operated by the Folsom Historical Society. Like Placerville, Folsom has had a varied history. Displays relate to all of Folsom's history: Indian life and culture, emigrants, gold rush, Pony Express, mining and the Sacramento Valley Railroad. Folsom also served for a few months as the terminus for the Pony Express. It also has a gift shop and an outside interpretive and educational center.

The museum is located at 823 Sutter Street. It is open all year, Tuesday through Sunday.

B. F. HASTINGS BUILDING, OLD SACRAMENTO, CALIFORNIA

The Hastings Building's construction began in 1852. It housed the California Supreme Court, California State Telegraph Company and the Alta California Telegraph and which served as agents for the Pony Express. It was also the terminus for the Pony Express for a time. Today it houses the Visitor Center, the Wells Fargo Museum which includes a small replica of the Wells Fargo stagecoach, gold scales and a safe, and information on the Pony Express.

296

The building is located at 1000 J Street at the intersection of 2nd and J streets. Across the street is the statue of the Pony Express Rider.

Also in old Sacramento are the **Sacramento History Museum** with its exhibits on the Indians, emigrants, gold rush and mining, and the Pony Express and the **State Railroad Museum**. **Sutter's Fort State Historic Site** and the main Wells Fargo office and museum are downtown. All are worth a visit.

Costa County Historical Society, Martinez, California

This is on the route that was used if the rider missed the riverboat. Part of their exhibits includes material on the Pony Express including a reproduction saddle and mochila.

It is located at 610 Main Street and is open Tuesday through Thursday.

Wells Fargo History Museum, San Francisco, California

The museum covers the period from 1848 to the present. Inside is an 1860 stagecoach, displays and lots of artifacts from the gold rush, including gold nuggets, letters, photos, and other aspects relating to Wells Fargo's history.

The museum is located in the present Wells Fargo Bank Building at 420 Montgomery Street. It is open weekdays.

For the armchair traveler many of these museums may have their own websites. There is a website dedicated to the Pony Express which provides a variety of information. It is associated with the National Pony Express Association.

www.xphomestation.com/npea

Chapter Nine

Additional Reading

For those interested in learning more about the history and lore of the Pony Express, there are a number of books that are available that will be discussed. Some are reprints of the old classics, while others are more recent works. There are a few books that are out of print and/ or difficult to find. As with other sesquicentennial celebrations, some older books may be made available. Some books were descriptions of journeys.

There are a number of books that were released around the turn of the twentieth century. Alexander Majors' *Seventy Years on the Frontier* was written as a biography and was first published in 1893. As a result, some parts of the book are not directly related to the Pony Express. However, because he was one of the founders of the enterprise, his whole life becomes important in understanding his role in it. He provides significant information about the Pony Express development and operations and even includes some information about some of the Pony Express riders with whom he was personally acquainted with. Some of these relationships were developed after the Pony Express era. It should be noted that Majors was assisted and encouraged by William "Buffalo Bill" Cody, the famous showman and Pony Express "rider." Cody also reportedly paid for the editing and publishing. However, it still provides some good information and is a good introduction.

William Lightfoot Visscher's *The Pony Express: A Thrilling and Truthful History* is considered to be one of the short classics. When it was first published in 1908 some of the Pony Express riders were still alive. It seems that parts of it were based on conversations with some of them, but actually a few may have been taken from other sources. In one way perhaps it includes more of the lore of the Pony Express.

Glenn Bradley's *The Story of the Pony Express* was first published in 1913. Since then it was been reprinted a number of times. It was one of the early books that successfully covered the history of the Pony Express. It was short and readable and in 1960 it was used as the official centennial history book. The 2003 reprint with the foreword by Tom Crews adds new information about the overland route between Sacramento and San Francisco.

Arthur Chapman wrote *The Pony Express: The Record of a Romantic Adventure in Business*. It was first published in 1932. His book provides another good review of the Pony Express and gives more detailed information. It provides the broad setting for its development and much supportive material. It is divided by chapters dealing with related aspects, such as California, land and sea communications, routes, organization, riders and equipment, stations, individual stories, problems and others. Some of the topics comprise more than one chapter. Because it was written almost eighty years ago, recent work and research has provided some new and differing information.

Saddle and Spurs: The Pony Express Saga was written by Raymond W. and Mary Lund Settle. It first appeared in 1955. This provides a good overall review of the appropriate topics covering the founders, the need, the organization, the send off, the riders, the route across, the problems and its downfall. Most of the information is still considered sound today.

Joseph J. Di Certo wrote *The Saga of the Pony Express*. It was published in 2002. It is another readable account of the Pony Express. It starts with the idea, moves to the founders and the organization and then starts across the expanse examining the route and providing detailed and relevant information. Various individuals associated with the Pony are discussed, and then it examines the Pony's fall. It also includes a list of riders and stations.

On the Winds of Destiny: A Biographical Look at Pony Express Riders was written by Jackie Lewin and Marilyn Taylor. It first appeared in 2002. Its approach to the Pony Express is different than most others. The title of the book suffices to describe its content. The book starts with a concise overview and summary of the Pony Express as well as a list of riders and stations, but the vast majority of the book is comprised of portraits and other photographs associated with the individuals and short biographical sketches of sixty-eight of the people who supervised or rode with the Pony Express.

One of the more recent books is *Orphans Preferred: The Twisted Truth and Lasting Legend of the Pony Express,* by Christopher Corbett. It was first published in 2003. This book is full of good readable information. The title tells it all. The first half deals with the Pony Express. Detailed and interesting information from a variety of sources is presented. Most of the topics from its founders and beginnings to the riders, stations, and problems, and its demise are all there. The later portion of the book has to do with more of the lore of the Pony Express including some of the individuals and old stories. For those especially interested in this aspect of Pony Express history, this book would be very enjoyable. Most of his sources are easy to discern.

Three other books that include some good primary source materials are worth noting. Parts of *Pioneering the West, 1846-1878: Major Howard Egan's Life* by Howard Egan and *The White Indian Boy* by Nicholas Wilson deal with experiences specifically related to the Pony Express. Egan served as one of the superintendents and opened the Egan's Trail, and Wilson was a rider. The majority of both books are about other topics dealing with the lives. Howard Driggs' *The Pony Express Goes Through: An American Saga Told by Its Heroes* recounts conversations with riders.

Two old books that are not specifically about the Pony Express but provide much information on the conditions encountered when crossing the continent are Mark Twain's *Roughing It* and Sir Richard Burton's *The City of the Saint and Across the Rocky Mountains to California.* Both give vivid accounts of their trip, however, Burton's is a daily account with much more detail. Both date from the Pony Express years. Reprints are still available or in local libraries.

There are probably many other good books. Each reader has his or her own interests and concerns. They will influence your selections, and remember, you really can't tell a book by its cover!

So get on your pony and go!!

BIBLIOGRAPHY

Footnotes denote book number and respective pages.

1. Benjamin, Israel Joseph. *Three Years in America*, Vol 2. (Introduction by Oscar Handlin, Translated by Charles Reznikoff). Philadelphia, 1956.
2. Bensen, Joe. *The Traveler's Guide to the Pony Express Trail.* Helena: Falcon Press, 1995.
3. Barry, Louise, ed., "Albert D. Richardson's Letter's on the Pike's Peak Gold Region," *Kansas Historical Quarterly*, Vol. 12, 1943:14-57.
4. Bloss, Roy S., *Pony Express: Fact & Fiction*. Concord: Contra Costa County Historical Society, 1991.
5. Bloss, Roy S. *Pony Express - The Great Gamble*. Berkeley: Howell-North, 1959.
6. Bradley, Glenn D. *The Story of the Pony Express: A Concise History: An Account of the Most Remarkable Mail Service Ever in Existence, and Its Place in History*. Chicago: A.C. McClug. 1913. (Reprint: Introduction by Tom Crews. James Stevenson Publisher, 2003.)
7. Bromley, George Tisdale. *The Long Ago and the Later On: or Reflections of Eighty Years*. San Francisco, Robertson, 1905. Reprint: Forgotten Books 2008.
8. Burton, Richard F. *The City of the Saints and Across the Rocky Mountains to California*, London: Longman, Green, Longman and Roberts, 1862.
9. Burton, Richard F., ed. Fawn McKay Brodie. *The City of the Saints and Across the Rocky Mountains to California*. New York: Alfred A. Knopf. 1963. (reprint of 1861)
10. Carlstrom, Jeffrey, and Cynthia Furse. *The History of Emigration Canyon: Gateway to Salt Lake Valley*. Logan: Utah State University Press, 2003.

11. Carter, Kate B. *Riders of the Pony Express*. Salt Lake City: Daughters of the Utah Pioneers, 1952.

12. Chapman, Arthur. *The Pony Express: The Record of a Romantic Adventure in Business*. (1932) Reprint. New York: Cooper Square Publishers, Inc., 1971.

13. Clark, C. M. *Journal, A Trip to Pike's Peak and Notes by the Way*. (Ed. Robert Greenwood) San Jose, CA: Talisman Press. 1958.

14. Corbett, Christopher. *Orphans Preferred: The Twisted Truth and Lasting Legend of the Pony Express*. New York: Broadway Books, 2003.

15. Cross, Ralph Herbert. *The Early Inns of California 1844-1869*. San Francisco: Cross & Brandt. 1954.

16. Di Certo, Joseph J. *The Saga of the Pony Express*. Missoula: Mountain Press Publishing Company, 2002.

17. Dickson III, Ephriam D. "On the Trail of Simpson's Illusive Photographer, 1858-59," 2009.

18. Driggs, Howard R. *The Old West Speaks*. Englewood Cliffs: Prentice-Hall. 1956.

19. Driggs, Howard. *The Pony Express Goes Through: An American Sage Told by Its Heroes*. Frederick A. Stokes Company. 1935.

20. Egan, Howard. *Pioneering the West, 1846-1878: Major Howard Egan's Diary*. Richmond, Utah,1917. (reprint: Council Press)

21. Fike, Richard E., and John W. Headly. *The Pony Express Stations of Utah in Historical Perspectives*. Washington, D.C.: Superintendent of Documents, U.S. Government Printing Office, 1979.

22. Findley, Rowe. "A Buckaroo Stew of Fact And Legend: The Pony Express," *National Geographic*, Vol. 158, No.1, July 1980, pp 44-71.

23. Franzwa, Gregory M. *Maps of the California Trail*. Tucson: The Patrice Press, 1999.

24. Franzwa, Gregory M. *Maps of the Oregon Trail*. Gerald: The Patrice Press, 1982.

25. Gilman, Musetta. *Pump on the Prairie*. Detroit: Harlo Press, 1975.

26. Godfrey, Anthony. *Historic Resource Study: Pony Express National Historic Trail*. Washington D.C.: United States Department of the Interior/National Park Service, 1994.

27. Godfrey, Anthony, and Roy Webb. *Pony Express*, Voyage of Discovery: the Story Behind the Scenery. KC Publications, Inc., 1999.

28. Haines, Aubrey, *Historic Sites Along the Oregon Trail*. Gerald: Patrice Press.1981.

29. Hardesty, Donald L. *The Pony Express in Central Nevada: Archeaological and Document Perspectives*. Reno: Bureau of Land Management, 1979.

30. "The Overland Pony Express," *Harpers Weekly*, November 2, 1867. Vol. XI, No 566, pp. 693-694.

31. Hill, William E. *Here Comes the Pony! The Story of the Pony Express*. Independence: Oregon-California Trails Association/ National Pony Express Trail Museum, 2006.

32. Hill, William E. *The California Trail, Yesterday and Today*. Boise: Tamarack Books, Inc. 1993.

33. Hill, William E. *The Mormon Trail, Yesterday and Today*. Logan: Utah University State Press, 1996.

34. Hill, William E. *The Oregon Trail, Yesterday and Today*. Caldwell: The Caxton Printers.1986.

35. Holmes, Louis A. *Fort McPherson, Nebraska, Fort Cottonwood, N.T. Guardian of the Tracks and Trails*. Lincoln: Johnsen Publishing Company, 1963.

36. Huffman, Ilene. *The Historical Patchwork of Woodlawn*. Huffman, 2006.

37. Jabusch, David M. and Susan C. *Pathway to Glory: The Pony Express and Stage Stations in Utah*. Salt Lake City: Treasure Press. 2007.

38. Jackson, Clarence S. *Picture Maker of the Old West: William H. Jackson*. New York: Bonanza Books. 1947.

39. Jackson, William Henry. *Time Exposure*. Tucson: The Patrice Press.1994.

40. Jensen, Lee. *The Pony Express: Illustrated with a Unique Collection of Historical Pictures*. New York: Grosset & Dunlap Publishers, 1955.

41. Kimball, Stanley B. *Historic Sites and Markers Along the Mormon and Other Historic Trails*. Urbana: University of Illinois Press, 1988.

42. Kimball, Stanley B. *Historic Resource Study: Mormon Pioneer National Historic Trail*. Washington, D.C.: U.S. Department of the Interior, 1991.

43. Lewin, Jacqueline, and Marilyn Taylor. *On the Winds of Destiny: A Biographical Look at Pony Express Riders*. St. Joe: Platte Purchase Publishers, 2002.

44. Majors, Alexander. *Seventy Years on the Frontier: Alexander Majors' Memoirs of a Lifetime on the Border*. Minneapolis, Ross & Haines, Inc., 1965.

45. Mason, Dorothy, Bureau of Land Management. *The Pony Express in Nevada*. Carson City: Nevada State Museum, 1996.

46. Mattes, Merrill. *The Great Platte River Road: The Covered Wagon Mainline via Fort Kearny to Fort Laramie*. Lincoln: The Nebraska State Historical Society, 1969.

47. Mattes, Merrill, and Paul Henderson. *The Pony Express: Across Nebraska from St. Joseph to Fort Laramie*. Gering: Courier Press, 1962.

48. Moeller, Bill, and Jan Moeller. *The Pony Express: a Photographic History*. Missoula: Mountain Press Publishing Company, 2002.

49. Monahan, Doris. *Julesburg and Fort Sedwick, Wicked City— Scandalous Fort*. Stering: Monahan. 2009.

50. Moody, Ralph. *Riders of the Pony Express*. Lincoln: University of Nebraska Press, 1958.

51. Moody, Ralph. *Stagecoach West*. Lincoln: University of Lincoln Press, 1998.

52. Nevin, David. *The Expressman*. New York: Time-Life, The Old West Books, 1974.

53. Petersen, Jesse G. *A Route for the Overland Stage. James H. Simpson's 1859 Trail Across the Great Basin*. Logan: Utah State University Press, 2008.

54. Rau, Margerat. *The Mail Must Go Through: The Story of the Pony Express*. Greensboro: Morgan Reynolds Publishing, 2005.

55. Reinfeld, Fred. *Pony Express*. Lincoln: University of Nebraska Press. Greensboro: Morgan Reynolds Publishing. 2005.

56. Root, Frank A. and Connelley, William Elsey. *The Overland Stage to California: Personal Reminiscences and Authentic History of the Great Overland Stage Line and Pony Express*. Topeka: Franck A. Root and William Elsey Connelley, 1901.

57. Root, George A. and Russell K. Hickman, "Part III-The Platte Route-Pike's Peak Express Companies," *Kansas Historical Quarterly*, February 1945, Vol. 14, No 8: pp 485-526.

58. Root, George A. and Russell K. Hickman, "Part IV-The Platte Route-Concluded. The Pony Express and Pacific Telegraph," *Kansas Historical Quarterly*, February 1946, Vol. 14, No 1: pp36-91.

59. Rottenberg, Dan. *Death of a Gunfighter: The Quest for Jack Slade, the West's Most Elusive Legend.* Yardley: Westholme Publishing. 2008.

60. *San Francisco Daily Evening Bulletin*, March, 1860- November, 1861. (various issues) photocopy from microfilm.

61. Settle, Raymond W., and Mary Lund Settle. *Saddle and Spurs.* Lincoln: University of Nebraska Press, 1972.

62. Settle, Raymond W., and Mary Lund Settle. *Empire on Wheels.* Stanford: Stanford University Press, 1949.

63. Scott, Edward B. *The Saga of Lake Tahoe: A Complete Documentation of Lake Tahoe's Development Over the Last One Hundred Years.* Vol. I. Crystal Bay, Lake Tahoe: Sierra –Tahoe Publishing Co., 1957.

64. Scott, Edward B. *The Saga of Lake Tahoe: A Complete Documentation of Lake Tahoe's Development Over the Last One Hundred Years.* Vol. II. Crystal Bay, Lake Tahoe: Sierra –Tahoe Publishing Co., 1973.

65. Service, Alex. *The Life and Letters of Casper Collins.* Casper: City of Casper. 2000

66. Simpson, James Hervey. *Report of the Explorations Across the Great Basin of the Territory of Utah for a Direct Wagon-Route from Camp Floyd To Genoa, in Carson Valley, in 1859.* Washington: Government Printing Office, 1876. [reprint. Reno: University of Nevada Press. 1983. Map included]

67. Spring, Agnes Wright. *Casper Collins: The Life and Times of an Indian Fighter of the Sixties.* New York: Columbia Press. 1927.

68. *St. Joseph Daily Gazette*, "Pony Express Edition" April 3, 1860. (Restored edition. Western Trails Enterprises, 1990.)

69. Tanner, Russel L. *Historical and Archaeologhical study of the Granger Stage Station, also known as the South Bend Stage*

Station, a way-station on the Overland Trail in Wyoming. Kymak Marook Heritage Research, LLC. Rock Springs, 2009.

70. Transierra Roisterous Alliance of Senior Humbugs. *Central Overland Route and Transcontinental Telegraph Through Nevada 1858-1868.* California, 1985.

71. Townley, John M. *The Pony Express Guidebook: Across Nevada with the Pony Express and Overland Stage Line.* Reno: Great Basin Studies Center. 1986.

72. Twain, Mark. *Roughing It.* Harper & Bros. 1872. (reprint. New York: Book of the Month Club)

73. Visscher, William Lightfoot. *The Pony Express: A Thrilling and Truthful History with other Sketches and Incidents of Those Stirring Times.* 1908. (reprint: Golden: Outbooks, 1980.)

74. Warren, Louis S. *Buffalo Bill's America. William Cody and the Wild West Show.* New Tork: Alfred A. Knopf. 2005.

75. Wetmore, Helen Cody and Zane Grey. *Last of the Great Scouts ("Buffalo Bill").* Grosset & Dunlap Publishers: New York. 1918.

76. Wilson, E. Nicholas. (& Howard R. Driggs.) *The White Indian Boy: The Story of Uncle Nick Among the Shoshones.* Yonkers: World Book Company, 1925.

77. Yancey, Diane. *Life on the Pony Express. San Diego: Lucent Books, 2001.*

PAMPHLETS –

"Hollenberg Station," Kansas State Historical Society.

"Pony Express National Historic Trail." Department of the Interior, National Park Service & U.S. Department of Agriculture, Forrest Service, Washington, DC.

"Rock Creek Station: A State Historic Park." Nebraska Game and Parks Commission.

"Sand Springs." U.S. Department of the Interior, Bureau of Land Management, 2001.

"The Mormon Trail: Fort Bridger to Salt Lake Valley," Utah Crossroads, 1997.

"Trailing the Pioneers: Pony Express – Utah Segment." Utah Crossroads, 2005.

"Trailing the Pioneers: Hiking: Mormon Flat to Mountain Dell." Utah Crossroads, 2005.

Acknowledgements

This project has in one sense been a project of a few years, but in another, it has been one spanning decades. Because of the overlapping of many of the other historic western trails, even when I was focused on one of those trails, I was coincidentally dealing with the Pony Express. Historically the Pony Express came relatively late in western trail history, and it happened to make use of segments of a number of other trails for much of its route. There were many people during that thirty year period that I researched those routes who helped me along the way and while I do not list them I want to at least acknowledge that fact. They provided me with much knowledge about the route and general information which provided a basis for my recent work on the Pony Express Trail.

As always, my appreciation and thanks go to many individuals, organizations and the various local, state and federal agencies. They have helped to preserve many of the sites and provided me with encouragement, information, and access.

Although the Pony Express Trail is now 150 years old, it was only designated a National Historic Trail in 1992. For those who worked to accomplish that, they all deserve acknowledgement. Even before that, many local, state and other federal agencies had been involved in preserving our history. Special thanks goes to the local property owners—the farmers, ranchers and their foremen, many of whom have been preserving the trail and our history for years without prodding by any government or organization, but simply because of their own interest and pride in our history. I am especially thankful to those who allowed me to access, wander on or guided me to places on their property, or on the public lands. It is unfortunate that some areas of the trail are now off-limits or behind locked gates because of either the misuse or vandalism by a few.

Over the years, more and more of the trail has been identified, marked, or re-marked. That makes following and researching it easier. Years ago people such as Paul Henderson, Merrill Mattes and Larry C. Bishop were involved in research, identifying and marking the trails and related historic sites. Some of their markings are still in existence. Earlier trail organizations placed monuments along the trail which, although some have been vandalized over the years, still stand. Many of Bishop's old iron stakes have found new company in the form of the aluminum stakes placed by Pony Express National Association.

It is always difficult to select those to thank, and this was especially true because of the time interruption in my work. Hopefully, for those I have not specifically acknowledged, they will understand and know that I am still very grateful. Some folks provided a small but important tidbit of information, while others gave much more information, and spent hours or provided access. Here are some of those individuals: Travis Boley, Jeff Burgess, Jude Carino, Peter Castagno, Ivy Collins, Bruce Cuthbertson, Ellery & Tom Damele, Orville Duden, Duane Durst, Tom Eckhoff, Neil & Sara Forgey, Rob & Martha Hellyer, Verl Hendrix, Bill Houston, Ilene Huffman, Eugene Hunt, Kyle Jones, Jolene Kaufman, Brian Kilthau, Wayne Koch, John & Cassandra Lancaster, Jackie Lewin, Joe Nardone, Diane Newborn, Dean Reasoner, Jack Rhodes, Ray Seifer, Haney Stevenson, Bob Summerville, Tena Sun, Kay Threlkeld and Rick Young.

To another group, the librarians, the unsung heroes are always helpful. From those in my own Centereach Middle Country Public Library to those in other communities, universities and archives across the country, their assistance is most appreciated.

And, of course, special thanks to my wife Jan who has since our honeymoon over the Santa Fe Trail accompanied me for the years of travels across the prairies, the deserts and the mountains. She endured all the bumps, dusty roads, river and creek crossings in all kinds of weather and waited "patiently" in the car ready to contact 911 or On Star if needed while I was out in the "wilds" looking for the right location. She is still my best admirer and my first critic.

The Author

William Hill is the author of several books on western trails, including *The Oregon Trail, Yesterday and Today, The Lewis and Clark Trail, Yesterday and Today* and *The Santa Fe Trail, Yesterday and Today*, all published by Caxton Press. He has devoted many years and traveled thousands of miles collecting material for his guides.

Born in Pennsylvania, Hill earned his B.A. in history from the University of Minnesota. He also attended Hofstra University, where he obtained his M.S. in secondary education and a C.A.S. in educational administration.

Hill's interest in the West dates back to childhood trips taken with his family. He is a member of the Lewis and Clark Trail Heritage Foundation, the Oregon-California Trails Association, the Santa Fe Trail Association, Western Writers of America and various historical associations.

Hill is now retired from teaching and he and his wife live in Centereach, New York.

INDEX

OTHER TITLES ABOUT
THE WEST
FROM
CAXTON PRESS

The Oregon Trail
Yesterday and Today
by William Hill
ISBN 0-87004-319-6, 179 pages, paper, $12.95

The Lewis and Clark Trail
Yesterday and Today
by William Hill
ISBN 978-0-87004-439-7, 300 pages, paper, $16.95

The Santa Fe Trail
Yesterday and Today
by William Hill
ISBN 0-87004-354-4, 260 pages, paper, $16.95

The Deadliest Indian War in the West
The Snake Conflict 1864-1868
by Gregory Michno
ISBN 978-0-87004-460-1, 450 pages, paper, $18.95

Massacre Along the Medicine Road
The Indian War of 1864 in Nebraska
by Ronald Becher
ISBN 0-87004-289-7, 500 pages, cloth, $32.95
ISBN 0-87004-387-0, 500 pages, paper, $22.95

For a free catalog of Caxton titles write to:

CAXTON PRESS
312 Main Street
Caldwell, Idaho 83605-3299

or

Visit our Internet web site:

www.caxtonpress.com

Caxton Press is a division of THE CAXTON PRINTERS, Ltd.